Wiring Your Digital Home

FOR

DUMMIES®

Wiring Your Digital Home For Dummies®

Cheat Sheet

Ohm's Law formula chart

The following figure shows a pie chart that makes it easy to determine the proper formula to use when calculating electrical measurements.

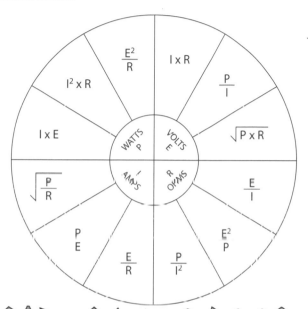

Ethernet cable terminations

The following lists describe the proper ways to wire the terminators for RJ45 Ethernet cable. To make a crossover cable for connecting like devices (such as two network interface cards) directly together, wire one plug to TA568A and the other end of the cable to TA568B. For normal straight-through cables, simply wire both end plugs of your cable the same way.

Wire a TA568A terminator according to the following color code:

- Pin 1: Green and white
- Pin 2: Green
- Pin 3: Orange and white
- Pin 4: Blue
- Pin 5: Blue and white
- Pin 6: Orange
- Pin 7: Brown and white
- Pin 8: Brown

Wire a TA568B terminator according to the following color code:

- Pin 1: Orange and white
- Pin 2: Orange
- Pin 3: Green and white
- Pin 4: Blue
- Pin 5: Blue and white
- Pin 6: Green
- Pin 7: Brown and white
- Pin 8: Brown

For Dummies: Bestselling Book Series for Beginners

Wiring Your Digital Home For Dummies®

Maximum breaker size for small power conductors

The small conductor rule limits the *maximum* breaker size allowed for copper wire to the sizes shown in the following list:

- ✔ AWG 14 copper wire: 15 amp breaker
- ✔ AWG 12 copper wire: 20 amp breaker
- ✔ AWG 10 copper wire: 30 amp breaker

Transformer terminal connections

The following figure shows the wiring diagram for the most common transformer you will encounter.

These transformers are reversible. You can power the H side and draw power from the X side or vice versa.

240/480 volt for 480 connect H2 to H3, H1 and H4 are 480 for 240 connect H1 to H3 and H2 to H4

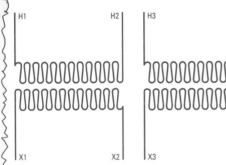

120/240 volt for 240 connect X2 to X3, X1 and X4 are 240 for 120 connect X1 to X3 and X2 to X4

Dual voltage motor connections and motor full load currents

The following figure shows the wiring diagram for a popular style of dual voltage electric motor and a full load current chart.

Capacitor start dual voltage motor connections

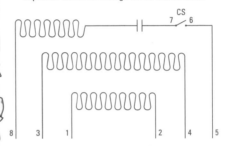

Voltage	Line 1	Line 2	Connect
High	1	4, 5	2, 3, 8
Low	1, 3, 8	2, 4, 5	None

Counterclockwise rotation facing terminal end to reverse rotation interchange leads 5 and 8

Horse-power	Voltage	
	115	230
1/8	4.4	2.2
1/4	5.8	2.9
1/3	7.2	3.6
1/2	9.8	4.9
3/4	13.8	6.9
1	16	8
1 1/2	20	10
2	24	12
3	34	17
5	56	28
7 1/2	80	40
10	100	50

Typical current (amps) required at listed AC voltage and horsepower rating

For Dummies: Bestselling Book Series for Beginners

Wiring Your Digital Home

FOR DUMMIES®

by Dennis C. Brewer and Paul A. Brewer

WILEY

Wiley Publishing, Inc.

Wiring Your Digital Home For Dummies®

Published by
Wiley Publishing, Inc.
111 River Street
Hoboken, NJ 07030-5774

www.wiley.com

For general information on our other products and services, please contact our Customer Care Department within the U.S. at 800-762-2974, outside the U.S. at 317-572-3993, or fax 317-572-4002.

For technical support, please visit www.wiley.com/techsupport.

Wiley also publishes its books in a variety of electronic formats. Some content that appears in print may not be available in electronic books.

Library of Congress Control Number: 2006926169

ISBN-13: 978-0-471-91830-1

ISBN-10: 0-471-91830-X

Manufactured in the United States of America

10 9 8 7 6 5 4 3 2 1

1O/RU/QZ/QW/IN

WILEY

About the Authors

Dennis C. Brewer is also the author of *Security Controls for Sarbanes-Oxley Section 404 IT Compliance: Authorization, Authentication, and Access* (Wiley). He earned a BSBA degree from Michigan Technological University and a Novell Network Engineer Certification, and he spent over a dozen years as an information technology specialist with the state of Michigan. Over the last ten years, Dennis has worked on networking and computer technology projects from the level of hands-on integration, maintenance, and operations to developing policy and charting future direction. He retired from his position as an information technology security solutions specialist in January 2006 from the state of Michigan, Department of Information Technology, Office of Enterprise Security. He currently operates his own IT consulting practice and works on additional book projects.

Dennis's on-the-ground and on-the-sea experience with electricity, wiring, building design, and construction, repairing, and maintenance includes 12 years in the U.S. Navy Reserve (where he attained the rank and rating of Chief Petty Officer, Interior Communications Electrician) and 12 years in the Michigan National Guard as a Combat Engineer Officer (which he retired from as a Captain in 1993).

Dennis currently resides in the quiet little town of Laurium, in the Upper Peninsula of Michigan, with his wife, Penny. Their shared hobbies and pastimes include reading, camping in the "little house," biking, walking when weather permits, and auto rides in sun, rain, sleet, or snow through the highways and byways of the Keweenaw peninsula (which almost always includes sightings of white-tailed deer, an occasional black bear or wolf, or a bald eagle busying itself "fishing" the mouth of the Eagle River, where it empties into Lake Superior). Dennis says, "There is nothing more rewarding than watching the sun set over the big lake after an engaging afternoon of writing, except for maybe helping someone install a home network!"

Paul A. Brewer has earned a state of Michigan Masters Electrician License and Michigan Residential Builders License. He studied electrical engineering at Michigan Technological University, in Houghton, Michigan. He is currently the vice president of the electrical contracting firm of All Systems Electric (run by his sons) located in Ishpeming, Michigan, and he also works on writing projects.

While in the U.S. Navy, Paul worked on electro-mechanical systems of the submarines of the Sunshine Squadron out of Key West Florida and later out of Charleston, South Carolina, as an Interior Communications Electrician Petty Officer Second Class. He also worked as an expediter for a general contractor and as an electrician in several states. For the final three years that Callahan Mining Company operated the Ropes Gold Mine near Ishpeming, he ran the electrical department for a developing underground mine; he also ran his own electrical contracting firm from 1976 to 2005. While at the Ropes Gold Mine, he designed and built an automatic control system that was CCTV monitored and could load skips by remote control. In addition, he maintained the high- and low-voltage distribution systems and the dewatering pumps as they advanced deeper with the mine's descent. In his contracting business, he has completed wiring projects that included department stores, offices, restaurants, homes, saw mills, and roller mills. On off-the-grid sites, he has installed generators, solar panels, and battery-powered inverter systems, which includes volunteering his time to the U.S. National Park of Isle Royal to install a solar-inverter–powered system on the beautiful island national park in Lake Superior.

Paul currently resides in the city of Ishpeming, Michigan, in the Upper Peninsula. He takes advantage of the area's seasonal amenities: skiing, skating, and — when the freeze precedes the snow — clears off the lake in front of his house to share the rink, where everyone is welcome to skate. Presque Isle Park in Marquette is a favorite place to ski in the winter. In the summer, he hits the rollerblade trails and concerts in the park. Paul says, "The park deer population in past years included two albino deer, which once cooperated by showing themselves when I took my only sister, Peggy, and her husband, Joe, to see them."

Dedication

Paul A. Brewer: I dedicate this book to our late brother, Edward Leslie Brewer. Ed, the oldest of us five children, was the spark that ignited our interest in the subject of electricity. As an extensive reader of all matters, Ed's knowledge of the electrical code book is best described as "a walking code book." When I first started in the business, he steered me to the right track by freely and enthusiastically giving me the code-compliant way to do a job. In later years, I still found good advice upon request and sometimes it came unsolicited. I do miss him.

Dennis C. Brewer: This book is dedicated to all those (too many to count or mention by name) who showed me how to actually do or make something with hand tools, power tools, and motorized equipment — particularly to my older brothers, Edward, Alfred, and Paul for their early encouragement toward learning to use tools and the trades. I also dedicate this book to those who want to learn how to do new things and pass that fresh knowledge, skill, or ability on to someone else who could benefit from the doing.

Authors' Acknowledgments

Paul A. Brewer: I would like to thank my family for their support, acknowledging my three beautiful daughters and their spouses: Joyce and Joe, Paula and Dave, and Sandy. I would especially thank my two sons, Gary (and his wife Lisa), and Ricky, who both by chance also happen to be electricians, for helping me with this book. I received help from many vendors; the vendors that went out of their way to be of assistance, include Rex TV, Midwest Security, and Wal-Mart, all of Marquette, MI. I want to thank the owners, as well as the contractors, of the many projects we wired and photographed. Our electrical suppliers were very helpful, especially Joe Rahoi at Prime Supply and Holly Bluebaugh, Scott Schwenke, and Paul Klarich at UP Electric Supply. I am grateful to my friend, John Wirtanen, for the entertaining tales he tells and also for the wisdom and water that I received at his establishment.

Dennis C. Brewer: Thanks to my wife, Penny, for her relentless patience and support; my friend Joe, for always asking the tough technical questions; my oldest son, Jason, for the inspiration to always do quality work; my youngest son, Justin, for pointing out that sometimes designs need to go a little bit outside of the lines; and my mother, Verna, for reminding me recently that finding the right answer to a problem is worth some degree of celebration.

I want to thank the many electrical, electronic, and networking product vendors and sales representatives who answered or found answers to my questions. They know who they are because I will give each of them a copy of this book!

From both authors: Thanks to our literary agent, Carole McClendon, at Waterside Productions for all of her valued assistance with this project. Special thanks goes to Melody Layne, acquisitions editor at John Wiley & Sons, for seeing the potential in this text to help readers, be they lay persons, architects, or contractors, to include the many benefits of the digital-age devices that surround us in the homes we love to live in and enjoy. Thanks to Jean Rogers, associate project editor, for her objective insight in improving every aspect of this text. We are particularly grateful to Keith Underdahl for his sharing his considerable knowledge of how to write *For Dummies* and his very valuable input into this text. We would also like to express our combined thanks to everyone else at Wiley Publishing for their excellent contributions in producing this book and for always being so pleasant to work with.

Publisher's Acknowledgments

We're proud of this book; please send us your comments through our online registration form located at www.dummies.com/register/.

Some of the people who helped bring this book to market include the following:

Acquisitions, Editorial, and Media Development

Associate Project Editor: Jean Rogers

Acquisitions Editor: Melody Layne

Copy Editor: Tonya Maddox Cupp

Technical Editor: Derek Cowburn

Editorial Manager: Leah Cameron

Media Development Specialists: Angela Denny, Kate Jenkins, Steven Kudirka, Kit Malone

Media Development Coordinator: Laura Atkinson

Media Project Supervisor: Laura Moss

Media Development Manager: Laura VanWinkle

Media Development Associate Producer: Richard Graves

Editorial Assistant: Amanda Foxworth

Sr. Editorial Assistant: Cherie Case

Cartoons: Rich Tennant (www.the5thwave.com)

Composition Services

Project Coordinators: Tera Knapp, Ryan Steffen

Layout and Graphics: Claudia Bell, Carl Byers, Brian Drumm, Lauren Goddard, Brooke Graczyk, Joyce Haughey, Stephanie D. Jumper, Heather Ryan

Special Art:

Proofreaders: Christine Pingleton, Charles Spencer, Jennifer Stanley

Indexer: Techbooks

Publishing and Editorial for Technology Dummies

> **Richard Swadley,** Vice President and Executive Group Publisher
>
> **Andy Cummings,** Vice President and Publisher
>
> **Mary Bednarek,** Executive Acquisitions Director
>
> **Mary C. Corder,** Editorial Director

Publishing for Consumer Dummies

> **Diane Graves Steele,** Vice President and Publisher
>
> **Joyce Pepple,** Acquisitions Director

Composition Services

> **Gerry Fahey,** Vice President of Production Services
>
> **Debbie Stailey,** Director of Composition Services

Contents at a Glance

Table of Contents

Introduction

• •

Thousands of years ago, a home was little more than a sheltered place in which to sleep. Later, indoor fireplaces and ovens allowed people to cook inside their homes. In recent centuries, homes sprouted washrooms and sinks, thanks to indoor plumbing, and in the last 100 years, electrical and telephone systems have become standard features.

Homes have come a long way since their humble beginnings as crude shelters. In the 21st century, digital lifestyles will influence home design as never before. The modern home is a place for high-fidelity entertainment, advanced communications, and automated convenience. This book shows you how to bring your home into the new millennium. We show you how to install whole-home remote controls, cable TV systems, computer networks, public address systems, multi-room sound, backup power, and the latest phone systems.

Wiring Your Digital Home For Dummies offers illustrations, diagrams, and job-site photographs to help you better understand the sometimes complex wiring topics. We've packed this book with practical advice on what to include in new-home designs and techniques that work whether you're building a new home or updating an existing one. Even if you're not a do-it-yourselfer, this book helps you better understand digital systems, allowing you to make more informed decisions as you work with your architect or builder.

About This Book

If you've ever started a sentence with, "I wish my home were wired for (insert fantasy here)," then *Wiring Your Digital Home For Dummies* is for you! This book is organized into parts and chapters, creating the framework that builds and binds the book together. You needn't approach the book in one single way — we expect that you will jump from section to section based upon your needs and plans.

We wrote this book both with the construction trade professional and the novice in mind. For the do-it-yourselfer, we've packed in lessons learned from a combined 80-plus years of working as electricians, technicians, and computer and networking geeks. We hope you can relate to these lessons as you complete your projects.

If you're a professional, *Wiring Your Digital Home For Dummies* provides a heads-up on features you may want to include in the next home you wire, and it gives some insights about what your residential customers will ask you to do in the days and years to come. For builders, architects, engineers, designers, and electricians, this book is not only a reference but also a marketing checklist. As a builder, use it to work with the buyer the next time you're asked to quote a price for a new home. Electrical contractors will want to use this book when working with the builder to offer options in the wiring contract.

Conventions Used in This Book

When we refer to or paraphrase some section of *the code,* we mean the National Electrical Code (NEC) sponsored by the National Fire Protection Association (NFPA). Often we use the word *must* without referring specifically to the code. This usually means either the code requires it or the circuit won't work correctly any other way. *Wiring to code* means meeting a minimum standard. Most of the time this minimum standard is sufficient.

In some cases, we refer you to helpful resources on the Internet. Web addresses are printed this way: `www.wiley.com`.

What You Don't Have to Read

It's perfectly okay to skip items you already know or don't care about. For example, if you already know the code inside and out, then you can probably skip stuff that is marked with the Code Stuff icon (although we think that a quick refresher is always a good idea).

In some cases we include sidebars, which provide nice-to-know information. Sidebars don't contain critical information, so you can safely skip them if they don't meet your current need.

And finally, it's a good idea to read all paragraphs marked with Warning icons. The information in those paragraphs is critical and will prevent mistakes that could cost you — or hurt you.

Foolish Assumptions

Whether you know nothing about wiring, everything about wiring, or you're somewhere in between, all we assume about you is that you want to better understand modern home wiring and how best to make it work with digital-age conveniences. You might be looking to build a new home or planning to upgrade your existing home. You might be an architect or engineer responsible for designing and selecting parts for someone else's home. You may be a builder or electrician looking to market digital-home features in your future jobs.

Whatever your reason for picking up this book, we think that when you're done reading you'll be in a better position to articulate and act on your own ideas and specific needs as you work to create your ideal digital home.

How This Book Is Organized

As electricians and technicians, we're very interested in the parts that make up the whole of the house wiring job. A home works well only when all its systems and subsystems work in harmony with one another. Every technical job eventually comes down to nuts and bolts, pieces and parts, step one followed by step two, and tab A going onto slot B. Our entire wired world is based on bringing the right parts together at the right time in the right way. Like wiring systems, this book is an assembly of parts that work together to make the whole. The parts, chapters, and topics break subjects down into bite-size pieces that you can easily use.

Although each part and chapter covers a unique topic, you may notice some overlapping subject material. We did this so you catch the complementary relationships between such things as (for example) security alarms and surveillance cameras.

Use the table of contents or index to skim for topics of immediate concern or to refresh yourself on information of interest after your first read. This book can be a valuable reference as you work though projects for many years to come. The table of contents, chapter titles, section headings, and icons help you quickly find the information you're seeking.

Part 1: Installing Power Distribution and Basic Wiring

Regardless of where your electrical power is coming from — a potato, a coin battery, or the power company — you need to get the power to the place that most needs it, and you must keep it under control at all times. The same goes for phone service and other systems. The chapters in Part I provide the groundwork for bringing the wires into your home and then distributing them to your various living spaces.

- **Chapter 1:** Use this chapter to reach out for your digital future and find inspiration for planning your new digital home or next remodeling project. This chapter also provides tips on selecting a contractor, and we show you which tools you'll need.

- **Chapter 2:** From the red tape of building permits to dealing with the power company, this chapter is all about getting services to your home, be it power, phone, cable, or Internet. We show you how to set up temporary services at a construction site, and how to install permanent service entrances and distribution panels for power, phone, and cable TV.

- **Chapter 3:** This chapter tells you how to get the right kind of wires to the lights, phones, TVs, and computers in every nook and cranny of your home.

- **Chapter 4:** Bare electrical wiring isn't pretty or safe. This chapter shows you how to make the final connections, install attractive trim, and make sure everything works perfectly.

- **Chapter 5:** Written for the control *enthusiast* in all of us, this chapter explains why you will need a 100-pocket vest to carry all of the remote controls for your home. No, not really. But Chapter 5 does help you get complete control of anything electrical, including lights and appliances.

Part II: Adding Communication, Audio, and Video Systems

Part II covers the convenience and luxury items that help you get the most enjoyment out of your investment.

- **Chapter 6:** In this chapter we chat with you about phone stuff, including traditional analog systems as well as digital, Internet-based phone systems. We show you how to install a home telephone exchange system that lets you make calls from the kitchen to the garage, and we show how to use your Internet service to affordably call distant relatives and friends. This is the quintessential chit-chat cheaply chapter.

- **Chapter 7:** This chapter discusses intercom systems that let you ask who's at the door while you're in the kitchen and push a button to let Mr. McMahon in with the million-dollar check, if it's really him.

- **Chapter 8:** This chapter is all about the wiring that brings entertainment to a video screen near you. We show how to run TV cable throughout the home while maintaining great video-signal strength. We also introduce home fiber optic services, which are becoming increasingly available.

✔ **Chapter 9:** Here we show you how to leverage the stereo players and receivers you own to bring wonderful stereo sound — including the controls for that sound — into every room.

✔ **Chapter 10:** This chapter details how to wire for and get the most enjoyment out of your theater and surround sound systems. In addition to dedicated home theaters, this chapter also helps you wire a multi-use family room

✔ **Chapter 11:** This chapter helps you select, wire, and place video cameras, which add to your home's convenience and security.

Part III: Installing Home Networks and Advanced Technology

This section covers the physical backbone and digital logic foundation for hooking up a modern automated home.

✔ **Chapter 12:** This chapter covers the installation of network wiring, routers, firewalls, and network hubs and switches to connect to the Internet.

✔ **Chapter 13:** Here we discuss the basics of integrating advanced controls and computer software to facilitate voice command and true automatic control of devices in your home.

Part IV: Security and Safety Systems

Part IV explains some ways to enhance the safety and security of your domicile by including alarm features and backup power.

✔ **Chapter 14:** Here we show you how to install security alarms and other safety features.

✔ **Chapter 15:** This chapter covers the installation of mechanical and solid-state backup systems to provide nonstop electrical power to critical systems, even in the event of a power outage. Earth-friendly sun- and wind-power backup systems are also covered briefly.

Part V: Extending Technology to Outdoor Living Spaces

Many people feel torn when they're inside watching a good movie and the weather outside is so inviting. Part V shows you how to move some of your entertainment technologies outside so you can enjoy the outdoors in new ways.

- ✔ **Chapter 16:** This information is all about bringing power and communications services beyond the confines of your home's wall to outbuildings and outdoor living spaces.

- ✔ **Chapter 17:** This chapter briefly covers some additional ways to bring network and other services to the outdoor landscape. We also show you how to build your own driveway traffic light as a just-for-fun project.

Part VI: The Part of Tens

Following the standard *For Dummies* roadmap, we included a Part of Tens. In fact, we liked the idea so much that we included three full chapters of Tens, making this really a Part of 30. These chapters are a ready reference long after you've read the rest of the book ten times.

- ✔ **Chapter 18:** This chapter takes you away on a World Wide Web search to ten of our favorite wiring and digital technology Web sites. Expect to find lots of great online information and links to even more helpful sites.

- ✔ **Chapter 19:** In this chapter we talk about the ten biggest wiring no-nos, so be sure to read this chapter before you pull your first foot of wire.

- ✔ **Chapter 20:** At some time in your life (if it hasn't happened already), you'll be inundated with requests for assistance. Someone is bound to ask you for help; you might even have a problem of your very own to solve. When that happens, bring Chapter 20 to the rescue with its ten universal troubleshooting tips.

Part VII: Appendixes

This part of the book contains the appendixes, which is where we stuck information that was important but didn't fit in the rest of the book.

- ✔ **Appendix A:** This appendix provides a list of product sources, showing you where to go to find the supplies you need for any wiring project.

- ✔ **Appendix B:** This appendix delves into electrical theory, wire properties, and provides ampacity tables from the National Electrical Code.

- ✔ **Appendix C:** This appendix gives you an overview of what's on the CD that's included with this book. It also provides installation instructions.

Icons Used in This Book

We use various icons in the margins to help organize some of the material and identify our intentions.

Whenever you see the Tip icon, it's our way of keeping your forehead somewhat rounded. If you don't read these tips, you may flatten your forehead with repeated smacking as you keep saying, "Now, why didn't I think of that?" Tips are our way of putting you and your project on the fast track to completion, with less effort and (hopefully) fewer mistakes.

If this book included quiz questions, paragraphs next to the Remember icon are the answers. We repeat these important things because they're worth remembering.

If you watch racing events, you're likely familiar with the caution flag. When this flag comes out, it's time to slow down and look for speed bumps, oil slicks, or debris ahead. The Warning icon is our caution flag. Think of these as must-read items. Once you read and understand these warnings, the green flag will be out for you on the next turn.

Sometimes you feel like you're in the know, and sometimes you don't. When you want to know more about the whys, hows, and wherefores of the technical side of home wiring, read these technical background and detail exposé items with wild-hearted expectation. Or feel free to skip them altogether.

Whenever you see this icon, pay particular attention to ensure that you follow the rules laid down by the building authority. In most cases the code we refer to is the NEC sponsored by the NFPA, which is adopted as the law of the land by code-enforcement authorities all over the United States (and even some other countries). We believe the code authors meant for you to do things the way they're explained in Code Stuff paragraphs. Whenever in doubt about a code question, check the latest code book or handbook, a licensed electrical professional, or consult with the governing code-enforcement authority.

Where to Go from Here

Although we don't recommend pulling out sections of the book to reorder the chapters, you can read them in any order you like. If you're a total wiring novice, you probably want to start with the first four chapters. They provide a foundation of knowledge, skills, and abilities that support the rest of the book (and the rest of your work). After that, follow your muse (or your immediate construction plans) to the topics that interest you most.

Part I
Installing Power Distribution and Basic Wiring

The 5th Wave   By Rich Tennant

"The kids are getting up right now. When we wired the house we added vibrating pager technology to their bunkbeds."

In this part . . .

This part discusses what you need to keep the electrons contained and under your control so you can do useful — and innovative and entertaining — things. The skilled wiring work basics covered in these chapters apply to the rest of the book. The information contained in these chapters proves to be useful for any home wiring project.

Chapter 1

Designing Your Digital Dream Home

Aesthetically, a digital home is a warm, welcoming abode — a place where you love to spend time and enjoy life with your family and close friends. The digital home has just the right lighting in every space, whether that space is used for reading, computing, or a favorite hobby. A digital home is a place where technology enhances and eases your lifestyle and maximizes the enjoyment of your surroundings. A modern digital home is a habitat where elements of shape, infrastructure, and control combine to meet your needs with a maximum of convenience.

Functionally, a digital home is one that takes full advantage of the latest technologies for electronics, networking, communications, and electromechanical devices. The well-wired contemporary digital home also anticipates coming advances and adapts easily to future changes. Each digital home is unique, tailored to the needs and desires of the individual homeowner; yet a well thought-out digital home contains wiring and electronic equipment that meets accepted standards of construction and design.

Are you ready to start planning your digital home? This chapter shows you some of the benefits of a digital home and gets you started with the designing and planning process. We go over some of the features you may want to incorporate and help you decide whether you want to be your own contractor.

Living on Digital Easy Street

Close your eyes and imagine yourself in the ultimate digital home. It's Saturday and no one has to go to work or school. You are awakened to a sun-drenched morning by the quietly rising sound of a string quartet playing a classic movement by Tchaikovsky. As you enter the bathroom, the lights come up to a warm glow automatically. The sink water is instantly warm with the first twist of the 24-carat gold-plated faucet as you wash your face and take care of dental hygiene. After you emerge from your shower, the rack-warmed towels are an arm's reach away.

The kitchen welcomes you with the fresh wafting aroma of Tanzanian pea-berry coffee, and your favorite morning news show tunes in on the flip-down television screen the instant you enter the breakfast nook. After the news, you walk out to the patio and read the newspaper editorials. As you leave the kitchen space, the TV turns off automatically. It is a sunny morning but still a little chilly outside, so you press a remote control button to light the gas fireplace and kick on its built-in circulation fan. As the rising sun warms the morning air, you press another button to turn off the fireplace.

It's a nice morning, so you pull out your hand-held computer and type a few e-mails, which you send via your wireless network. Later, you use the PC workstation in your kitchen to copy some digital photos from your camera and send them to grandma in Arizona. While online, you check the local Doppler weather radar image to see if any clouds are in the area. There are none, so you decide to take a walk in the park.

When you return home in the evening, you find that the microwave has just cooked a light dinner moments before your return. Later, you watch a newly released DVD in your home theater. After the movie the auto-vac-bot begins its quest for stray popcorn fragments, gliding almost silently across the floor. Lights in rooms and hallways sense your presence and automatically turn on and off as you pass through, ready to turn in for the night.

The scenario presented here illustrates just some of the possibilities of the modern digital home. Your dream home may look a little different, but with proper planning the possibilities are virtually limitless. The next few sections help you start your plan for your own digital home.

Planning Your Digital Dream Home

It may seem easier to design and build your digital dream home from the ground up, but any home can be adapted to include modern wiring, controls, appliances, computers, and other technology. As you start planning your digital home, you need to consider several factors:

- ✔ **Budget:** What can you afford? Does your home have enough space for the features you want?

- ✔ **Features:** Make a list of the features you want.

- ✔ **Appliance locations and sizes:** Choose where you want certain appliances, and determine what size each appliance should be.

- ✔ **Outlets:** Determine the type, location, and number of outlets you need before construction begins.

Define your requirements in writing to help focus you and your contractor on meeting the design objectives. Page though this book chapter by chapter, taking note of the items you want to include in your own digital home. Also, go through each room in your home (or your home plan) and make a list of features you want in each of those rooms. Be specific in your plan, because it influences the wiring installed in each room.

Designing for new construction

When building new homes, contractors often tend to do things the way they have done them in previous homes. As the homeowner of a new house — or a do-it-yourselfer building your own home — it is absolutely critical that you

- ✔ Include your digital home plans in the design specifications.

- ✔ Communicate to everyone involved the need for neatness and attention to detail.

For example, wiring runs should be made so that they minimize *crosstalk* (interference between power supply wires and communication wires). Different wiring types should have adequate separation, particularly on long parallel runs.

The *NEC (National Electrical Code)* requires a minimum separation of 4" between communication cables and open conductor power wires. (*Open conductor* is a wiring system used prior to the 1950s and is often referred to as *knob and tube wiring.*) To minimize crosstalk, however, we recommend at least 6" between communication cables and any type of power wires. More separation is better.

Remodeling an existing residence

Homeowners often undertake remodeling projects involving one or two rooms. If you're planning a project, consider rewiring and including additional elements that can take advantage of newer technology.

The demolition and removal of old wiring, fixtures, and equipment is an added cost to consider when undertaking a remodeling project. If you abandon wires because they cannot be fully removed, take extra care to ensure that those abandoned wires cannot be accidentally reenergized later. To do this, cut the wires off flush with the box surface they protrude through, or cut them off in a few places along their route.

When planning your remodeling project, schedule the work so that one trade is not too far ahead of or behind the others. If you're working with a contractor, make sure he takes this into account. For example, the rough-in wiring must be done and the boxes mounted before new drywall is started. Pay close attention to the timeline and to job dependencies.

Completing single-focus projects

You may not have the time or budget to build, remodel, or upgrade your entire home to accommodate a digital lifestyle all at once. Instead, you may want to focus on one living space or one project at a time. Perhaps you have become serious about getting all the value possible from your home computers and want to build a home network to share Internet connections, printers, and fax services. Or maybe you're not satisfied with only two separate smoke alarms in the whole house. Situations like this make for perfect single-focus projects. You can complete many a project without major destruction and reconstruction. We show you some of these projects in Chapters 11 and 17.

Regardless of your project scope, include

- ✔ Starting with the floor plan, then onto the fixture, appliance, and furniture layouts, in that order, to determine where the wiring infrastructure will go.
- ✔ Separating different wiring types.
- ✔ Planning routes for power and communication cabling before drilling.

- ✔ Specifying exact locations for appliances, utilities, services, and outlet boxes.
- ✔ Planning racks, shelves, and mountings.
- ✔ Purchasing or gathering the required tools and equipment.
- ✔ Accounting for any job dependencies and the necessary work sequence.
- ✔ Determining how your plan alternatives affect the overall budget.
- ✔ Visiting the site often to ensure your plans are being implemented properly.

Choosing the Contractor — or Being Your Own

When using a professional contractor, the most important thing (besides writing the check) is knowing what you want included in your home and articulating your needs accurately to a reputable builder or contractor. Defining the work is the same whether you decide to go the do-it-yourself route or hire a contractor. And, of course, you need to choose a competent contractor.

Selecting a contractor

"How," you wonder, "can I be sure I am choosing the right builder or contractor for my project?" Thanks for asking! Table 1-1 offers some of the things to consider asking or finding out about your prospective contractor.

Table 1-1	Interviewing a Prospective Contractor	
Question	*Answer You Want*	*Why*
How long have you been in your business or trade?	Since the earth cooled.	Generally, you want to hire a contractor with some experience in the business. Proceed with caution if the contractor has fewer than four years' experience.
Do you have worker's compensation and liability insurance?	Yes.	If he doesn't have insurance and his workers are injured on your premises, you may become liable.

(continued)

Table 1-1 *(continued)*

Question	Answer You Want	Why
What's your experience with similar projects?	I've done jobs similar to this one.	When a contractor has done a job similar to your project before, his learning from experience should benefit your project.
Can you provide industry, trade, and customer references?	You betcha.	If others speak well of the contractor's work and performance, you are more likely to get your project done to your satisfaction.
Can I see examples of prior work?	Uh huh.	This one really separates the ho hum contractors from the ones whose attention to detail is unparalleled. If the contracting firm is willing to show you prior work and let you be in the same space as prior customers, you can expect a great finish on your project as well.
Are you a member of a professional organization or trade association?	Yep.	You would prefer a contactor who's learning from others in the trade and makes a contribution to the greater good.
What's your community involvement?	I'm heavily involved.	Having a contractor willing to giving something back shows that she is concerned with more than making a profit and realizes that all the work she does benefits the community.
Can I inspect your vehicle? (Okay, you don't really ask this.)	Huh?	What's the general appearance of the contractor's equipment, vehicles, tools, and employees? If the things you *can* see aren't up to par, those things you *can't* see after installation have little chance of being done in a neat, orderly, and workmanlike manner.

Question	Answer You Want	Why
Do you have all the required licenses?	Oh yes.	States differ in what type of work requires a license. The license process is designed to provide some level of assurance that the license holder will do work that is safe and up to current building and electrical codes.
Has anyone ever complained about your work?	No. (Or "Yes, once, and we solved the problem.")	You don't want to be the next in a long string of complaints. Choose a contractor who stands behind his work and satisfies his prior customers.
Where are your positive attitude and amiable manner?	You could ask outright, but you're likelier to see the answer just by watching.	The look of a can-do attitude can mean a number of things, none of them good. If you want to fight, you hire a boxer; your contractor should be amiable and respect you as a valued customer.

These questions will help you start evaluating a contractor or builder, but may not include everything that is important to you, so add to it if needed. High-quality builders, remodeling contractors, and electrical contractors are proud of the work they do and are not offended if you check them out. Do your homework so you won't become the next horror story on the pages of contractor dissatisfaction.

Show me the cost

Get an estimate from more than one contractor if you lack trusted recommendations, especially on expensive projects. An estimate considerably lower than another is usually a red flag; the lowest estimate may not be the best choice. The chosen contractor should give you a written contract detailing the work to be done. Avoid the contractor who says, "Oh, I didn't know you wanted x, y, and z done, too. That's going to cost an arm and a leg." Know his schedule before you sign — when he will start and when he expects to finish.

Find out what your state laws are regarding worker's compensation. If the contractor on your project doesn't have insurance, you may become liable for any on-the-job injuries experienced by workers on your project.

Being your own contractor

Doing major construction work is not for the timid . . . well, not for the *too* timid, anyway. If you already have the skills and some experience, the decision to be your own contractor may be easier. If this is your first construction or remodeling project and you are willing to learn, the knowledge you gain will lead to increased confidence tackling future projects as well. The bottom line is this: Can you cheerfully take full responsibility for the outcome? If so, then you are ready to begin.

Adequate preparation is often the only thing that separates the professional from the do-it-yourselfer. One expects a professional electrician or network installer to come to a job site equipped with the time, talent, tools, pieces (screws, nails, brackets, and the like), and important parts needed to get the job done in one quick visit. The do-it-yourselfer, on the other hand, usually has to run to the hardware store often for special tools or extra parts.

Careful planning can prevent delays. Visualize yourself doing the work one step at a time. Collect all of the tools and equipment you need beforehand, along with the components, wire, hardware, and other things you need to finish the task. Use your project plan to make a list of the things you need, and check the items off the list as you buy them.

Gathering Tools and Equipment

You're going to need a lot of tools — some basic, some specialized — to complete your project. Some of these tools are worth owning so they're readily available for minor repairs. You may want to rent more expensive, seldom-used power equipment, especially in the case of specialty tools like heavy-duty cement saws or core drills. The following sections list some of the hand tools, power tools, and test equipment that you need as you build and maintain your digital home.

Hand tools

Acquiring more hand tools is usually a good thing, because they typically get used a lot. Before you become your own contractor you will need to own or have access to a basic issue of hand tools, including

- 8" diagonal wire cutter
- 9" lineman's pliers
- Stubby and long-handled screwdrivers for each of the following sizes: #2 phillips, ⅛", ¼", and ⅜" flat-blade
- Wire stripper
- Cable stripper
- Hack saw and assorted blades
- Hole saw
- RJ-45 (Ethernet cable) crimper/cutter
- RG-6 (coaxial TV cable) crimper
- Bubble level
- Folding ruler and tape measure

Power tools

In addition to a basic set of hand tools, you need some power tools. Power tools can be expensive, but the ones listed here are used so frequently that you should own them.

- **Drill:** Look for a drill that can make it through 2" × 4" framing and 2" × 8" floor joists. A right-angle power drill is best because the right angle gives you leverage against the twisting action, making drilling easier and safer.

- **Hammer drill:** This comes in handy when mounting service panels and backboards to masonry or concrete. If you don't want to invest in a hammer drill, you can also use a .20-caliber power fastener.

- **Circular saw:** Find a saw with comfortable grips for both hands so you can easily control the cut.

- **Rechargeable battery-powered screw gun:** This tool is handy for drilling screws to quickly mount junction boxes and other items. Make sure you have an assortment of driver tips, including a lot of extra Phillips head tips; they are used most frequently.

- **Reciprocating saw:** With a reciprocating saw and carbide blades, many tough cutting jobs become no more difficult than cutting cold butter.

- **Expendable items:** Shop for drill bits, assorted machine bits, and ¾", 1", and 1½" ship augers. To drill though floor joists purchase 1½", 2", and 2½" self-feed bits. You also need extra hack saw blades, work gloves, eye protection (goggles or a clear face mask), HEPA dust mask and filters, and a fully stocked first-aid kit.

Test equipment

You need a multimeter, and need to decide between digital and analog:

- ✔ **Digital multimeters** come with a selector switch to measure AC/DC voltages, ohms, or low-amperage currents. This version is inexpensive and popular.

- ✔ **Analog multimeters** come with a selector switch for measuring voltage, ohms, and current. Analog makes a better troubleshooting tool, partly because you don't have to constantly digest the changing digits.

You also need these goodies:

- ✔ Neon test light
- ✔ Low-voltage test light/continuity tester
- ✔ Category 5 network cable tester

Chapter 2

Bringing In the Services

· ·

· ·

*I*f you want to fill your home with a lot of cool digital gadgets, it goes without saying that your house must be connected to an electrical power source. Technology doesn't run on magic beans.

You have to equip your home with an electrical distribution system to support your digital lifestyle. The distribution system — generally referred to as your *electrical service* — receives big power from the utility company (unless you use an alternative power source) and splits it into usable chunks. You must choose the service's location and proper size, and then get all the required permits. Other considerations, such as whether you install overhead or underground service, may be up to you or your power company.

This chapter helps you plan for and install your electrical service. It also introduces the equipment you'll use, explains some electrical terms, and looks at how electrical power is produced and sent to your home.

Understanding the Power You Need

As you probably already know, most electricity is generated at power plants. Those plants typically run on coal, natural gas, nuclear power, hydroelectric generators, or hamster wheels. The electricity is transmitted to your local power company, which then distributes it to individual customers like yourself. Most likely, your home is fed by 60-cycle 120/240-volt *alternating current (AC)*. What does this mean? Read on.

Alternating stuff

When a power plant generates power, it does so by rotating a magnet so that it passes by a coil. The voltage rises as the magnet nears the coil, then decays as the magnet continues past the coil. As the magnet's opposite pole nears the coil, the voltage builds in the opposite direction. (Voltage is explained in the next section.) The voltage mimics a sine wave like the one illustrated in Figure 2-1, and is said to be *alternating current* because it alternates between positive and negative; first the electrons flow in one direction through the circuit and then in the opposite direction. When the current alternates 60 times per second, it is called *60 cycle.* By the way, these cycles are also called *Hertz,* after the German physicist Heinrich Hertz, who was the first person to artificially produce radio waves.

Current that doesn't alternate between poles is called *direct current (DC).* DC power flows in one direction. The current from a battery (from the one in your car to the one in your iPod) is direct current.

Transforming current with transformers

When AC comes from the power company, it's sent in thousands of volts. Devices called *transformers* step that power down to the 120/240-volt power used in your home. These transformers work on a simple ratio. A transformer with 100 turns on the input coil (primary) and 10 turns on the output coil (secondary) has a 10:1 step-down ratio. For every 10 volts fed into the primary, you get 1 volt out of the secondary. Transformers are *reversible,* meaning that a transformer with a 10:1 ratio can step voltage up from 1 volt to 10 volts.

Because electricity has to travel long distances before getting to your home, the power company uses transformers to lessen line loss. Most power is generated at 15–25 kilovolts (KV) and stepped as high as 236 KV for transmission over long distances. The very high voltage is stepped down to a few thousand volts in residential areas, and then further stepped down to 120/240 volts at or near your home. If 236 volts are lost over the lines of the 236 KV system, this represents a line loss of 1/10 of 1 percent. But if the system were a straight 240 volts from the supply to the point of use, you would wind up with only 4 volts in your home.

So, your power company supplies your home with transformed AC power. However, most of the digital stuff in your home runs on DC power. This is why you usually plug them into your AC power outlets with *AC adapters,* which are power cords with small rectangular blocks on them. The block on an AC adapter includes a transformer that steps down the 120-volt AC wall power to a lower voltage, which varies depending on the device. The AC adapter also includes a device called a *rectifier,* which converts AC voltage to DC voltage.

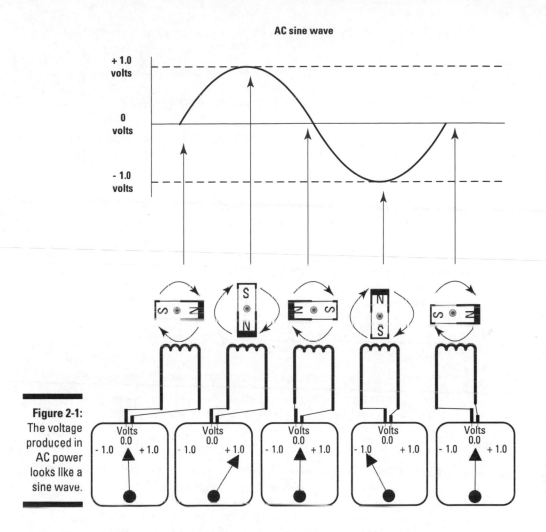

Figure 2-1:
The voltage produced in AC power looks like a sine wave.

Amps and volts and other terms

Making the permanent connection to the electricity supplied by your power company happens just once, so getting it done right is important. We recommend that you invest some time in getting familiar with the terms and equipment you need to do the job properly. It's good to know this stuff, even if an electrical contractor is doing the work for you, because you want to make sure that you get an installation that will meet your home's needs. Some of the electrical terms you'll encounter include:

- **Amps:** Short for *amperes,* a measurement of electrical current flow. Amps measure the amount of current a conductor can carry. The measurement also specifies the size (electrical capacity) of electrical items, such as a 100-amp panel or a 20-amp breaker.

- **AWG (American wire gauge):** The diameter of a wire. Wire diameter is also expressed as the Brown and Sharpe Wire Gauge (B&S). To determine the actual diameter of a wire in *mils* (a mil is 0.001 inch) use $5 \times 92^{(36-AWG)/39}$. For sizes 1/0 through 4/0 use -1 to -4.

- **CMA (circular mil area):** The wire's diameter is expressed in mils squared. CMA helps determine how much current a conductor can carry.

- **Breaker:** Common term for a circuit breaker. Circuit breakers close and open circuits. Circuit breakers have current ratings in amps to denote how many amps are allowed to pass before the breaker is tripped. When a breaker *trips,* the circuit is open and no current flows.

- **Conduit or cable:** The medium by which you bring power from point to point. Conduits or cables contain *conductors* (wires) that actually carry the power.

- **Current:** The flow of electrical energy, as measured in amps.

- **Distribution panel:** The equipment that parcels out power to different circuits and locations. This panel is also sometimes called a *breaker panel* or *service panel*.

- **Fuse:** Works like a circuit breaker, but is a one-time-use device.

- **Ground:** Earth or connected to earth; this term also refers to the bare ground conductors or wires with green insulation on the conductors. The ground wires aren't intended for carrying any current unless there's a fault condition. A ground wire's purpose is threefold: to ensure the breaker trips on a fault condition; to divert lightning strikes to ground; and to protect the equipment user from becoming the path to ground.

- **Grounded:** Denotes something connected to ground. The white or neutral conductor is referred to as the *grounded conductor* because the neutral conductor is the only current-carrying conductor connected to ground in the service-entrance panel. The difference between the *ground wire* and the *grounded conductor* (or neutral wire) is that when everything is working normally, the neutral wire carries the return current and the ground wire carries no current at all.

- **Grounding:** The process or action of connecting to ground.

- ✔ **Junction:** The point where wires or cables are joined together. Junctions are located in junction boxes with the exception of some outdoor cables. Overhead services cables for example connect to the home's entrance cables without using a junction box.

- ✔ **Meter:** Watt-hour meter. The power company uses this device to measure your home's power usage. Test meters also measure volts (voltmeter), amps (ammeter), ohms (ohmmeter), or power factor meter.

- ✔ **Meter socket:** The box the power company uses to plug in its usage meter.

- ✔ **Power:** The product of volts multiplied by amps expressed in *watts (W)* or *volt amps (VA)*. The ungrounded conductors that carry power are also sometimes called the *power wires* or *energized conductors*.

- ✔ **Service:** The conductors and equipment bringing power from the utility to the premises' service disconnect.

- ✔ **Service disconnect:** The one to six disconnects that interrupt all power from the power company. This is usually a single main circuit breaker in the service panel. If any disconnect is installed ahead of the service panel, this disconnect then becomes the service disconnect and the service panel becomes a branch panel.

- ✔ **VA (volt amps):** Measurement of power. VA is the product of volts times amps.

- ✔ **Volt:** The international measurement of electrical potential. One volt is the measurement of the electromotive force necessary to carry one amp of current across a resistance of one ohm.

- ✔ **Watt:** The product of volts times amps in a DC circuit. In an AC circuit, wattage is the product of volts times amps times the power factor.

Fluorescent lights and rotating equipment

As we mention in this chapter, 60-cycle AC voltage actually goes to 0 volts 60 times per second. When 60-cycle AC voltage is used to power *filament lights* (standard light bulbs), the filament doesn't cool off fast enough to go completely dark. In early U.S. systems that used 25-cycle current, a flicker could easily be seen in filament bulbs; 60-cycle AC current is too fast for the eye to detect a flicker in filament lights.

Unlike filament lights, fluorescent lights actually go out when the cycle crosses 0. When fluorescent lights illuminate rotating equipment — like in a workshop or manufacturing plant — a *strobe condition* can occur. (This effect is similar to what you see in movies when wheels or propeller blades seem to be turning backwards. When this happens in movies, the frame speed is nearly matched with the cycle of the rotating item.) A rotating piece of equipment under a fluorescent light can appear to be standing still when it is, in fact, turning. If you illuminate your work area with fluorescent lights, either take extra care around spinning tools and equipment or consider using filament lights instead.

Meeting Power Company and Code Requirements

You're going to have to jump through some hoops to get power to your home. We've worked in various jurisdictions all over the United States, and the only thing they have in common is that they're all different. The only way to sort out your exact requirements is to make phone calls or personal visits to your power company's building code office and meet with the building inspectors. The following sections help you ask the right questions of the regulatory officials when you talk to them.

Getting permitted

A homeowner can do his own wiring in his own home without hiring a licensed electrical contractor. In most areas, or *jurisdictions,* the owner must be living in the home or intend to live in the home. Minor electrical work — such as replacing a single outlet or installing a new ceiling fan — doesn't require a permit in most jurisdictions. But if you do more extensive work, you're usually required to get a permit. The process usually goes as follows:

1. **Find the authority that has jurisdiction, which can be your**

   - Township
   - City
   - County
   - State
   - Tribe

   The quickest way to find the right jurisdiction is to start at the lowest level, either township or city. If they don't perform the inspections they can refer you to who does. The power company serving your area may know this information.

2. **You fill out the required form and take it, or mail it, along with the permit fee, to the authority.**

   Some jurisdictions have the forms available online.

3. **The authority reviews the form, accepts your money, and issues the permit.**

   Mailed permits are sometimes returned for additional information. Make sure you fill in the form completely.

Some jurisdictions have a flat fee for a new construction home-wiring project. In some jurisdictions, you have to itemize the number of circuits, receptacles, fixtures, and so forth to determine the inspection fee.

4. **The electrical inspector visits your project site and checks the work.**

   If a discrepancy (code violation) is found, you're notified in person, by phone, or in writing; you're told how and when to correct the problem. A new home may have four or more inspections, one each for temporary power, electrical service, electrical rough in, and electrical final (trim out). Each of these inspections may require one or more follow-up inspections, extending the total to eight or more.

Installing in light of code requirements

When you install electrical service for a home, whether it's new construction or an upgrade, the electrical code requires that you do a *load calculation* to determine the correct size for your electrical service. Most jurisdictions don't enforce this requirement, but for safety's sake it's worth doing. The minimum service size allowed to supply a residence is one that carries a total electrical load of 100 amps. With all the circuits needed in a modern home, we recommend installing a 200-amp service panel with 40 circuits unless the load calculations require a larger one.

Load is calculated in *volt amps (VA)*, which is the product of volts times amps. For a residence, the load calculation includes a general lighting load of 3 VA per square foot of habitable space, plus any additional loads present. For the service load, the first 3,000 VA are calculated at 100-percent usage and any remaining load is calculated at 35-percent usage. The usage percentages are called *demand factors*. Demand factors are applied because it's unlikely everything will be on at the same time. If the load calculation is in excess of 120,000 VA, the demand factor is 25 percent for the remainder of the load in excess of 120,000 VA. You must also add in a minimum small-appliance load of 3,000 VA for the kitchen and 1,500 VA for the laundry. The results are added to determine the total calculated load.

Table 2-1 shows a sample load calculation for a 2,000-square-foot home. As you can see in the table, the total calculated load is 19,125 VA. To determine the minimum amperage you need for your electrical service, divide the calculated VA load by 240, which is typical residential voltage:

19,125 VA ÷ 240 volts = 79.69 amps

The sample load calculation in Table 2-1 calculates 2,000 square feet at 3 VA per square foot equaling 6,000 VA and adds the two kitchen circuits (3,000 VA plus the 1,500 VA laundry circuit). All of these total 10,500 VA. By code, only the first 3,000 VA of this 10,500 load is calculated at 100-percent usage. By using the allowed demand factor, the remaining 7,500 VA is calculated at 35 percent adding 2,625 VA to the load and yielding a subtotal load of 5,625 VA.

In addition to the calculations, we have included an 8,000-VA load for the electric range and a 5,500-VA load for the electric dryer. Adding these loads brings a total of 19,125 VA. If the range or dryer were gas, you'd eliminate them from the calculation. If your project has any additional loads, such as a furnace or air conditioner, they have to be added to the load calculation.

Table 2-1	Sample Service Load Calculation
Service Calculation	*Volt Amps*
2,000 × 3 VA	6,000
Kitchen Appliance	3,000
Laundry	1,500
Total	**10,500**
First 3,000 VA 100%	3,000
10,500 − 3,000 at 35%	2,625
Load	5,625
Range	8,000
Dryer	5,500
Total Calculated Load	**19,125**
19,125 VA ÷ 240 volts	79.69 amps

As you can see, the 2,000-square-foot home in Table 2-1 needs at least (a rounded-up-to) 80-amp service. Code requires at least a 100-amp service for residences. Code also dictates the minimum number of circuits required to serve the 2,000-square-foot load calculation. Using the code requirements for circuit calculation for 2000 square feet at 3 VA per square foot requires a minimum of four 15-amp 2-wire circuits or three 20-amp 2-wire circuits. Doing the math for the 15-amp circuits: 2,000 × 3 = 6,000 VA ÷ 120 volts = 50 amps. 50 amps ÷ 15 = 3⅓, so round up the result to 4 circuits. Doing the calculations for the 20-amp circuits, the steps are: 6,000 VA ÷ 120 = 2.5; round up the result to 3 circuits.

Some electrical contractors do use the result of these calculations to wire the home, and why not — it's code. But it is also doing a job on the cheap. Remember, the code is a minimum. We believe it is much better to have more circuits than the required minimum. Some electrical inspectors say that you can only have 11 receptacles on a 20-amp circuit and 8 on a 15-amp circuit. But that confuses commercial requirements with residential requirements. For commercial buildings whose load is unknown, the receptacle load is calculated at 180 VA per receptacle. Residences have no limit to the number of receptacles you can put on a circuit. You need only provide at least the calculated minimum number of circuits as explained earlier in this chapter.

For a 2000-square-foot home, code requires you to have

- Three or four general lighting circuits to supply lights and receptacles
- Two 20-amp circuits to serve the 3,000-VA kitchen receptacles
- One 20-amp circuit to supply the 1,500-VA laundry receptacle(s)
- One 20-amp circuit to supply the bathroom receptacle(s). (This circuit, although required, doesn't have to be included separately in the load calculation.) This circuit can serve one or more receptacles; it can also be used to serve more than one bathroom.

These minimum circuits are required by code. In Chapter 3, we talk about why we recommend many more circuits than the required minimum.

Choosing a circuit panel

Manufacturers produce residential panels in various sizes, including 100-, 125-, 150-, and 200-amp versions. The 100- and 200-amp panels are the most popular. It is usually cost-effective to choose a 200-amp panel, especially if you envision a lot of electrical expansion in your home later. The 100-amp panels have a maximum of 32 circuit-breaker spaces, and the 200-amp panels have up to 40 spaces. These panels are equipped with a main circuit breaker; if the panel's main breaker turns off all the power in the residence, or if it's one of up to six such panels in a group that does it, it must be marked as a *service disconnect*. If they're sub-panels, a *MAIN* marking label is appropriate.

The electrical code limits the number of circuits in a panel to 42. Here we mean a circuit is a space where a single pole breaker can be installed. For a single-phase system, if more than 40 spaces are required, you must install more panels. The largest three-phase panel has 42 circuit spaces. The code also requires that all power be turned off with no more than six hand operations. Additionally, these disconnects are required to be grouped for one occupancy. The electrical code doesn't define an occupancy, which assumes the word is commonly defined. We take *occupancy* to mean an independent dwelling unit, such as a single-family house or an apartment.

Figure 2-2 shows a Square D 200-amp 40-circuit panel. Over the years, many manufacturers and styles have come and gone, but Square D uses the same breaker and panel style that they introduced many years ago. We like the consistency of this company. A new Square D breaker made today will fit in panels that were installed 40 years ago.

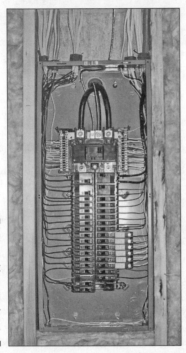

Figure 2-2:
Square D
circuit
panels have
changed
little over
the years.

Very large houses commonly have panels in scattered locations. By code, the disconnects for these remote panels must be grouped and marked as service disconnects, and each disconnect must be marked for the location it serves. At some accessible location inside or outside the home there must be one to six marked service disconnects that turn off all the power to the home. The main breakers in any remote panels shouldn't be marked as service disconnects. They must be marked with information that states from what source panel they're fed.

Choosing a distribution-panel location

Your distribution panel should be somewhere both safe and convenient. It should not be blocked by obstructions, not only because you need to access it easily during installation and maintenance, but also because you may need to access it quickly in an emergency.

Building codes make the following requirements for panel location:

- The area in which the panel is located must have at least 6½' of headroom. If the top of the panel exceeds 6½', the clear working-space requirement is extended to the top of the panel.

- There must be at least 30" of clear wall space from the floor to the ceiling. (Don't worry, the panel doesn't have to be centered.)

- Pipes or ducts may not run above or below the panel.

- If something has to be run over the panel, it must be beyond the front of the panel. To clarify: If a 4"-deep panel is mounted to the wall and a pipe has to be run over the panel area, the pipe must be more than 4" away from the wall and be higher than 6½'. If necessary, you can install a false ceiling so long as the required 6½' of headroom is maintained.

- The floor space must be clear to 3' in front of the panel. The combination with the 30" above and the 6½' height defines a clear working area that is 30" wide by 3' deep by 6½' tall.

- The area must be lit.

- The panel can't be in a bathroom. Code defines a bathroom as an area with a basin and one or more of the following: a toilet, a tub, or a shower. You can't install the panel in a clothes closet.

Normally, the panel's main breaker serves as the service disconnect. If so, the conductors feeding the panel are service-entrance conductors. By code, service-entrance conductors have to be terminated in the panel as near as possible to their point of entry to the building. This usually dictates that the panel be installed on an outside wall or on a stub or partition wall that connects to an outside wall. Service-entrance conductors can be run on the surface outside of a building to any necessary distance, and then brought into a building and terminated in the panel.

The power company usually overfuses the service-entrance conductors. Their fuse is sized to protect their transformer, not your service-entrance conductors. If your service-entrance conductors become shorted, they're likely to burn before the power company's fuse blows. Code considers service-entrance conductors to be outside of the building if they're encased in 2" of concrete. In a basement or on-slab construction, you can run the conductors below the slab to a central location remote from the meter location.

Installing Electrical Services

Electrical service can be installed underground or overhead, both of which we cover here. We believe the electrical service should be inconspicuous and not detract from the aesthetics of the house exterior, which means we generally favor underground service. The next few sections describe some considerations for service installation, whether you're setting up temporary service during construction or permanent service for the residence.

Setting up temporary service

When you build a new house, the first electrical consideration is temporary power. Temporary power can be overhead or underground. You and the power company generally determine which. It's not uncommon to have overhead service for your temporary electricity and underground service for the permanent installation. In some areas, the power company will supply and install the temporary power for a fee. Their fees are usually quite reasonable.

Figure 2-3 shows a typical temporary electrical-service assembly. This particular one only has a few receptacles. On a busy site, we run a portable cord from the main service panel to a freestanding panel that has a dozen or so receptacles, as shown in Figure 2-4. The freestanding panel can be located somewhere within the site.

Figure 2-3:
Temporary
service
panels
usually look
something
like this.

When you add up the cost of a temporary service panel using new equipment, the power company hook-up charges, and the permit fee, you are usually looking at a cost of several hundred dollars. Consider these alternatives:

- ✓ If your project is in a site that has a next-door neighbor, buy power from that neighbor. It would be unusual for you to use more than a couple of dollars' worth of electricity per month as you build the house.

- ✓ Check with an electrical contractor to see if rental equipment is available.

- ✓ Use a portable generator.

Looking up to overhead electrical service

The best overhead service is a *mast service* through the roof. In most cases, mast-type service has a mast through the roof and a cable from the meter socket into the panel. By code, the power-company connection to the house must be below the service-entrance fitting. This code requirement often isn't enforced, but is very important to observe. When the mast goes through the roof, this requirement is always met because the power company has no choice but to connect to the mast below the service head. If the overhead service doesn't penetrate the roof, the power company often anchors the service drop from the pole above the service head.

Figure 2-4:
A freestanding panel inside the work site gives your crew more flexibility.

The power company typically puts a drip loop in the conductors to prevent rain from following the conductors to the meter socket. Unfortunately, the insulated surface of the entrance cable acts like a hose, especially if the service drop is anchored above the service head. Small voids in the stranded conductors allow water to run into the meter socket. Eventually this water can get into the service panel, fouling the breakers and causing rust both in the circuit breakers and the panel housing. When the power company installs your service, try to ensure that they anchor the service drop below the service head.

Overhead service is usually either 100- or 200-amp service. An experienced electrician requires about 7 hours of labor to install 100-amp service, and an additional 3 hours for 200-amp service. If this is your first installation, don't feel bad if it takes you about twice as long to do the installation.

When installing the service, follow these general tips:

- Installing the conduit hub backward on top of the service panel moves the conduit about ½" farther from the wall. This may reduce the amount of drilling you have to do and generally makes the job easier.

- When using aluminum conductors, use #2 wire for 100-amp service or 4/0 for 200-amp service. For copper conductors, reduce the wire size by one size. Aluminum is a lot cheaper than copper, but copper is a better conductor.

- If your 200-amp service is connected to a mast, the mast will usually be a 2" conduit. You can use *Rigid Metal Conduit (RMC)* or *Intermediate Metal Conduit (IMC)* conduit. IMC is about ⅓ lighter than RMC, costs less, has a thinner wall, a larger inside diameter, and a higher *tensile* (harder to bend) strength. But RMC is made of mild steel, making it much easier to thread with a hand-held pipe threader.

- You can connect 100-amp service to a mast conduit as small as 1¼", although many contractors simply use 2" conduit for all masts.

- If your mast is 75' or more from the service pole, use at least 2" conduit. If the pole is 150' away or more, use a 2½" conduit. This prevents the mast bending in high winds.

- Choose a meter socket that matches your service size (100- or 200-amp). Most power companies no longer provide a meter socket, so you may have to buy your own. Most power companies have a list of meter sockets they find suitable. Make sure you heed any special height requirements from the power company for the meter socket.

Some wire assemblies, such as Sweetbriar assemblies, are *Underground Residential Distribution (URD)* twisted-wire assemblies sized as 4/0-4/0-2/0. This means that the power and ground conductors are 4/0 and the neutral conductor is 2/0. The smaller neutral is justified because the neutral in a

120/240-volt or 120/208-volt system only carries the imbalance of the load between the phase conductors. Any 240-volt load, such as an electric range or dryer, contributes no current to the neutral conductor.

✔ Don't use an outdoor disconnect if you can avoid it. Outdoor disconnects are an inconvenience and possibly subject to vandalism. Sure, you can lock an outdoor disconnect, but at some point the key will probably get lost.

Figure 2-5 shows a typical overhead 200-amp electrical service. In this depiction the service panel is in the basement. It could just as easily be installed in the wall behind the meter socket.

TIP

If the service panel is installed on the wall behind the meter socket, stagger the panel one stud cavity to either side of the meter socket. You usually have no good way to come out of the back of the meter socket directly into the service panel if both are mounted back to back.

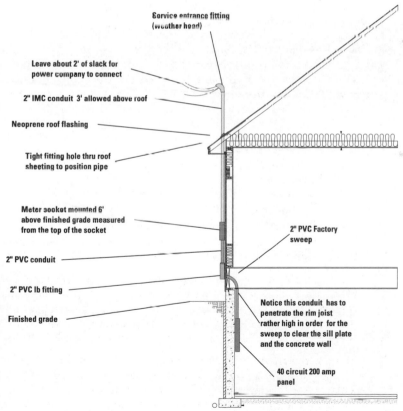

Service entrance fitting (weather head)

Leave about 2' of slack for power company to connect

2" IMC conduit 3' allowed above roof

Neoprene roof flashing

Tight fitting hole thru roof sheeting to position pipe

Meter socket mounted 6' above finished grade measured from the top of the socket

2" PVC Factory sweep

2" PVC conduit

2" PVC lb fitting

Notice this conduit has to penetrate the rim joist rather high in order for the sweep to clear the sill plate and the concrete wall

Finished grade

40 circuit 200 amp panel

Figure 2-5:
This overhead electrical service is a typical arrangement.

In Figure 2-5 you see the three conductors with about 2' of slack. The wire slack allows the power company to connect to your service. The conductors leave the conduit through a rainproof cap called a *weather head* or *service-entrance fitting,* which clamps to the conduit and has insulated holes for the conductors to pass through. The Neoprene roof flashing fits tightly to the conduit and is cemented to the roofing. The flashing is slipped over the conduit before the weather head is installed. Below the meter socket, the 2" *polyvinyl chloride (PVC)* conduit is glued to a 90° fitting called an *LB.* The *L* stands for 90 degree and the *B* denotes the cover is on the back. You could use *LR,* a 90° fitting with the cover on the right. The LL has the cover on the left. Getting the heavy conductors in either of these fittings is impossible. The 2" PVC sweep is a factory-made 90° elbow.

In Figure 2-5, the tight-fitting hole through the roof sheeting holds the mast in place. Code requires that a conduit be secured within 3' of a box or fitting. For this reason you can only have 3' of mast projecting above the roof surface. If the mast extends higher than that, you must secure it with a *guy wire* (attached high on the mast and anchored to the roof).

Because the mast connects to the socket by a threaded hub, a support on the wall is not required. However, some inspectors require an additional support anyway. The conduit from the bottom of the socket to the panel is 2" PVC conduit. Using service-entrance cable instead of PVC is less expensive and a lot less labor intensive. If this is a traffic area or the cable could be otherwise damaged, PVC is a better choice.

Going underground

Underground electrical service is the cleanest looking, because you don't have unsightly cables dangling between a utility pole and your house. Installing it is easier, too. Unlike overhead electrical service, high winds, ice, snow, and falling trees don't affect underground service.

In most jurisdictions, the power company does the rest once these things are completed:

- The underground meter socket *(pedestal)* is installed. (The meter socket extends from about 18" below grade to about 5' above grade.)
- The conductors are connected from the meter socket to the panel and inspected.

In addition, the power company usually also brings in the underground phone and TV cable. If the utility company doesn't install the underground service laterals, you have to trench from the utility underground source to your socket location and install your own laterals. (The *electrical service lateral* is the buried wire that brings power from the utility's transformer to your meter socket.) The electrical code requires a depth of 18", but we recommend a depth of 24" or more. In most cases the phone and cable companies supply wire, but you have to install. In addition to the wires, you have to bury a caution tape 12" above the service lateral conductors. This tape is like what you see all over the latest TV police dramas, except that it's red and marked, "Danger buried power lines."

The electrical service conductors will be AWG 2 for 100-amp service or AWG 4/0 for 200-amp service. These lateral conductors must be approved for direct burial, with markings on the wire indicating this approval. We recommend a wire assembly called Sweetbriar, which is a 4/0-4/0-2/0 URD twisted three-wire assembly. Sweetbriar assemblies are described in the previous section.

Mount the underground meter socket in accordance with power company specifications. Underground meter socket mounting height can vary from 2' to 6', depending on the utility company's wishes. Figure 2-6 shows the layout of a typical underground service installation. As you can see, the house looks a lot nicer without an overhead cable and mast.

Not shown on the underground service detail are the service lateral conductors running 24" below the grade line. On this detail we're using 4/0 service entrance *style U cable (SEU)*. This cable requires a 1½" 2-screw connector on the back of the socket where the cable leaves. It also requires the same connector where it enters the top of the panel. We point out in Figure 2-6 the steps for making a recess behind the meter socket to accommodate the connector and making a hole through the rim joist that fits the SEU cable. This recess allows the panel to mount flush to the wall.

Connecting the electrical distribution panel

After the overhead or underground service is in place, your next step is to connect the service to your electrical-service disconnect. In most cases, the main breaker in the distribution panel is actually the service disconnect. The disconnect must have the neutral conductor connected to ground. This is the only place where the neutral wire should be grounded.

- **Power wires:** The voltage across these two wires (usually black or red) is 240 volts to supply large loads, such as a range or a clothes dryer. The voltage between either of these power wires and the neutral wire is 120 volts.

- **Neutral wire:** Always white, this wire provides a return path for the 120-volt loads that aren't balanced across the loading of the two power wires.

- **Ground wire:** Either bare or green, this wire carries fault currents back to the neutral in the panel and trips the breaker when a fault, or short, is present. We cover grounding in more detail in the next section.

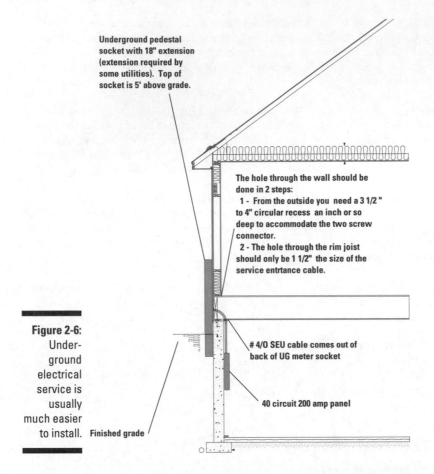

Underground pedestal socket with 18" extension (extension required by some utilities). Top of socket is 5' above grade.

The hole through the wall should be done in 2 steps:
 1 - From the outside you need a 3 1/2 " to 4" circular recess an inch or so deep to accommodate the two screw connector.
 2 - The hole through the rim joist should only be 1 1/2" the size of the service entrtance cable.

4/0 SEU cable comes out of back of UG meter socket

40 circuit 200 amp panel

Finished grade

Figure 2-6:
Under-
ground
electrical
service is
usually
much easier
to install.

After the service disconnect, the system changes from a three-wire system to a four-wire system: two power wires, a neutral, and a ground. Each of the four wires serves a specific purpose:

If the service panel is mounted on a concrete wall, a backboard may be installed to make panel installation easier. This backboard should be treated plywood if there's a chance that the wall could become damp. The branch circuit wires *(home runs)* must be secured within 12" of the panel. In some jurisdictions, you may be allowed to install a pair of 2" PVC conduits into the ceiling space to accommodate the branch circuit wires.

Residential voltages of the past

When electrical service was first installed to residences in the United States, the service usually supplied 100 volts. In the early 1900s, 220-volt service was introduced to serve large power loads such as electric stoves and water heaters. These systems retained 110-volt service by center tapping a 220-volt transformer and running three wires to the home, giving the configuration you see in Figure 2-7. Other early power systems supplied 115/230-volt or 117/235-volt service. Many U.S. homes still only have two-wire 120-volt service. Most of these were installed prior to the 1950s.

A careful reader may notice that we use 110- and 120-volt references interchangeably. Also, when working with older appliances and equipment, you may see markings that rate the devices for older voltage systems. Fortunately, if you need to connect a 110-volt appliance to 120 volts, or a 220-volt item to 240 volts, doing so is perfectly safe.

If the premises are to be equipped with a backup generator that powers the whole house, the wiring from the meter socket must terminate in a service-rated transfer switch, which then offers separate connections from back-up power or normal power to the service panel. The transfer switch's main breaker becomes the service-entrance disconnect. From the transfer switch to the main distribution panel, four wires must be run because now the neutral and ground have to be separate conductors according to code. The distribution panel inside the house becomes a subpanel, and its main breaker can't be labeled as a service-entrance disconnect.

Grounding your service

The subject of electrical system grounding is the most confusing and misunderstood subject in electrical wiring. Here we explain a little about panel grounding. We think it's important, when explaining, to start at the transformer (like the one shown in Figure 2-7) serving the house to get a complete picture.

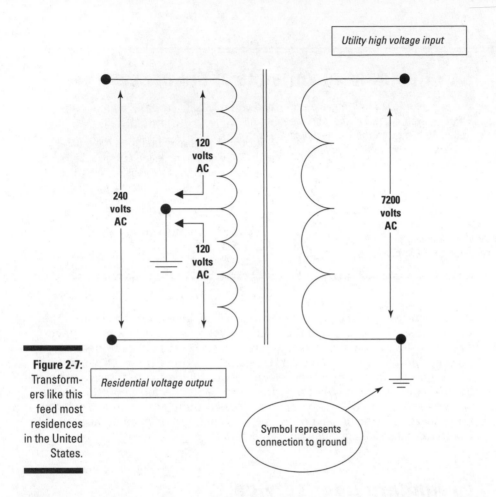

Utility high voltage input

120
volts
AC

240
volts
AC

120
volts
AC

7200
volts
AC

Residential voltage output

Symbol represents connection to ground

Figure 2-7: Transformers like this feed most residences in the United States.

REMEMBER

The center tap on the transformer shown in Figure 2-7 is grounded at the service-entrance panel and is called the *neutral.* Just to make things confusing, this neutral at this point is also the ground. As we mention earlier in this chapter, this grounding of the neutral is *only* true at the service-disconnecting equipment. In the wiring system beyond the service entrance, the wiring changes to a four-wire system.

If the service disconnect is also the main panel breaker, the neutral (white wire) from any light, receptacle, or appliance is connected to this neutral/ ground wire. All green or bare conductors from any of the circuits are also connected to this neutral/ground connection point. Because so many conductors must connect to the service-entrance neutral/ground, a connection strip or bar with many terminals is usually used. You may even have multiple bars connected by jumper wires to provide a sufficient number of connection locations for the incoming neutral and ground wires. A filled 40-circuit panel would have to accommodate a total of 80: 40 grounds and 40 neutral wires.

The neutral is a current-carrying conductor. The ground wire doesn't carry any current under normal conditions. The ground wire only carries fault current if a grounded part comes in contact with an energized conductor. Current flow on the ground will clear as soon as the circuit breaker trips. When anything is required to be grounded, it has to be solidly connected to the neutral/ground on the service disconnect. Electrical code requires this point to be grounded by one of the allowable methods:

- If you have a municipal water system that uses metal piping (it seems every municipal system in the U.S. does), you have to connect the ground to the piping system if there is more than 10' of buried piping. This is a good ground. Your grounding electrode conductor has to be connected within 5' of where this piping enters the building. Continuity of the grounding path cannot depend on water meters or filters, which means you have to install jumpers around these removable items. The 4 AWG or 6 AWG jumper is connected to a ground pipe clamp on either side of such items.

  Connecting to water pipes does have one potential drawback. In a residential neighborhood, it connects you to your neighbors' electrical service if they're connected to the same power company transformer. If a neighbor experiences an open neutral condition, the water piping to your house becomes that neighbor's neutral. Of course, the opposite is also true. Plumbers see sparks or get shocked when working on these energized pipes. In northern climates when welders are used to thaw frozen pipes, wiring connected to these pipes (like yours) can burn. If the person sent to thaw the frozen pipes asks you to unplug the TV, you may be in trouble.

- If you have a pump instead of city water, your piping from the pump to the house is probably plastic. In this case, the electrical code allows you to use an 8' ground rod that tests 25 ohms' resistance or less for a ground. Without the test you can just use two 8' ground rods driven 6' apart to ground the service disconnect neutral. Electrical code also requires you to use ground rods to augment the city water piping system.

  If a pair of ground rods is your only connection to earth, you're at risk of being electrocuted during a lightning storm, a power-company transformer failure, or an accidental contact between your service drop and the high voltage lines. In such an instance, anything connected to the service ground — such as the piping in your house — can become energized. Although these events are rare, you should be aware of the risk.

If your water is supplied by a well, you probably have 30' to several hundred feet of well casing in contact with the earth. That is a good ground. If lighting strikes, it could find the well casing via the wiring to the pump and burn the pump motor and controls. If you have a good ground available on your site (such as a metal well casing or any large amount of metal in direct contact with the earth), use it. If connecting to a well casing, you should run an AWG 6 or larger bare wire to the well casing. Run this wire in the trench along with the plastic water piping and pump power supply cables. The best way to connect the ground wire to the casing is an exothermic weld. The next-best connection is a terminal lug connected with a self-drilling/tapping screw.

Chapter 3

Roughing In the Wiring

In This Chapter

▶ Planning the wiring job

▶ Understanding codes and standards for electrical installations

▶ Installing electrical boxes

▶ Drilling joists and framing

▶ Running the wires

As you can tell by the title, this chapter is all about running the rough wiring for your digital home. The *rough wiring* includes the wiring and parts inside the walls that are eventually hidden behind drywall and plaster. Rough wiring connects the electrical service entrance (see Chapter 2) to the various switches and receptacles in your home. (The rough wiring also includes specialized wiring for cable TVs, telephones, computer networks, and sound systems, but we cover those subjects in more detail in later chapters.) When your home is complete, you won't see the rough wiring, but you'll appreciate the benefits of a high-quality wiring job every day.

If you're going to tackle the wiring job yourself, this chapter guides you through the process. If you plan to hire a contractor, you should understand the rough-in wiring — know how it works and how it should be installed. This chapter takes you through the planning and installation of rough-in wiring of your home's electrical system. For now, we focus on drilling home runs, carefully selecting locations for components, and mounting boxes and wiring.

Laying Out Receptacles (Legally)

Whether you're building a new home or retrofitting an existing house, your wiring job should start with the floor plan. Carefully consider how each room in the home will be used. Where will appliances, lights, and desks be? The following sections guide you through the special considerations involved in planning and installing receptacles. As always, special attention is paid to code compliance to ensure that your home is safe and passes inspection.

Spacing receptacles

The *National Electrical Code (NEC)* requires that no spot along a wall be more than 6' from a receptacle. For example, the first receptacle in any room must be 6' or less from the door. The next receptacle on the wall must be 12' or less from the first receptacle, and so on, continuing along the perimeter of the room.

This spacing is often called the *Six-Foot Rule.* Some people take this literally and place a receptacle every 6', which may be overkill in most rooms. To eliminate confusion, we call it the *Six- to Twelve-Foot Rule.* Of course, code dictates only minimum requirements; in most situations we recommend placing receptacles about 8' to 10' apart. Other code requirements include

- ✔ In any habitable room, any wall space that is 2' or longer must have a receptacle.

- ✔ Rooms not designed for habitation — closets, pantries, and so forth — aren't required to have receptacles, but you may include some.

- ✔ Hallways 10' or longer are required to have a single receptacle.

- ✔ No spot along the wall above kitchen counters may be farther than 2' from a receptacle. The maximum space between above-counter receptacles is 4'. Any isolated counter space 12" or wider must have a receptacle. A break in the counter space — such as a sink — counts as the start of a new space. At least one receptacle must be within 2' of the sink.

- ✔ At least two circuits must be dedicated to supplying the kitchen and dining room receptacles, and these receptacle circuits can't supply any lighting circuits or receptacles in other locations.

- ✔ Receptacles must be as evenly spaced as possible.

We recommend paying special attention to symmetry when installing receptacles. For example, try to space outlets evenly on either side of a window. Also consider special needs in every space, such as furniture placement. For example, in Figure 3-1 a 2" × 6" framing extension was added to the normal support framing; the quad receptacle box was moved 5½" to the left to accommodate future furniture placement. The loose Cat 5 network cables will be stapled to the framing on the right later, before the wallboard is added. The receptacle box is mounted by driving nails through the angled-edge flanges and into the stud.

Underwriters Laboratory (UL) — the organization that tests and sets standards for electrical devices — requires that household appliances have cords at least 6' long. An exception to this is kitchen appliances, which may have 2' cords. Consider this limitation when spacing your outlets.

Figure 3-1:
Spacing is an important considera-tion when installing receptacles.

When to use GFI receptacles

Ground Fault Interrupter (GFI) receptacles are also sometimes called *Ground Fault Circuit Interrupter (GFCI)* outlets. A *GFI* is a safety receptacle that opens the circuit if 5 *milliamps (mA)* or more of the current on the power conductor is *bleeding,* or running, to ground and not traveling back on the neutral con-ductor. The electronics in the GFI monitor the current on both the power and neutral conductors for an equal load.

Milliamps is abbreviated as mA; 1 milliamp equals ½,₀₀₀ of 1 amp.

If someone comes in contact with the power from a GFI receptacle, some cur-rent may travel through his body to ground. If this current reaches 5 mA, the GFI immediately trips and the power is cut off. Although 5 mA provides a pretty hefty shock, it shouldn't be fatal. The 5-mA level is used because a healthy person can withstand a 10-mA shock for about 10 seconds and survive.

Some people believe that GFIs are solely for personal protection. Just because a circuit is GFI protected doesn't necessarily make it human safe. Some GFIs have higher current ratings and are designed to protect heavy electrical equipment. Be cautious: Always test GFIs before betting your life on them.

Silent C

Like most electrical trade professionals, we prefer to drop the *C* from the GFCI acronym and just call it *GFI*. Besides, one letter saves the publisher some ink.

GFI-protected receptacles are required in places with significant grounding and shock hazards. You must use GFIs in the

- ✔ **Kitchen:** Above-counter receptacles in kitchens must be GFI protected. The kitchen receptacles require their own circuit(s), and can have no other outlets.

- ✔ **Bathroom:** Bathrooms are required to have a GFI within 36" of the vanity. The bathroom receptacles must be GFI protected and require their own circuit(s), and can have no other outlets outside the bathroom. Figure 3-2 shows a GFI receptacle installed on the side of a vanity. Note that this outlet is positioned so it won't interfere with a large mirror or medicine cabinet. The box was mounted at 38" measured from the floor to the bottom of the box.

- ✔ **Basement and exterior:** All basement receptacles and exterior receptacles must be GFI protected. Finished basement areas such as family rooms do not require GFI protection for receptacles.

- ✔ **Wet-bar sink:** Here, the receptacles are installed for countertop use within 6' of the outside edge of a wet-bar sink.

- ✔ **Crawl space:** Receptacles at or below grade level must be GFI protected.

- ✔ **Garage, tool shed, storage area, and similar on- or below-grade structures not intended for habitation:** An inaccessible receptacle, such as for a garage door opener installed in the overhead, is exempt.

A change that was introduced in the 2002 code is that an appliance-garage receptacle doesn't count as a counter receptacle for spacing but can be connected to the kitchen-required small-appliance circuit. An *appliance garage* is a section of cabinetry built between the upper and lower kitchen cabinet to conceal and *park* various appliances, such as a toaster or coffee maker, when not in use. We generally install a quad receptacle inside the appliance garage. The appliance garage has a roll-up door. The code requires you have at least two circuits to supply the kitchen and dining room receptacle circuits. These circuits can't supply other outlets in other locations, nor can they supply lighting.

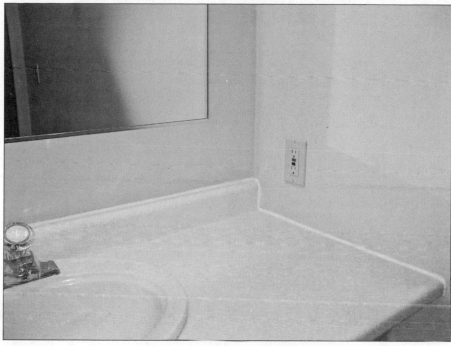

Figure 3-2:
Bathrooms must have a GFI outlet within 36" of the vanity.

Figure 3-3 shows a sketch of an appliance garage. Although two duplex receptacles are in the appliance garage, you must install a receptacle on both sides of the appliance garage within 2', as shown. These receptacles must be GFI protected.

Code lets you replace a two-prong receptacle with a GFI receptacle without having a ground wire present. This allows you to plug in *grounded* (three-prong) plugs. Installing a GFI receptacle to get a third prong doesn't give you a grounded receptacle. You only have a grounded receptacle if a continuous wire runs from the receptacle ground screw terminal to the ground bar in the service panel. If this connection isn't present, using a surge-protected outlet-strip at a receptacle without the ground wire doesn't give you surge protection. In this case you should install surge protection at the service panel to protect the whole house.

Figure 3-4 shows a panel surge protector next to a double Decora switch for size comparison. This surge protector costs about $50.

Figure 3-3:
An
appliance
garage.

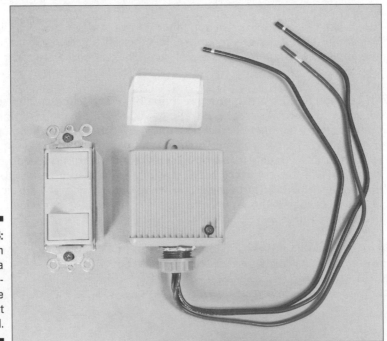

Figure 3-4:
You can
install a
whole-
house surge
protector at
your panel.

Setting box heights

Once you've figured out where you want to install receptacles, the next step is to decide how high you want to mount the boxes. Traditionally, outlets are placed relatively low, where they are less visible, but sometimes you may want to mount them a bit higher.

The electrical code doesn't specify a height for receptacle boxes, except to say that they have to be less than 5½' above the finished floor. Receptacles above kitchen counter tops may be no more than 20" above the counter top. This requirement is a change in the 2002 code. Earlier codes set the above-counter distance at 18". The earlier 18" requirement didn't allow for the installation of multi-outlet strips installed on the bottoms of upper cabinets. Wiremold makes a product perfect for this use. Its outlet assembly — shown in Figure 3-5 — is similar to a computer power strip, but it lacks a cord. Wiremold strips are available in a variety of sizes and outlet spacings.

In older houses that had to be retrofitted for electricity, the receptacles were usually cut into the baseboards. The baseboards of these older homes were frequently solid wood between 6" and 10" tall. The ¾"-thick baseboards provided a rock-solid mounting point for receptacle boxes. In later homes that were wired during construction, outlets were usually placed about 12" above the floor. If your project has existing receptacles, you may want to match the height of the existing receptacles. If there aren't too many existing receptacles, you may want to abandon or ignore them and chose a different mounting height. A height of 12" is typical but not mandatory.

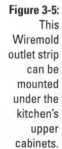

Figure 3-5: This Wiremold outlet strip can be mounted under the kitchen's upper cabinets.

Figure 3-6 shows a new receptacle cut into a wall at a higher level than the baseboard receptacles, which were installed in 1920. If the baseboards are painted, the original receptacle could be removed and the hole simply patched. But the room in Figure 3-5 is quarter-sawn oak paneling from floor to ceiling, and a patch would have been less appealing than simply leaving the outlet in place.

Switch boxes are usually mounted at about 4' above the floor. Thermostat boxes can be mounted at 5'. For commercial wiring, the *American Disabilities Act (ADA)* requires that receptacles be mounted at least 18" above the floor, and switches must be mounted so handles are no higher than 48". You don't have to meet these requirements in your own home. The electrical code requires that switches and circuit breakers used as switches be located so you can operate them from an accessible location: Install them so the switch handle is 6' 7" or less from the floor.

Most of the figures in this book show the receptacle boxes mounted 16" high, and switches and kitchen-counter receptacle boxes mounted 48" high. These measurements are from the rough flooring to the bottom of the electrical box. For an 8' ceiling, some drywall installers prefer that switches be mounted at a distance of 48⅝" between the ceiling and the top of the box, so that they only have to cut the lower sheet of drywall when the 4' × 8' or 4' × 12' sheets are hung horizontally.

Figure 3-6:
The lower baseboard receptacle was originally installed in 1920.

Making sure the box is flush

When you mount a receptacle in a switch box, the electrical code requires that each box extend out through the building's wall finish to within ¼" of being flush with the drywall surface. The box should be set exactly even with, or back slightly from, the finished surface to ensure that the finish plate sits flat on the wall. Before applying the drywall or other finish, check each box with a straight edge and a level to ensure that they are, uh, straight and level.

If the stud is slightly twisted or angled, the box may stick out from the drywall even if the measurement at the point of attachment is correct. Dealing with these kinds of problems is easier if you do so before hanging the drywall. Watch for this when checking your boxes, and adjust their mounting as necessary.

Mounting boxes during rewiring projects

Installing boxes as part of a rewiring project can be a little tricky, because there's usually wall finish in the way. This means you have to spend some extra time finding the hidden wall studs, and then carefully cutting holes in the finish so the new boxes can be mounted.

We recommend that you cut the openings so that one side of the box is ½" or less away from the stud. This way the box can be mounted directly to the framing using drywall screws through the side of the box. Cutting slightly away from the stud makes the box angle in slightly, helping make it flush with the wall surface. This is especially helpful if the stud is angled slightly, which is a common problem.

To install a box in an existing finished wall, follow these steps:

1. **Locate the stud using a stud finder, and then approximate and mark its center.**

2. **Mark the top and bottom of the box on the wall, using the actual box as a template.**

3. **Drill a pilot hole about 2" away from the stud center.**

   You know the drill: Wear eye protection before you start and make sure you're very careful while using power tools.

4. **Use a reciprocating saw to slowly cut along the top line of the box toward the stud.**

   Hold the reciprocating saw with the blade tip angled toward the stud. Use a 14-teeth-per-inch blade to ensure a clean cut. When the cut is near the stud, you should be able to feel the stud — first turn the saw off, and then angle the blade toward the stud.

5. Once you locate the stud, saw within ¼" of it.

6. For the bottom of the box, repeat steps 3 through 5.

7. Use the box as a template again to draw the complete box cutout on the wall.

8. Drill a ¼" hole at the side away from the stud.

9. Make the vertical cut for the far end of the box away from the stud.

It is especially important in lath-plaster walls to make the far vertical cut first. If you cut the vertical on the stud side first, the lath will flap with the motions of the saw blade and make it very difficult to cut.

10. Make the vertical cut on the stud side and remove the loose wall piece.

You'll probably also have to drill a hole here to begin the saw cut.

The finished hole should be ¹⁄₁₆" larger than the box. If you need to install a second box such as a cable TV or phone wall jack, it is easy to do that in the same opening between the two studs, on the opposite stud.

Depending on the type of finish used on the wall, you may need to take extra care to avoid damaging the finish. This is especially true when you're cutting into a finish that you won't retouch, such as paneling or tile. Different types of finish call for different precautions:

- **Paneling:** Make a ⅛"-deep cut with a utility knife on the horizontal plane, across the grain. This keeps the paneling from chipping as you saw. Saw on the inside of the knife cut.

- **Tile:** Cover the area beyond the cut with duct tape, using the tape as the cutting guide. Keep the saw shoe firmly against the tile surface.

- **Painted plaster:** Hold the shoe slightly away from the surface to prevent marring the paint. Don't use tape for protection on painted plaster walls because the paint will come off with the tape.

Old-work boxes have flanges on the front to fasten to wall surfaces. We think they're okay for phone or TV cable wiring, but we don't recommend them for switches or electrical receptacles. A box fastened to the framing is a far superior mounting method, and can stand the greater force of plugging in cords. Stud-mounted boxes are also easier to trim to the wall.

In Figure 3-7, the three-gang switch box and the central vacuum outlet were mounted to the stud on the right. For the receptacle, a 2 × 4 was screwed to the door framing to provide a secure mounting some distance away for that box to clear the 4" wide trim. On this second-floor installation, the wires were fished down the wall from the attic.

Figure 3-7:
Take extra care when installing new boxes during rewiring projects.

Calculating box fill

As you plan and install the boxes that hold your home's switches and receptacles, you need to calculate *box fill,* the space in cubic inches that devices and wires need inside the box. Receptacle and switch boxes come in various sizes, so make sure you choose boxes big enough to hold everything you plan to stuff inside.

Count the number of wires that will be in the box:

- Each insulated wire counts as one wire equivalent.

- All bare wires (ground wires) added together count as one wire equivalent, whether there are 1 or 100 ground wires.

- Each device (switch or receptacle) counts as two wire equivalents.

   Table 3-1 lists the number of cubic inches filled by common wire sizes used in home wiring. You can see by the table that a wire equivalent for 14 AWG wire is 2 cubic inches while a wire equivalent for 6 AWG is 5 cubic inches. The larger the wire size you are using, the larger the required box.

Table 3-1	Box Fill Ratings for Common Wire
American Wire Gage (AWG)	*Cubic Inches of Box Fill (per Conductor)*
14 AWG	2 cubic inches
12 AWG	2.25 cubic inches
10 AWG	2.5 cubic inches
8 AWG	3.0 cubic inches
6 AWG	5.0 cubic inches

For example, assume you have a box that contains a 14/2 cable with ground, as well as a 14/3 cable with ground. (14/2 means the cable contains two insulated 14 AWG conductors; 14/3 means the cable has three insulated conductors.) This gives a total of five insulated conductors, two bare grounds, and one receptacle. All the bare grounds count as one wire. The receptacle counts as two wires. Each insulated conductor counts as one wire equivalent.

```
5 Insulated Conductors + 1 Ground Wire + 2 Receptacles = 8
          Wire Equivalents
```

This example box is filled with eight wire equivalents. Multiply the wire equivalents by the cubic inch capacity required for 14 AWG wire:

```
8 × 2 cubic inches = 16 cubic inches
```

For this example, you need to use a box that has a minimum volume of 16 cubic inches. When in doubt, err on the side of providing a little extra space.

Drilling Holes for Wiring

When you've decided where and how high to mount your switch and receptacle boxes, it's time to drill some *wiring holes*.

Drilling the framing

We recommend running your wires about 4" above where you plan to mount your receptacle boxes. This means that if you plan to install your receptacle boxes 16" above the floor, add 4" for the box, plus the 4"-space above the box; you should drill the holes 24" above the floor.

While you're at it, follow these guidelines when drilling your holes:

✔ Make sure that all of your wire holes are drilled at the same height. Measure them if necessary. Also take care to avoid drilling at an angle; the straighter the holes, the easier it is to pull the wires through. Drill each hole so the distance from the front of the stud is the same on every stud.

✔ Run all wires at right angles to or parallel to framing. Don't run wires at angles between wall studs, floor framing, or ceiling framing, and don't drill angled holes. Most often you're running wiring at right angles to the framing members to get to a wall cavity some distance away. Once you reach a wall cavity where a box is needed, then you make a 90° angle within that stud to reach the box.

✔ Drill to fit the stud.

   • In a 2" × 4" wall stud, drill wire holes in the center of the 4" face of the stud.

   • In a 2" × 6" wall stud, the hole must be at least 1¼" back from the wall face.

✔ The hole size depends on how many wires you intend to run in the hole, including electric, phone, cable, and special communication systems. In Chapters 7 and 9 we discuss which wires shouldn't run parallel to power wires, but in general you should avoid running computer network and amplifier-input cables right next to power wires. If the hole will need to accommodate a single three-wire cable, use a ¾" drill bit.

The electrical code requires the wire be supported within 12" of where the wire enters the box. By giving 4" of clearance between the wire run and the box, you have enough room to staple the wire to the wall stud just above the box.

✔ When installing wire runs under tall windows, drill through the studs below the window rough in, or go up and over the window framing. For windows that go very low to the floor or for doors, you have no choice but to go up and over the frame.

Be diligent about drilling holes in the center of 2" × 4" studs, and at least 1¼" back on wider studs. This lessens the chance of a drywall nail or screw puncturing a wire and causing a short in the circuit. On specialty walls such as those using 2" × 2" studs or ¾" stripping on foundation walls, use steel plates to protect the wires if you can't meet the 1¼" setback. These plates are commonly known as *nail plates*. A standard nail plate is 1½" × 3" 14-gauge steel plate. Plumbers also use nail plates to protect copper and plastic piping from damage by drywall mounting nails.

Drilling joists

In homes with basements, most of the wiring home runs are run in holes drilled in the floor joists. *Home runs* are the supply wires that travel from the first load on the circuit back to the electrical panel. If your home doesn't have a basement, all of the home runs come out of the top of the panel and run along the top of the lower cord of the roof trusses. In multi-story buildings, the joists between floors are drilled to provide home runs.

When drilling joists, follow these basic rules:

- Drill holes large enough to easily accommodate all the wires you need to pull through, while also drilling as few holes as possible to avoid weakening the joists.

- As with holes drilled in wall studs, holes in joists should be in a straight line.

- In 2" × x" lumber floor joists, leave 2" from the bottom of the drilled hole to the lower edge of the joist.

- In manufactured joists, follow the manufacturer's drilling specifications. Manufactured joists usually have 1½" to 3½" flanges on the top and bottom, attached to a web of ⅜" *oriented strand board (OSB)* ranging from 10" to 20" high. Most manufacturers allow a 1½" hole anywhere on the web, and a 2" hole no closer than 12" to the end support. Larger holes must be farther away from the weight-bearing end of the joist. While drilling down through a floor supported by manufactured joists, *don't* drill through manufactured joist flanges.

Your electrical inspector probably won't worry too much about holes drilled in manufactured trusses, but your framing inspector will.

- In both lumber and manufactured joists, drill the holes low for wires crossing the joist, and run the wires high, 1" or so from the floor for the wires running parallel along the joists. This keeps the wires away from any additional holes you may have to drill later.

- If the joists are open frame, no need to drill. Staple the wires to the top of the bottom cord of the joists on the cross-joist runs and to either side on parallel runs.

Some electrical inspectors will lower, or *derate,* the rated capacity of grouped conductors. This is because grouped conductors heat each other up, making them unable to carry their rated current without overheating. After 10 or 20 years of overheating, the insulation can become brittle and break off if the conductor is bent. The National Electrical Code requires electrical conductors that are grouped together to be derated to a lower amperage capacity.

Table B. 310.11 of the 2002 code lists derating factors based on wire capacity and grouping. In reality, heating is seldom a problem because most loads are *transient,* meaning that not all conductors in a bundled group will carry their full loads at the same time. Using the code 50-percent table for load diversity and having fewer than 40 conductors, you can have 15 amps on a 14 AWG conductor and 18 amps on a 12 AWG wire. Still, keep this in mind when planning your wire runs. Avoid grouping conductors that carry heavy or continuous loads.

TECHNICAL STUFF

Running wires for rewiring

For rewiring, the receptacle wires should go from box to box, just as in new construction. We covered rewiring box mounting in the "Mounting boxes during rewiring" section. Once the box opening is cut, you still have to get wires to it before mounting the box. For homes that have a crawl space or basement, locate the stud cavity that you cut into for a box and then drill a hole up through the flooring and the wall-framing bottom plate. You have to be quite exact here. If you miss, you'll drill a hole up through the finished floor and ruin it, whether the floor is carpeted, tiled, or hardwood.

To validate your measurement for partition walls, try our method:

1. **Using a wire coat hanger in place of a drill bit, drill a hole from upstairs to locate the place in the basement to drill up.**

   The makeshift drill bit is an 8"- or 10"-long piece of the straight part of a wire clothes hanger. This 3/16" wire drills a hole surprisingly well, and because a wire hanger is smooth, it won't catch carpet threads and cause a run. When drilling through hardwood flooring, we pull the quarter-round molding slightly away from the baseboard and drill between it and the baseboard so we don't leave a little hole in the floor.

2. **Remove the drill motor and leave the hanger protruding 6" so you can easily locate the wire marker in the basement.**

3. **Calculate the distance from your marker. If you drilled the hole straight, measure the distance from the marker to the stud cavity center and drill up from the basement.**

4. **Run the wires and mount the boxes.**

When drilling to wire a box on the inside of an exterior wall on an old construction, you usually have to drill through an 8 × 8 timber at an angle to wind up in the wall cavity. If you drill at too low an angle, you'll drill through the siding. If you drill at too steep an angle, you'll drill through the floor. All we can say is review your trigonometry and measure twice, drill once.

If you have no access from below, the wires have to be fished down from the attic or upper crawl space. You can still use the wire hanger to locate the stud cavity. Here the hanger has to be long enough to be seen through the insulation. The hole you make in the ceiling can be patched with a drop of plaster or spackling compound.

Rather than run wires from box to box, some electricians install a powered junction in an accessible area and then branch out to each receptacle. This layout resembles a star or a spoked wheel. This method saves a little wire, but it seems messy.

Pulling Wires

So you've mounted your switch and receptacle boxes, you've planned your wire runs, and you've drilled all of your holes. But you look at your progress thus far and think, "Something's missing. . . ."

Wires! Yes, it's time to pull some wires through the holes that you carefully drilled in your studs and joists. Running wires is a big job, but it can be accomplished by following these basic steps:

1. **Pull the conductors from box to box.**

   As you pull the wires, you might have to mark some of them. The best way to mark wires is to simply write on the wire jacket with a ballpoint pen or permanent marker. Remember that the first 8" or so of sheathing is going to be removed. You remove 3' or 4' of the protective sheathing at the panel. Some electricians *ring cut* the cable's protective sheathing and slip it off, and then slip it back over the black (or red) conductor after rough in to retain the previous marking. You don't need to identify the grounds because they ultimately all connect together. Neutrals also usually don't need to be identified, except in the case of AFI and GFI circuits at the panel.

2. **Cut the wires at each box.**

   Cut the wires so there's at least 6" — and preferably 8" — of free conductor extending from the face of each box.

3. **After pulling a single room, go back and strip each conductor's outer sheathing.**

   Code requires that the protective sheathing surrounding the insulation on the conductors extend ¼" into the box. This prevents chaffing between the box and the sheath from harming the conductor insulation.

4. **Insert the wires into the boxes.**

5. **Secure the wires, with one staple, directly above each box.**

   The staple must be within 12" of the box.

6. **If you haven't already, mark each wire's use.**

   You may have to mark some of the wires again if you marked them earlier. Marking isn't necessary for just the power in and power out at most receptacles. Marking is useful for a feed through GFI or some of the switching.

Don't try to save wire as you run it. Code requires at least 6" of slack. If you wind up with a foot of slack rather than 6" to 8", that's okay. A little extra length allows you to easily install the wires onto the receptacles a few inches away from freshly painted walls. You can easily push the slack back into the box after connecting the receptacle. Of course, you can only do this if the box has sufficient volume, which is covered in the earlier section, "Calculating box fill."

Figure 3-8 shows a roughed-in box. Notice that the slack in one of the wire sets is about 8", and the other wire has about 12" of slack. The wires running to the switch box (not shown) have to run over the right side because the box is as deep as the stud and the wire has no room to run behind the box.

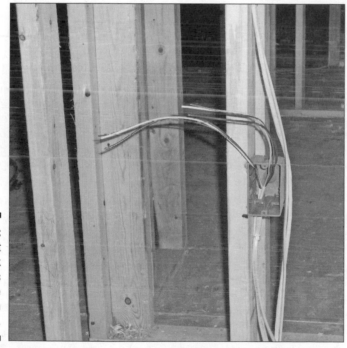

Figure 3-8:
Leaving a lot of slack makes receptacle installation easier.

Wiring to Code

It should go without saying that the National Electrical Code (NEC) has a few things to say about how a home should and shouldn't be wired. It's impossible for us to tell you every single code requirement here, so spend time studying the actual code to make sure you do the job right. Remember, the NEC isn't just a bunch of arbitrary requirements designed to make your life more difficult as an installer; the guidelines are designed to make your house as safe as possible. We recommend using the Handbook of the NEC Codebook. It has the complete code text in addition to explanatory notes and diagrams.

In this section, we highlight a few specific requirements to keep in mind as you rough in your wires. Earlier sections in this chapter detail code requirements for locating and installing switch and receptacle boxes. Other wiring requirements include:

✔ **Bedrooms:** Arc Fault Interrupter (AFI) circuits are only required on bedroom circuits. An AFI is a circuit breaker that monitors the current; it recognizes the characteristics of an electric arc and trips when it detects one. Brush motors like those found in vacuums, mixers, or drills produce an arc when running. Sometimes false tripping can occur if using these types of devices on AFI breaker-controlled circuits. We recommend that the bedroom hall receptacle(s) be supplied by non-AFI circuits to power vacuum cleaners for cleaning the bedrooms if false tripping occurs.

✔ **Smoke detectors:** If a smoke detector is installed in a bedroom, it must be on an AFI circuit. Of course, smoke detectors must also have battery backup power as well. The electrical code doesn't specify where smoke detectors should be placed, but building codes usually require them in all bedrooms and bedroom hallways. Consider using one or more combination carbon monoxide-smoke detectors. Make sure the interconnect feature works with your smoke detectors.

Smoke detector systems are required to have an interconnect feature. If one detects smoke, all interconnected detectors sound an alarm. The interconnect wire is usually orange, which should be connected to the red conductor on a three-conductor cable.

✔ **Bathroom, laundry, kitchen, or dining-room receptacle circuits:** All of these circuits must be supplied by 12 AWG wire. This is also true of any receptacle circuit that will have more than a 12-amp load. Lighting circuits in these locations can be wired with 14 AWG wire.

✔ **GFI wiring:** When pulling the wires, the power wires at a box can usually be marked with the letter *P* — except when the wiring connects a GFI receptacle to a second receptacle. On a GFI feed-through system, the power-in wire connects to the line terminal, and the power-out wire connects to the load terminals on the GFI receptacle. It is important to identify the in-out wires at rough in so the GFI is connected properly.

✔ **Existing wiring:** The electrical code doesn't mandate that you bring an existing residence up to code. It only requires that any new work you do conforms. However, the existing wiring in your home isn't immune from scrutiny. If an electrical inspector finds something she considers hazardous, she may instruct you to correct the problem. Such problems may include bare wires, open splices, or extension cords used for permanent wiring. If you refuse to solve these problems, the inspector can order the power company to disconnect your power.

✔ **Existing receptacles:** If you plan to replace a receptacle in a kitchen, bathroom, garage, or other location where a GFI outlet is required, you must replace the outlet with a GFI unit. This is true even if the old receptacle was installed before GFI outlets were required. If the house uses older two-wire conductors, mark the new GFI receptacle with **No ground is present.** You can feed other three-prong receptacles from this ungrounded two-wire circuit. They will be ground-fault protected, but mark them with **No ground is present**; **GFCI protected.**

Diagramming

Diagrams are a crucial part of your wiring plan. You may draw up the diagrams yourself, or a contractor, electrician, or designer may provide them. In any case, it's important that you know how to read and use wiring diagrams. Figure 3-9 shows a few of the common symbols used on electrical diagrams and blueprints — for a more complete listing, see Color Plate 6 in the color insert pages in this book.

Figure 3-9: Wiring diagrams use these common symbols.

Symbol	Description
⊐⊙	Duplex receptacle
⟷$	Single pole switch
⟷$³	Switch w/superscript # 3 or 4 way

Figure 3-10 shows a basic wiring diagram for a bedroom with nine receptacles. The receptacles are indicated by the standard receptacle symbol, which looks like a circle with two legs. The home run, which goes to the panel, connects to the receptacle behind the door. This wall is long enough that the receptacle is mounted beyond the *door swing,* meaning you can see it when the door is open. On a shorter wall, the door may hide this outlet, making it essentially useless. But as stated earlier in this chapter, any wall longer than 2' in a habitable room must have an outlet by code.

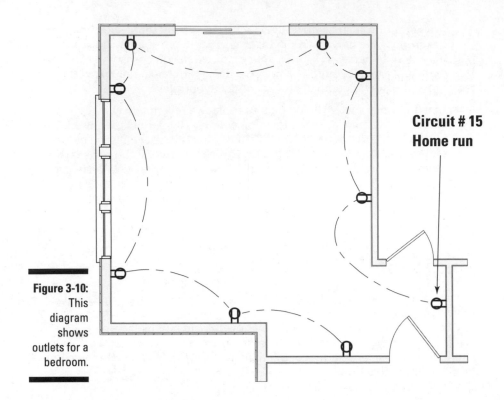

Circuit # 15 Home run

The wiring from the home-run receptacle goes up and over the doorway during rough in to connect to the other receptacles in the room. Each receptacle is connected to the next in turn. The wire run ends at the receptacle on the left side of the bedroom door.

As you run the wires, mark your progress on your diagram or blueprint. After you make a few runs, draw lines from point to point on your diagram to remind you what's done and what isn't. Include in your markings the kind of wire you used. We use this system:

- ✔ Cross the line at a right angle with a long line for a power wire.

- ✔ Cross the line about half the length for a neutral (white) wire. For instance, two longs and a short indicate the connecting wire is a three-conductor wire.

- ✔ Don't mark for the ground. For simplification it is convention to omit grounds in diagramming for wiring, understanding that ground wires must be present.

This helps make sure the circuits are complete. On your documents, feel free to get as elaborate or colorful as you want.

Some diagrams may look simple even though they involve rather complex wiring. Figure 3-11 is typical of what you may see on an electrical blueprint for lighting. Some electricians wire these lights just the way they're shown, but this is a mistake. This consumes a lot of time. This type of diagram is intended to simply convey which switches control which fixtures.

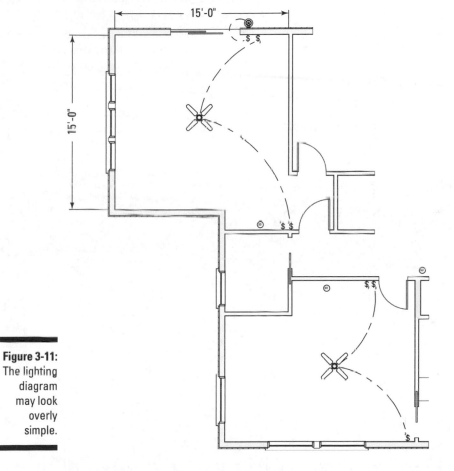

Figure 3-11:
The lighting diagram may look overly simple.

Figure 3-12 looks a bit more complex because it conveys a lot more information. This diagram shows wiring both for lighting and smoke detectors. Note the following elements in Figure 3-12:

✔ Power wires are indicated by the letter *P.*

✔ The switched wire is indicated by the letter *S.*

✔ The wires marked as 14-3 are 14-3 Romex. This is a 14-gauge, three-conductor wire. The 14-3s serve three functions:

- Those to the paddle fans are switch legs. The black brings power to the light, the red powers the fan from the wall-mounted speed control, and the white is a common neutral for both fan and light.

- Those between smoke detectors power the detectors on the black and white, and the red enables the interconnect feature.

- Those between the three-way switches are the three-way interconnects. The red and white are the travelers, and the black is the common. (See Chapter 4 for more about three-way switches.)

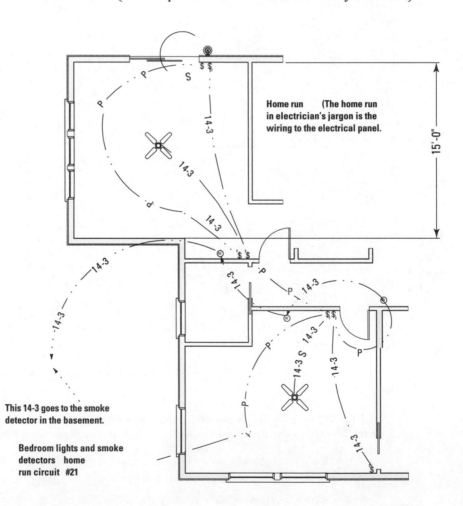

Figure 3-12:
This diagram shows all the light wiring.

This 14-3 goes to the smoke detector in the basement.

Bedroom lights and smoke detectors home run circuit #21

Wiring the rest of the house

The previous sections focused on two bedrooms. Now you will look at the remainder of this house. The home of interest is a 2,000-square-foot home. For an experienced electrician this will require about 140 hours to rough in and 55 hours to trim it out.

Turn to the color insert pages in this book and check out Color Plate 8 to see a whole-house wiring diagram. A circuit number labels each fixture or receptacle and some switches, indicating which circuit breaker controls this circuit. The switches that don't have a circuit number don't have a power wire — mostly three- and four-way switches. This circuit numbering is what a designer would typically include on a blueprint. The electrician would bring the home run to where it is indicated and then run a wire in the easiest or shortest route from that point to all of the boxes with the same number. In many cases the electrician may change the indicated home-run box if he discovers a better alternative.

The living room of this house has three floor receptacles. Floor receptacles require a special box and cover, which come in different styles for carpet, tile, and wood floors.

Wiring dryers and ranges

Wiring standards for ranges and dryers have changed in recent years. During World War II, they dropped to three circuits in an effort to conserve copper. The third conductor — the white or bare wire, depending on the type of cable used — served as both a ground and a neutral. In any other wiring system this arrangement is prohibited. Although there were never any problems with this wiring method, folks stuck on technicalities wanted the standard changed back to four wires, and in 1999 they got their way. Now any new residential construction requires a four-wire feeder to a range or dryer and a four-prong receptacle for each.

If you're replacing the service panel on a three-wire configuration, the local authority may require you to update three-wire power plugs to four-wire plugs. Any new installation of a 240-volt circuit — whether the home is existing or new construction — must use a four-wire configuration. The plugs in question are

- A 40-amp circuit — usually for an electric range — requires 8-3 Romex with a ground.

- A 30-amp circuit — usually for an electric dryer — requires 10 3 Romex with a ground.

- These 30-amp and 50-amp 240-volt receptacles require two-gang boxes for four-prong receptacles.

Figure 3-13 shows a three-prong plug for an electric range. This picture was taken through the range's bottom drawer opening. This opening is typically 7" high and 19" wide. Notice that the receptacle is to the right of center to help it clear the cable going into the stove-junction box. Notice that the box needs to be mounted 3–4" from the floor to allow the cord to be easily plugged in. The install for a four-prong, 50-amp cord is better if the box is mounted so the receptacle can be mounted horizontally.

Figure 3-14 shows a modern range connected to a three-wire pigtail. In this photo the ground (neutral) is disconnected to reveal the strap that connects the ground to the stove body. This connector strap must be in place with a three-wire connection. In a four-wire connection the bonding strap must be disconnected. If in doubt, have an electrician help with the installation. Rather than cutting or removing this strap, we suggest you just disconnect it from the neutral terminal and leave it attached to the ground screw. If this range is ever reinstalled on a three-wire system it may prompt an installer to reconnect it properly.

Wiring closets

The electrical code has special rules about clearance on closet lights. A major concern with closet lights is that an item on a shelf may tip against an exposed lamp and cause a fire. To light a narrow closet, we recommend installing a florescent strip fixture above the closet door. We recommend a 4'-long fixture because the 48" bulbs are usually cheaper than 24" or 36" bulbs.

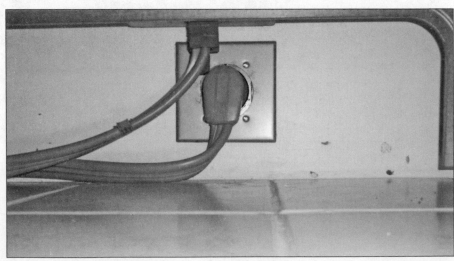

Figure 3-13:
A typical 240-volt receptacle for an electric range.

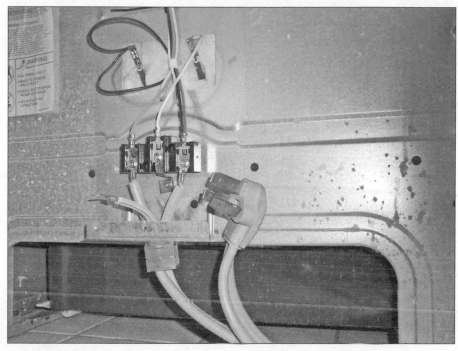

Figure 3-14:
Make sure
the bonding
strap is in
place for
three-wire
installations.

A florescent fixture must have at least 6" of clearance from a storage area, while an incandescent light must have 12" of clearance. For a walk-in closet, a center ceiling fixture with 12" of clearance from the shelf is permitted and is probably a better choice.

The closet lighting can be fed from the nearest receptacle. We recommend placing the switch outside the closet and controlling it with a pilot switch like the one shown in the color insert pages in this book as Color Plate 1. Don't confuse a pilot switch with a lighted switch. The handle is lighted on a *pilot switch* when the light is turned on. The handle of a lighted switch is lighted when the light is turned off. The installation for this type requires that you have a neutral in the switch box to provide the return path for the pilot light.

Chapter 4

Trimming Your Home's Electrical System

Throughout this book, we show you all the ins and outs of a digital home's advanced electrical systems. Most of the wires, junction boxes, breaker panels, and other parts are vital yet ugly, so they remain hidden. When people actually use the electrical system, they mainly flip the system's switches and plug items into the receptacles.

This chapter is about your electrical system's public face: the switches and power receptacles you use every day. We start by helping you pick components that complement your home's décor. Then we show you how to properly install those components so they're safe and ready to use. Selecting and installing switches and receptacles is often called the *trim-out phase* of construction, because these parts are an integral part of your home's cosmetic trim.

Selecting Device Styles and Colors

Your first step as you trim out your home's electrical system is to choose the color and style of your visible devices. These visible devices include switches, receptacles, and sensors. The least expensive choices are, of course, the old standby toggle-type light switch and the ubiquitous standard oval duplex receptacle. It's hard to go wrong with the same parts that are found in zillions of homes around the country.

Pre-marking pays off

When wires are marked in an understandable way, connecting them properly to switches and receptacles is easy and even fun. As we describe in Chapter 3, things can get messy when you are installing wiring, but the job will be easier if you spend some time before you start running the wires taking careful notes and labeling every single wire. Don't fear being redundant.

The time you spend organizing, marking, and understanding everything during the rough-in phase will save you a lot of time during the trim-out phase. After the drywall and finish are in place, whatever is behind them can quickly become a mystery. Unraveling that mystery can take a lot of time and create headaches, unless you're working with good notes and clear markings.

You may, however, want to spruce up your home with more decorative switches and receptacles. Many are now available in the *decorator* style of design, which features rectangular receptacles and paddle switches rather than toggle switches. Decorator components usually cost about twice as much as standard components.

Color Plate 2 (turn to the color insert pages in this book) shows receptacles and switches from the Decora collection by Leviton. Most *ground fault interrupt (GFI)* receptacles are decorator design. We think decorator-style components are a better choice than the old standby styles. Paddle-style switches are easy to operate even when your hands are full, and many dimmer switches are only made in decorator style.

In addition to standard and decorator devices, many more expensive specialty devices are available. One style features a snap-on cover requiring no screws. Spend some time at your local electrical supplier to see what wiring devices are available.

After choosing a style for the switches and receptacles, you should choose a color. The standard colors are brown, white, ivory, and almond. Almond seems to be the most popular color right now, followed closely by white and ivory. Ten years ago, ivory was predominant. Many more colors are available, but it may be hard to find special devices in a specific color. For instance, a specific dimmer, fan-speed control, or volume control may be offered in only one of the standard colors.

Most people choose one color and use it throughout the home, but this convention isn't written in stone. For example, almond-colored components might look great in the kitchen and living room, but almond might be too pale against the paint in the dining room. For certain rooms, you may want to customize the switches and receptacles by painting them or by covering them with contact paper or wall paper.

Working with Receptacles and Switches

In this section, we describe installing the actual device you've chosen in the previous section. We go through the various connection details with diagrams and photos. We supply some time estimates to give you some idea of how much time this phase of your project will consume.

Installing receptacles and GFIs

Installing duplex receptacles should be a breeze. Most jurisdictions have no standard for how duplex receptacles should be installed, but in some jurisdictions, the inspectors require the receptacle to be installed with the ground terminal up; see Figure 4-2, later in this chapter. The logic is that if a piece of metal falls on the outlet between the receptacle and a plug, it can bridge across the hot and neutral contacts if the outlet is installed ground down. We think this is nonsense. One manufacturer offers a four-outlet receptacle with one outlet ground up, one ground down, and two horizontal opposite to each other. Most 15-amp and 20-amp angled cord ends have the cord hang properly if the receptacle is installed ground down. We also believe that standard receptacles look better with the ground installed down.

Figure 4-1 shows a Bryant quad receptacle. This is an Underwriters Laboratory-listed wiring device. As you can see, a receptacle is oriented with the ground terminal up, down, right, and left: You have four mounting options. This wiring device mounts on a 4" × 4" box. With the adapter to the right of the quad receptacle, it can be mounted on one of the following:

  ✔ **Single-gang box:** Designed for a single standard receptacle or switch
  ✔ **Two-gang box:** Designed to hold two standard receptacles or switches

Because of the multiple receptacle orientations, this receptacle can accommodate several plug-in adapters and still leave receptacles free.

Figure 4-1:
Quadplex
receptacles
can be
installed at
all possible
angles.

All 30-amp and 50-amp angle cord ends hang properly when the receptacle is installed ground up. The 125-volt, 15-amp, and 20-amp cord ends may be manufactured with *ground-up* or *ground-down orientation*. For permanently installed appliances such as washers and gas dryers, you have to check your appliance's cord orientation. The great majority of 15-amp and 20-amp cord plugs are oriented properly if the receptacle is installed with the ground terminal down. The receptacles for these appliances should be installed about 40" measured to the top of the box. At this height the appliance hides the receptacle and the receptacle is high enough to be reached.

Figure 4-2 is a photo of a 50-amp and a 15-amp receptacle installed with the ground terminals oriented up. You can see the 50-amp cord is hanging properly and the 15 amp cord isn't. The 15-amp receptacle should have been installed with the ground terminal oriented down to make the installation look better. A careful look at the 50-amp receptacle reveals the manufacturer's engraved name upside down. The point is to get you to think of the total picture and get the installation correct the first time; consider what comes next.

An industrious, experienced electrician with a screw gun can install up to 30 receptacles in an hour. A novice or first-timer who can install five receptacles in an hour is doing pretty well, because experience and skill greatly affect labor time. If you can install 15 receptacles per hour, it takes about 5 hours to trim out a 2,000-square-foot home. The trim-out time includes installing switches, receptacles, TV and phone jacks, lights, trimming the electrical panel, and making final connections to mechanical systems such as a furnace and air conditioner.

Figure 4-2:
Install
receptacles
with proper
cord
orientation
for neatness.

If the outlets were roughed in properly (by *properly* we mean that enough slack is present and the conductors are plainly marked so that the trim out is just a simple repetitive exercise for each one; see Chapter 3), installing a receptacle is a simple matter of following these steps:

1. **Connect the two white conductors in each box to the neutral terminals on the receptacle.**

   The neutral terminals usually have white or silver screws.

   Most receptacles have two sets of wires roughed into the receptacle box, because power receptacles are usually *daisy chained* together. One set of conductors brings in power from the previous outlet in the chain, and the other set sends the power on to the next receptacle.

2. **Connect the two black conductors to the power terminals on the receptacle.**

   The power terminals usually have darker or brass screws.

3. **Wrap one of the green (or bare) wires around the receptacle's ground terminal screw.**

   When you wrap the ground wire around the ground terminal, wrap it so a tail about 3" long sticks out.

4. **Connect the other green wire to the ground wire's tail using a yellow wire nut.**

   Wrap the wire so that when you tighten the screw, it draws the wire tighter, rather than pushing the wire out from under the screw.

   Wrapping both ground wires around the ground terminal's screw is against code. Alternatively, you can connect the two green (or bare) ground wires along with a *pigtail* (a short piece of green or bare wire) and wire nut, and then connect the single pigtail wire to the ground terminal on the receptacle. Whatever method you choose, make sure the ground wires are connected solidly through to the next box.

5. **Cut the blue wire!** *Cut the blue wire!!*

   Just kidding. There shouldn't be a blue wire, but if there is, don't cut it.

If you install a GFI receptacle with only one power and one neutral wire, simply connect the power-supply wire to the line terminals on the receptacle. If the GFI receptacle is protecting downstream standard receptacles, the wires feeding the standard receptacles must be connected to the GFI outlet's load-side terminals. These downstream load wires should be marked during rough in. A daisy-chain electrical circuit is said to be *directional*. Power flows from a power source to outlet 1, 2, and so on. In a 15-outlet chain, outlet 15 is downstream of outlet 14. Outlets 2 through 15 are downstream of outlet 1. When standard outlets are properly connected downstream of the load terminals of a GFI-protected outlet, the downstream outlets are also GFI protected and are labeled as such.

The simple way to mark downstream load wires is to strip both the white and black wires ¾" during rough in. Connect these load wires to the GFI before stripping the line (power) wires to avoid getting them mixed up. Alternatively, you may want to mark the line and load wires with mailing labels.

The electrical inspector is probably going to use a tester like the one shown in Figure 4-3 to make sure the GFIs and receptacles are connected properly. Two GFI receptacles appear nearby in the figure. The face-down receptacle shows yellow tape with a warning from the manufacturer prompting you to connect the device properly.

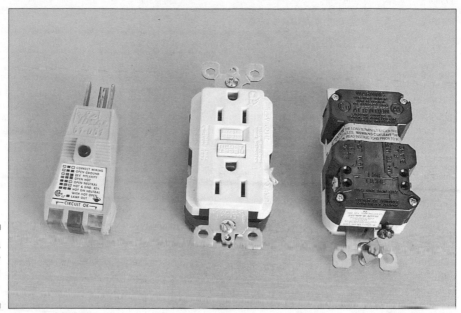

Figure 4-3: A GFI tester and two GFI receptacles

Installing switches

The first time you install a switch and everything works properly when you try it, a smile will probably appear across your face. Connecting every wire in a four-gang switch box to the correct terminal when nothing is marked can be a challenge for any electrician. Don't do that to yourself. When you rough in the switch boxes, install and connect every wire that you can. Visualize the plaster in place and imagine the passage of time between rough in and trim out. This can be a month or more, so connecting what can be connected and marking wires will save you a lot of headaches later.

Make some wiring rules and keep to them consistently. For example, in most wiring scenarios, the power wire should go on top, but on a single-pole (On-Off) switch, it makes no difference. Additional rules that we suggest are in Table 4-1. The next few sections describe how to install the most common types of switches used in your home.

Table 4-1	Author-Recommended Wiring Rules
What You See	*What It Means*
Two wires	A single-pole switch.
Three wires	A three-way switch.

(continued)

Table 4-1 *(continued)*

What You See	What It Means
Four wires	A four-way switch.
Four-gang box	Four groups of wires, each arranged in the four spaces of the box where switches are installed later.
Fan-speed switch	Two wires and may need additional marking to avoid confusing it with a single-pole switch.
Switch nearest the door trim	Should operate the light in the space you are facing toward or in the direction ahead of you.
Switch adjacent to one nearest door	Should operate the light in the hall outside the room.
Any remaining switches	Should operate lighting and devices in order of importance or frequency of use.

In the 2002 code, most lights or fixtures are called *luminaires*. Luminaires are described as fully completed light units. A porcelain lamp holder, for example, is not a luminaire until you screw in the light bulb.

Single-pole switches

Single-pole switches are the easiest to install. This assumes, of course, that you understand that a neutral wire goes to the light fixture and completes the circuit. Not counting the ground wire, you must connect only two wires, and it doesn't matter which goes where. One wire is the power source and the other brings power to the light. When you turn on the switch, both wires are energized.

A single-pole switch wiring has two wiring options. The circuit wires (hot and neutral) can be brought into the light-fixture box or to the switch box. Generally, bringing the circuit into the switch box is easier. This is especially true for multiple-gang switch boxes and multiple light fixtures controlled by the same switch.

Three-way switches

Suppose you want to control a single light fixture from both ends of a hallway. You can do this by installing three-way switches at each end of the hallway. Three-way switch wiring has five popular wiring layout options, three of which we will consider here.

The circuit for a three-way switch normally requires four wires:

> ✔ **Black:** Power
>
> ✔ **White:** Neutral or, sometimes, *traveler*
>
> ✔ **Green or bare:** Ground
>
> ✔ **Red:** Traveler

Three-way switches are technically single-pole double-throw switches, or *double-on with no off position.*

Figure 4-4 shows the wiring diagram for a three-way switch circuit. The ground (green or bare) wire is omitted both in the text and the diagram for clarity. Bear in mind the ground wires are always connected together and connected to all wiring device ground terminals.

To wire the three-way circuit shown in Figure 4-4, follow these steps.

1. **Install a two-conductor cable (14-2 Romex with ground) between the light fixture and the first three-way switch.**

   This switch is called switch number 1 in Figure 4-4.

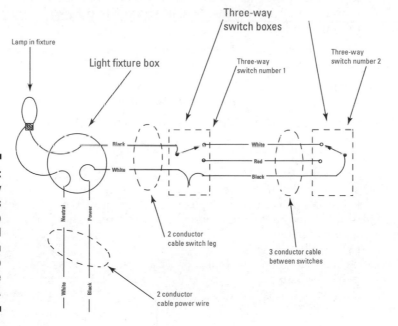

Figure 4-4: Three-way switches allow you to control lights from two separate locations.

2. **Install three-conductor cable (14-3 Romex with ground) from the first three-way switch to the second three-way switch in the circuit.**

   This switch is called switch number 2 in Figure 4-4.

3. **Connect the red and white wires to the brass screws on each three-way switch assembly, as shown in Figure 4-4.**

   • In the second three-way switch, you've connected the red and white travelers to the traveler terminal screws. You have one wire left to connect (the black wire) and one terminal left to connect it to (the common terminal).

   • In the first three-way switch, you've connected the travelers to the two traveler terminal screws.

   The brass terminal screws are called the *traveler terminals* and the common terminal screw is usually dark brown on a three-way switch. In any case, two screws are colored the same *(travelers)* and one is colored different *(common)*.

4. **On the remaining switch terminal (common), connect either one of the wires of the two-conductor cable from the light.**

   The remaining wire of this two-conductor cable connects to the black of the three-conductor from the second three-way switch.

   On this switch wiring setup, you have a two-conductor cable bringing power into the light-fixture box, in addition to the two-conductor cable from the three-way switch.

5. **At the fixture box, connect the white power wire (neutral) to the fixture's white (neutral).**

6. **Connect, with a wire connector, the black power wire to the white wire that runs to the first three-way switch.**

7. **Connect the one remaining wire (black) to the fixture's black wire.**

   This is the black of the cable that runs to the first three-way switch.

In the preceding steps, you used the white wires as travelers and to bring power from the fixture to the first three-way switch. Whenever you use a white wire as a power wire (not a neutral), mark it with colored electrical tape — any color but green — or color it with a permanent marker — again, any color but green.

Keep in mind the common terminal on a three-way switch is always connected within the switch to one or the other traveler terminals. From the common terminal in the figure, you see an arrow close (not connected) to a traveler terminal.

This shows the common flips from one traveler to the other traveler when the switch is operated. In one position it connects to one of the traveler terminals and operates the switch, and the common is connected to the other traveler. We describe this switch elsewhere as a *double on*.

If reading the following paragraph doesn't turn on the light (pardon the pun), draw this diagram on paper and follow the text. Picture power connected to one of the three-way switch commons. The three-way switch connects this power to one of the travelers. If the other three-way switch is connected to the same traveler that connects to the light, the circuit is complete and the light comes on. If the opposite switch is moved to its alternate position, the light goes out.

The travelers are like two roads going to the same place. Moving the three-way switches is analogous to events. In the spring you can't take the lower (red) road because the bridge washed out. In the winter you can't take the high (white) road because an avalanche took out the road. The light is on when a continuous path goes from the power wire through the switches, then through the lamp back to the neutral.

✔ The three-way switch diagram in Figure 4-4 shows both commons on the three-way switches connecting the commons to the whites. You can see that if one of the three-way switches is operated, there's no longer a circuit. Now one of the commons will be connected to the red. Further, you can see the circuit to the light fixture can be restored by operating either switch. You can also see that the circuit still behaves the same by connecting the travelers on the opposite switch common terminals. It doesn't matter which traveler color connects to which screw, it still works the same.

In some wiring schemes the switch box may have a red wire bringing power up to the light. In these cases, you have to distinguish this red power wire from the red traveler wire. Just stripping the red power wire back ¾" should be sufficient, or you can mark the switch-leg red wire with black tape. If you do neither, remember the red traveler will be running with the white traveler (part of the same Romex) from the other switch.

✔ The second wiring layout for three-way switches, shown in Figure 4-5, brings the electrical circuit to the first three-way switch. The power neutral would connect to the white wire going to the fixture box. In the fixture box, the power neutral connects to the lamp neutral. The black circuit wire connects to the black of the three conductor to the second three-way switch. Everything else is the same.

✔ The third variation, shown in Figure 4-6, brings power to the second three-way switch in a very different way than the previous two layouts. In this scheme, the traveler wires are going to be black and red, so you can use the white wire as neutral. We seldom use this layout, but it's nice when the first three-way switch and the fixture are far from the second three-way switch, and the first three-way switch's area has no power.

As briefly mentioned earlier, other wiring schemes bring the three-conductor wires though the fixture box(es). We never use these messy and complicated wiring layouts. The numerous connections waste time and increase the possibility of errors. A wiring problem usually involves removing a light fixture or paddle fan to solve the problem.

There is a three-way wiring layout that connects power to the travelers. The power to the loads is taken from the three-way commons. This system works, but as the different three-way switches are turned on, the load's neutral and hot wires are swapped. That is, in one position, one conductor is neutral; in the next position, the same wire is hot. Don't use this switching arrangement! It is a code violation. Before four-conductor cable was readily available, this wiring was often used to have power for a receptacle and three-way switching at a remote location by just running three-wire cable.

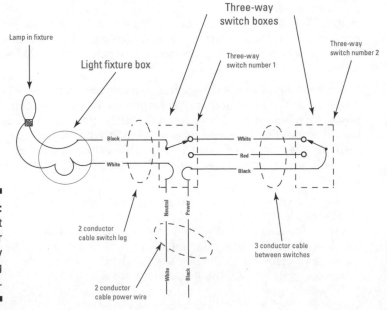

Figure 4-5:
The most popular three-way wiring layout.

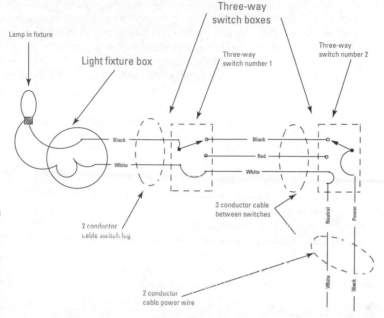

Three-way
switch boxes

Light fixture box

Three-way
switch number 1

Three-way
switch number 2

Lamp in fixture

Black

White

Black

Red

White

3 conductor cable
between switches

Neutral

Power

Figure 4-6:
Another
three-way
wiring
layout.

2 conductor
cable switch leg

2 conductor
cable power wire

White

Black

Four-way switches

After you understand how three-way switches work, wiring four-way switches
is a piece of cake. Three-way switches allow you to control light from two
locations. *Four-way switches* are used to control lights from three or more
locations.

Four-way switches have four terminals and are always used in conjunction
with and in between (electrically) two three-way switches. You can install any
number of four-way switches in a circuit between the two three-way switches.
Four-way switches come in two types:

- **Through wired:** This is the most common. The pair of travelers from
  one three-way switch connect to one end of a four-way switch, and then
  the pair of travelers connected to the other end of the four-way switch
  run to the next switch in the circuit (whether it's a three- or four-way
  switch).

- **Cross wired:** On a cross-wired four-way switch, one three-way switch's
  traveler pair goes on one side of the four-way switch, and the travelers
  from the other three-or four-way switch connect to the other side.
  Although the travelers are red and white just like connections on a
  three way switch, the colors are less important than the proper pairing.

Figure 4-7 shows a four-way switch wiring layout. The wiring schematic is the same whether through wired or cross wired — you just have to identify which switch type you have to properly connect it. The manufacturer usually helps by marking one traveler pair one color and the other pair another color. To reiterate, our terminology here of a *pair* is the red and white (travelers) from one location. In the explanation we consider a four-way switch connected between two three-way switches.

The three-conductor cable from the first three-way switch goes to the four-way switch location. From there, a second three-conductor cable goes to the second three-way switch location. A quick mental drill: If you connect the two three-conductor cables together, color to color, in this four-way box, you have the three-way wiring working. In a sense, all a four-way wiring and switch does is connect the travelers in to the travelers out. With the four-way switch in one position the connection is color to color. In the other position the colors are reversed. In the four-way box, the black wire in connects to the black wire out — not to the switch at all. The four-way switch in one position connects the red traveler in to the red traveler out and the white in to the white out. In the alternative position, it connects the red traveler in to the white traveler out and the white traveler in to the red traveler out.

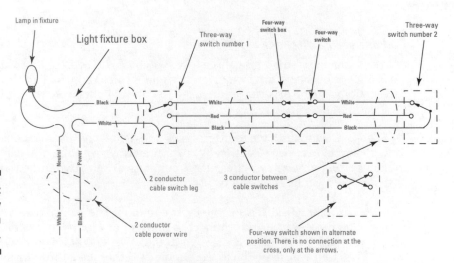

Figure 4-7:
Four-way
switch
wiring.

Pilot switches

Pilot switches have a pilot light built into the switch, illuminating when the load (a light or fan, for example) is turned on. They can be used on single-pole, three-way and four-way switching arrangements.

> ✔ A single-pole pilot switch outside a closet can remind you to turn off the closet light.
>
> ✔ An entry-porch switch may control exterior lights, and a pilot switch reminds you when the exterior lights are on.
>
> ✔ A pilot switch can control the lights in a basement, crawl space, or attic.
>
> ✔ You may also want to install a pilot switch for equipment that normally doesn't give a visual clue when it's on, such as heat tape.

The single-pole pilot switch is just like a standard single-pole switch, except that now it matters where the power and load (light) wires are connected. The wiring scheme for both single-pole and three-way systems requires a neutral at the pilot switch location. The three-way pilot wiring requires the pilot neutral be connected to the power neutral wire for that circuit. A three-way pilot switch can only be used on one of the two three-way locations. In both instances, when you bring a neutral to the switch box, you also bring the power wire to that box.

Lighted switches

Lighted switches illuminate when the light (load) is turned off and are available in single-pole, three-way, and four-way configurations. A lighted switch doesn't require a neutral. Lighted switches can be installed on any single-pole switch, three-way switch arrangement, or four-way switch wiring scheme. You don't have to use lighted switches at every switch location in three-way and four-way schemes.

Lighted switches are most useful in areas that are normally dark. For example, an interior bathroom or hallway may be dimly lit even in the middle of a sunny day, which makes a lighted switch helpful. Lighted switches let you find the switch in the dark. Install these lighted switches anywhere that finding a switch in the dark is a problem. On a three-way or four-way wiring scheme with all lighted switches installed in all locations, all switches illuminate when the light is turned off.

Dimmer switches

You can install *dimmer switches* on any incandescent lighting system. Most dimmers change the incoming AC voltage to DC and then vary the value of the DC voltage. For this reason, you shouldn't connect a dimmer to a receptacle. If you plug a device such a cell phone charger into a dimmer-controlled receptacle, it could burn out the dimmer and may damage the charger. Dimmers can be used to vary the speed of AC-DC brush motors like those in electric drills and fans. Generally, however, you should reserve dimmer switches solely for use with incandescent lights.

Dimmers are generally available for 600- to 2000-watt applications. If you want to control a fixture with a dozen 60-watt lamps, a standard 600-watt dimmer won't suffice. Always use a dimmer rated for larger wattage than you need. This reduces heat in the switch, making the dimmer last longer. Higher-wattage dimmers have cooling fins, which you can usually remove to fit the dimmer into a multiple-gang switch arrangement. Of course, removing a fin reduces the dimmer's wattage capacity. If you're going to dim a lot of watts, wire to a single-gang location.

Dimmers are made in single-pole, three-way, four-way, and multiple-switch versions. Some of these have full-range dimming in all locations. Special dimmers can dim low-voltage and fluorescent lighting. To dim fluorescent lighting, the fixture must have a dimming ballast that matches the dimmer. Some of the specialty dimmers are very sensitive to lightning, which of course is just another reason to install surge protection at your home's service panel.

Timer switches

Timer switches come in various types. These switches are generally a single-pole Decora design and fit in a one-gang switch box.

Check the load and type rating to make sure the timer is adequate for your application. For example, some timer switches are for incandescent loads only, while others will control lights or motors.

Some common uses for specific timer switch types include

- ✔ **Interval:** Turns on a load for a specific time interval. Commonly used to control a heat lamp or fan.

- ✔ **Time delay:** Can have delays ranging from two minutes to an hour. Turns on instantly, but delays turning off after you move the switch to the off position.

- ✔ **Variable countdown:** Usually just a rotary knob that you can set for times from a few minutes to many hours. You've probably seen these in motel bathrooms to control the heat lamp.

- ✔ **Programmable:** Can be set on intervals within a 24-hour cycle. Although it has indoor uses such as office lighting and fans, it's most often used for outdoor lighting.

If you want outdoor lights to come on at dusk, we recommend installing a photo sensor along with the timer. For example, suppose you want the lights to come on at dusk and turn off at midnight, and then turn back on at 6:00 AM and stay on until dawn. Set a programmable timer to turn on at 6:00 AM and turn off at midnight. When used with a photo sensor, the lights are only on during the dark times between 6:00 AM and midnight.

Infrared sensors

Infrared sensors, occupancy sensors, and *motion sensors* are all different names for the same device. These sensors act like switches that turn on when you or your pet squirrel walks into the sensor's field of detection. The sensors most often control incandescent or fluorescent lighting, and some are rated to control motors. These devices add convenience and should save power, especially in areas where lights tend to be left on unnecessarily. Some motion sensors have ambient light sensors and don't turn on if the area is already lighted from windows or a skylight.

Many fixtures have built-in motion and light sensors. Some also have built-in overrides that allow you to turn on the light whether motion is detected or not.

X10 devices

X10 devices are remote-controlled devices that work using a line carrier signal sent through your home's existing wiring. (See Chapter 5 for more about X10 devices; see Chapter 13 for computer control of X10 devices.) An X10 transmitter can be a wired-in switch, a plug-in unit, or a hand-held transmitter. The transmitter must be powered, but it doesn't need to be wired directly to a receiver in the traditional sense. The transmitter sends control signals to receivers over the existing house wiring, meaning that one transmitter can control almost any light or device in your home. The transmitter can even be a hand-held universal remote control like the one you use for your TV. Likewise, a programmable garage-door opener can be programmed to turn on driveway lights. Both the receiver and transmitter must use the same side, or *leg,* of the home's breaker panel. If not on the same panel leg, a signal bridge is sometimes needed.

A variety of programmable X10 controllers and timers are available. They can control lights, alarms, lawn sprinklers, and many other devices. Because X10 devices use existing wiring, you can use them in new construction as well as in retrofit installations. A single receiver such as a single pole switch can cost about $20, and a transmitter can be double that amount.

Flushing and Leveling Electrical Devices

As you're installing switches and receptacles in your digital home, you want to make sure that each device is *flush* (seats properly) and *level* (straight), making it look like the professional installation that it is. Although even an experienced builder may not identify trim that's not quite level or flush, the human eye perceives the problems and feels a little uncomfortable in the room.

Flushing and leveling start during the rough-in phase of construction. During rough in, make sure that every box is level and doesn't protrude past the surface of the drywall. Sometimes the drywall hanger can knock the box out of level. The screws that mount switches and receptacles in the boxes are slotted, allowing for a small degree of leveling adjustment. For single- and two-gang installs, these slots can facilitate a lot of adjustment. For three-gang or larger boxes, the degree of adjustment is limited. In all cases, tighten the screws until the plaster ears on each switch or receptacle exert a slight amount of pressure on the finished wall surface.

On a four-gang switch box, for example, the switches all have to line up with screw holes in the trim plate. Moving the switches into alignment when the screws are too tight is tough, and they needn't be excessively tight. With the plate in place and all screws started but not tightened, check the leveling of the trim plate. At this point, you can still level the plate by putting the edge of your screwdriver against the edge of the plate and bumping it with the palm of your hand. Be careful not to damage the finished surface. Once leveled, finish tightening the screws. Don't make them too tight; plastic trim plates break easily.

No matter how hard you try, after installing the drywall you may notice that some box edges protrude from the wall. Don't fret! Try this remedy:

1. **Insert a narrow screwdriver near the top of the box between the box and the drywall, and then locate the nail securing the box to the stud.**

2. **With the end of the screwdriver against the nail, hit the screwdriver with a hammer and drive the nail back slightly.**

3. **Repeat this on the bottom nail, moving each nail until the box is flush.**

   If the box breaks loose from the nail, use a few drywall screws through the side of the box to refasten it to the wall stud.

If you use plastic boxes in accordance with article 314.43 of the 2002 electrical code, you must cover any screw heads inside the box with some insulating material or tape. This prevents the conductors from contacting the screws. You can also cut the entire side from a broken box and slide it between the screw heads and wires to satisfy the code requirement.

On a multiple-gang box that is protruding slightly, a hold-it can be used. A *hold-it* is a piece of sheet metal shaped like the letter F. You insert this piece of metal between the outside edge of the box and the drywall with the longest side up. Installing it long-side up prevents it from falling into the wall cavity if the pressure on the sheet metal is less than the pull of gravity. The box is pushed back slightly more than flush and the two tabs of the hold-it are folded into the box, thus holding the box flush.

By code, the maximum allowable gap between a box edge and plaster, drywall, or plasterboard is ⅛". If you find the gap too large for your trim plates to cover, check your local supplier for oversized trim plates. The oversized trim plates also help cover drywall goofs.

Testing Your Installations

After all the switches and receptacles are installed, everything must be tested. Obviously, check all the lights to make sure they work. Check all of three-way and four-way switch locations to make sure they work as intended. Use a receptacle tester that has a GFI trip tester to determine whether the wiring was done properly. At this point, you should be ready for a perfect final inspection.

Although the receptacle test is referred to as a *polarity test,* AC voltage has no polarity. The test checks the connection of the hot conductor in relation to the receptacle's neutral and ground terminals and indicates whether a neutral or ground is *open* (disconnected or broken). If the hot is open, the test indicates nothing — the lights on the tester won't light up.

Figure 4-8 shows a receptacle tester. This particular tester also checks GFI receptacles, which is a feature you should look for. The GFI tester duplicates the function of the test button on the GFI receptacle. Perform this test not only on GFI outlets, but any receptacle that feeds through the GFI. The GFI test won't work if the ground wire path is open.

Figure 4-8:
Receptacle
and GFI
tester
close up.

Chapter 5

Controlling Your Life Remotely

In This Chapter

▶ Understanding remote controls

▶ Using X10, RF, IR, and UPB to control power to lights and devices

▶ Timing appliances and saving energy

ifty years ago, remote controls were almost unheard of. But as years passed, handheld remotes started controlling various devices. The Zenith Space Command introduced many people to TV remotes, using sound waves to change the channel or adjust volume from across the living room. Remotes used low-power radios to open or close garage doors. Later, TV and home electronics remotes used *infrared (IR)* light waves to provide remote control.

Remote controls aren't just for garage door openers and VCRs anymore. You can control your entire home using remote control systems. Imagine being able to turn on any light or adjust the temperature without moving from your chair. This chapter introduces some of the remote control technologies available for your digital home. It also shows you some of the handy automation features that help make your home safer, more energy efficient, and easier to live in.

Controlling Your Gadgets Remotely

Remote controls don't have to be just for home electronics or specific appliances. If an item in your home is powered by electricity, it can probably be controlled remotely. For instance, in addition to describing IR and radio frequency remotes, the following sections explain motion sensors, which can turn on lights or security cameras. The technology called X10, which we also explain here, can control lights and other devices.

Infrared and radio frequency remotes

You probably already have a lot of remote controls in your home, such as handheld IR remote controls for TVs, VCRs, stereos, CD players, and DVD players. You may also have manufacturer-provided IR remote controls for ceiling fans, gas fireplaces, window blinds, air conditioners, and heaters. Other remotes — such as garage door openers — use *radio frequencies (RF)* to provide control. The remote shown in Figure 5-1 controls a ceiling fan, and although it provides remote control, it's actually hard-wired to the fan assembly.

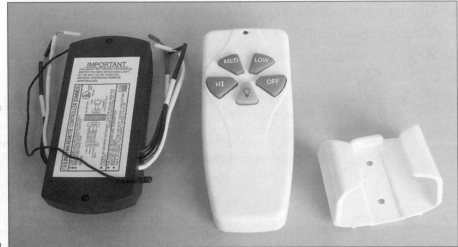

Figure 5-1:
This manufac-
turer-
supplied
remote
controls a
ceiling fan.

If you encounter poor signal reception between a handheld IR remote and its receiver, you can install a repeater. *Repeaters* act like mirrors that let you see around corners, allowing the IR wave to reflect around corners.

RF remotes work through low-density walls, but may not penetrate concrete. The transmitter's strength determines its operating range. Most handheld RF remotes work to a distance of about 100'.

Motion sensors

One of the most commonly used lighting controls is the misnamed *motion sensor.* These devices, which actually detect body heat, are often used with outdoor lighting, but a variety of motion switches designed for indoor use are available. These indoor motion sensors are useful in areas where

✔ You tend to leave lights on.

✔ Manually turning lights on or off is inconvenient.

Motion sensors directly replace standard single-pole switches. Many motion sensors can work without a neutral wire present in the switch box. They generally have a 180-degree sensing field of view that covers an area about 20' × 20'.

Most motion sensors also have automatic *ambient light sensors* built-in, meaning that if the area is lit with sufficient natural light, the sensor will not turn the lights on. Most sensors include a manual override so they can work like a standard toggle switch when needed.

X10 remotes and devices

Wouldn't it be cool to turn on the kitchen light from your bed so you don't trip when you get up for your 3 a.m. drink of water? If you think this kind of control is only possible if you can train your dog to flip light switches with his nose, think again. A technology called *X10* allows you to control any device in your home using your existing electrical system. With X10 you can turn on the lawn sprinkler or the sauna stove, dim the lights, and change the TV channel, all with the same handheld remote control. You can also program X10 devices to act automatically. For example, you can set the central vacuum system to automatically turn off when the doorbell or the phone rings. Some X10 controllers have an "all lights on or off" feature. Many X10 devices can be programmed using computer software.

As we describe in Chapter 4, residential electrical systems in the United States use 60-cycle *alternating current (AC)*. This means that the voltage cycles through zero 60 times per second. When the voltage is at zero, X10 devices use the wires to transmit control commands from controllers to receivers in your lights and receptacles. The X10 system uses 16 numbered addresses (1 through 16) and the first 16 letters (A through P) of the alphabet. This gives the system its capacity of 256 addresses (16 × 16). Each address can control an unlimited number of devices.

You may encounter a few X10 technology limitations:

✔ **Poor signal reliability:** You may find that commands are successfully transmitted only about 90 percent of the time, depending on where you are in your home.

- ✔ **Time delays:** You may encounter a half-second delay between pushing the On button and seeing the light come on.

- ✔ **Cross talk with neighbors:** With only 256 X10 addresses available, your neighbor's X10 may inadvertently control your lights.

- ✔ **Line noise:** Electrical line noise may degrade X10 signal strength. Amplifiers and line couplers are available to help address this problem.

- ✔ **No feedback:** When you operate an X10 device remotely and out of sight or hearing, you don't get any feedback that lets you know whether your command was successfully received. There are now some controllers on the market that have feedback features.

Selecting X10 devices

You may use X10–controlled relays, switches, receptacles, dimmers, or plug-in modules to actually provide control. Once the controlling devices are wired or plugged in, you just have to choose how to control them. You need two basic components:

- ✔ **Transmitter:** The transmitter sends your control input to the receiver. It can be wired, or it can use IR or RF signals to transmit commands to a plugged-in receiver/transmitter.

- ✔ **Receiver:** The receiver is connected to your electrical system. It receives control signals from the X10 transmitter and initiates some action. This could be turning on or off a load or dimming a light, for example.

Figure 5-2 shows an inexpensive handheld X10 RF remote and *receiver/transmitter (transceiver)*. The transceiver is shown straight on and from the back. The key-chain RF transmitter can be set to control two X10 addresses. This unit receives an RF signal and transmits an X10 signal. The right-side view shows the plug-in and the unit's receptacle. This RF handheld remote sends on or off signals to the X10 transceiver. The transceiver plugs into an outlet and sends an X10 signal over the house wiring to control anything you have set to its address. It also turns on or off its own built-in receptacle.

Figure 5-3 shows seven assorted X10 devices, each of which is numbered. These devices each have some unique features:

- ✔ **Device 1:** This transmitter just plugs into a standard receptacle. The transmitter has 16 buttons and 16 letter positions, allowing control of 256 X10 addresses.

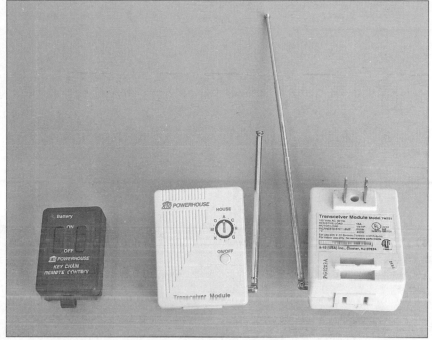

Figure 5-2:
X10
controllers
can use IR
or RF to
control the
systems in
your home.

🖒 **Device 2:** These three-way switches can replace a standard single-pole or three-way switch. Once you install a switch, just set the switch and a transmitter to one of the 256 available addresses.

🖒 **Device 3:** This fixture module is designed to mount in a box . This module has dimming capabilities.

🖒 **Device 4:** This appliance module plugs into a receptacle, and then you plug an appliance or lamp into the module. Set the address code on the front of the module and control it with any X10 transmitter set to the same code.

🖒 **Device 5:** An X10 signal controls relay operation for this plug-in relay module. We have used these to enable remote opening of garage doors that did not come equipped with remote openers. For garage door opening and closing on commercial garage doors that have separate buttons for up and down, the installation requires two relays. Relays can also be set for momentary operation. In the momentary operation mode, the relay closes when it receives an on signal and then immediately turns off. This mimics a person pushing a doorbell or a garage door opener, and then releasing it.

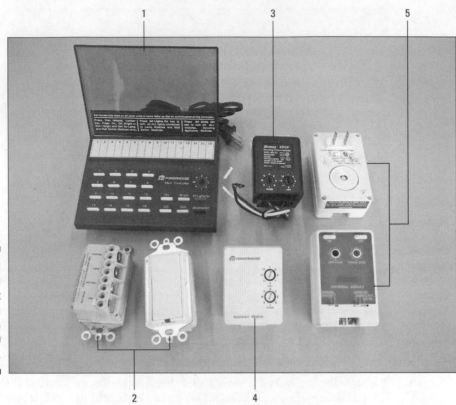

Figure 5-3:
Control
almost
anything in
the home
with X10
devices.

Retrofitting X10 in older homes

New homes aren't the only places where X10 can be used. These devices can be easily used in any home that has AC electricity.

Color Plate 3 (shown in the color insert pages in this book) shows an example of an older home upgraded with X10 devices. In the figure, you can see a wall fixture that was installed about 90 years ago — it's the light fixture on the right side, just above the globe. This is one of three similar fixtures in a library finished with quarter-sawn oak paneling and beams. Each of the two lamps on the light fixtures was originally controlled by a separate pull chain. Lighting all three wall fixtures required walking around the room and pulling all six chains. By simply removing the fixtures and installing a fixture module connected to the existing wiring, X10 gives full on, off, and dimming control of these three fixtures from one location.

Beyond X10

Due to the limitations of X10 devices, a California company called Powerline Control Systems (PCS) has developed a new product using a new proprietary power-line communication technology, the *Universal Powerline Bus (UPB)*. This system has a total of 62,500 addresses, which should eliminate the problem of cross talk. The reliability of UPB is said to be near 100 percent.

The devices themselves have some programmable features. They can be used on X10 systems without interfering with X10 operations. The UPB system doesn't have as many devices or interfaces available as does X10, but the list is growing. At the time of this writing, UPB devices cost more than similar X10 devices, but that too may change.

The paddle fan in the same room (see Color Plate 3) has two X10 controls installed in the fan's hanger box. One control dims the light or turns it on and off. The second control is wired to turn the paddle fan on and off. We installed a four-button wall transmitter to control the fan, the fan's light, and the three light fixtures along the wall. X10 allowed us to update the electrical controls without damaging the beautiful and expensive oak paneling.

Controlling X10 away from home

Once you have X10 controls in place, you can add a phone interface to control any X10 device from any touchtone phone, including cordless and cell phones.

One such interface is called TeleMaster, which costs about $150. This unit simply plugs in to an existing phone jack and a 120V outlet. With this TeleMaster interface, you can call home as you return from vacation or work. Press a couple of phone buttons on the phone to turn on the air conditioner and warm the hot tub. Access to the TeleMaster is restricted by a four-digit security code. Normal phone calling to and from your home is unchanged. You can set up this interface so that when the phone rings, lamps in your home flash on and off, thereby giving a visual indication to someone with a hearing impairment.

The only real drawback to a system like the TeleMaster is that it doesn't provide any feedback. For example, if you use it to turn on the hot tub, how do you know that it really turned on before you step in? Without any kind of feedback, you don't. Still, this is definitely a great way to add high-tech remote control to your digital home.

Using Timers for Around-the-Clock Control

Timers are a great way to add convenience and save money. A thermostat set to change the temperature in your home at certain times (for example, to lower the thermostat to 65° after 10:00 p.m. and to raise it back up to 72° at 7:00 a.m.) can save money on your utility bill for heating and cooling. When using timers to heat or cool a large area, you may need to add some recovery time to the time settings, so that the desired temperature is reached at the right time. Adding a timer to turn off the water heater overnight can also save money.

Be aware that big changes in temperature may involve an hour or two recovery time, depending on the outside temperature. If you are heading out to your secluded mountain cabin, we suggest making the call earlier than usual.

You can also add programmable timers to control repetitive tasks — for example, to set the outdoor lighting to come on at 6:00 p.m. and turn off at midnight.

- ✔ **Countdown timer:** This simple type is often used with heat lamps.

- ✔ **Seven-day timer:** Figure 5-4 shows this timer, which replaces a single-pole or three-way switch. This timer doesn't require a neutral to be present, but it does require a battery. A manual override allows local control, but is a little bit clumsy to access.

Many timers are just single-pole switches. Some others require a neutral wire or batteries. When installing new wiring, make sure you have a neutral wire in any box where you intend to install a timer. If your project is a retrofit and no neutral is present, use a mechanical or battery timer or choose a type of timer that doesn't require a neutral wire. A good alternative is to use an X10 or UPB timer that is remote from the usage location where a neutral is present. One manufacturer offers a digital alarm clock that plugs in to a standard receptacle. This clock controls up to four X10 addresses and costs about $30.

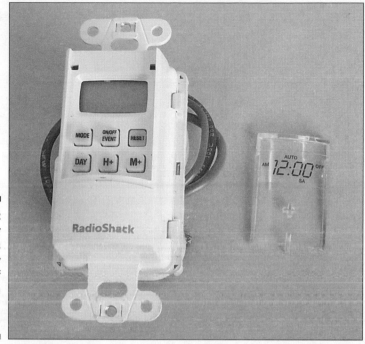

Figure 5-4:
This timer
brings
a handy
level of
automation
to your
home.

Part II
Adding Communication, Audio, and Video Systems

The 5th Wave   By Rich Tennant

"I think I've fixed the intercom. Just remember to speak into the ceiling fan when the doorbell rings."

In this part . . .

In kindergarten you found out everything you need to know about empty soup cans, string, and mirrors. In this part you discover how to wire for phones, PA systems, TV, stereo sound, and video cameras.

The chapters in this part show you how to hook into the step-saving features provided by installing intercoms and video surveillance systems, as well as how to lay out and wire theater-quality sound systems. This part also contains some very helpful information about using remote controls to operate nearly any electrical device in your home.

Chapter 6

Wiring Your Home Phone System

Many of the digital home features described in this book — like security and surveillance systems, intercoms, networks, and remotely controlled lights — may seem high tech and thrilling. These systems are exciting, and you may install some of them based on your individual budget and needs. In addition to digital home upgrades, you can upgrade your phone system. Telephones became ubiquitous in American homes over the last century, though some households have gotten rid of their traditional landline phones in favor of cell phones. This chapter assumes that your home has or will have a traditional landline phone system with at least one line and a local exchange number.

But just because phones have been around for a long time doesn't mean that your system has to use old-fashioned technology or outdated wiring design. A modern home phone system can incorporate many advanced features that were only a dream just a few years ago.

In this chapter, we cover the basic things you need to know before wiring or rewiring your home for phone service. We also cover some more advanced options to the basic single-phone interface: multi-line systems, facsimile (fax) installations, in-home phone exchanges, *Voice over Internet Protocol (VoIP),* and even videoconferencing. So sit back and get ready to let your fingers do the walking into your future possibilities with plain old telephone system and its new pals.

Wiring Your Phone Service

Every home needs at least one phone connection to the outside world — you know, for ordering pizza or calling 911. The digital home requires additional phone lines and features for staying connected and in control whether you're away from home or tucked into bed. The type of phone service interface your home uses depends a lot on the *Telco* (local telephone company) that supplies your service. *Plain old telephone service (POTS)* comes to your house from the phone company's switch using a pair of copper wires. The wires usually run fewer than seven miles from the Telco's switch location to your house.

Some phone companies in major markets offer fiber optic service for phone and high-speed data services right to your home. Fiber optic links exchange data digitally, whereas older copper-wire systems exchange analog data. You need a conversion device to use conventional analog phone sets with digital fiber optic networks. See Chapter 8 for more information on bringing fiber optic phone and digital services into your home.

Planning service entrances

Your phone service — whether copper wire or fiber optic — must enter the house somewhere. This entrance can either be overhead or underground. The method is sometimes dictated by the home's location; most new housing subdivisions prefer, or even require, underground services for all utilities.

The wires to connect your home to the phone system are usually supplied by the service provider.

- **Overhead service:** The provider usually supplies all the cable and their technicians install the phone wires to the customer's home, at least as far as the network interface device box.

- **Underground phone service:** You or your builder will have to check with your local service provider to see who supplies the service wire and who's responsible for installing it.

Identifying the demarcation point

The *demarcation point* is where the phone company line(s) connects to your home's internal wiring. Usually this point is inside a *demarc box* or *Network Interface Device (NID)*. Unless you have a maintenance contract with your Telco, the demarcation point is also the dividing point of wiring responsibility. Before the demarcation point, the phone company is responsible for maintaining and repairing the wiring. After the demarcation point, the wiring is your responsibility.

Using overhead service entrances

If you have overhead service, the phone company will probably install a demarcation box outside your home. Figure 6-1 shows a typical demarc box connected to a house. Notice the grounding tab mounted vertically in the center-left portion of the box. On the upper-right side of the box, a one-line interface jack is already mounted in the box. The NID also requires a grounding connection running as straight as possible to the electrical service entrance grounding point with at least a 14-gauge, insulated grounding copper (stranded or solid) wire listed by *Underwriters Laboratory (UL)* as suitable for grounding. The ground wire should be guarded from potential damage using conduit. If using metal conduit, ground both ends of the metal conduit. In this case, using PVC schedule 40 conduit is probably better.

Figuro 6 1: A demarcation box for overhead service usually looks like this.

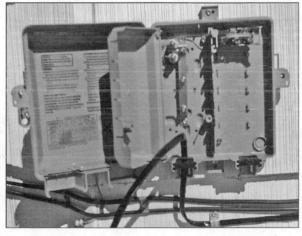

The phone company typically installs only a two-line NID at the demarcation box. If your system needs to grow beyond two lines at some point, the Telco may want to come back and install a second NID. This can be unsightly. We recommend

 ✔ Choosing one of these options:

   • Buy and install your own six-line NID.

   • Insist the phone company use an NID with spaces for more than two lines.

 ✔ Insisting the phone company install a four- or six-pair entrance cable to match the NID capacity.

Figure 6-2 shows a six-place NID box with two lines fully installed on the right side. In this case, the Telco used Category 3 cable to run to a punch-down block inside the house, which connects the phone extension home runs inside the house. In Figure 6-2, notice the cable from the phone pole and the gray ground conductor coming out of the Telco's side (the left) of the NID box. All of the homeowner's wiring comes out of the box's right side.

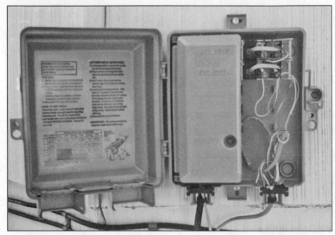

Figure 6-2:
Two lines have been installed in this six-place NID box.

If you look closely at the picture in Figures 6-1 and 6-2, you notice that the interface between the Telco and the customer sides is a standard RJ-11 jack. (*RJ* is short for *Registered Jack.*) If you're having trouble with your phone and want to know whether the problem is in the phone company line or with the house wiring, disconnect one of the RJ-11 plugs in the NID box and insert a standard phone cord attached to a phone. If you hear a dial tone and can make calls from the NID box, then the problem is with your wiring or phone sets inside the house.

Dealing with underground service entrances

Many newer homes have underground utility service rather than overhead. The photo in Figure 6-3 shows a pedestal meter socket, which brings power into the home from underground. On the right of this meter socket is the TV cable interface box. On the left of the meter socket is the phone interface box. The phone and cable companies that installed these interfaces did a marginal job of bringing their underground cables to their respective boxes. The lines are susceptible to damage from snow blowers, lawn mowers, or other hazards.

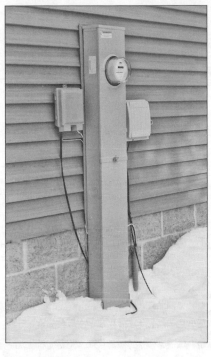

Figure 6-3:
These sloppy cable TV and phone installations are susceptible to damage.

A neater and more professional-looking installation than the one shown in Figure 6-3 has the following:

- ✔ Both interface boxes on the same side of the meter post.
- ✔ A protective conduit extending up the wall to just below the interface boxes.
- ✔ A conduit T connection on the top of the extended conduit.
- ✔ A conduit below grade to protect the cables both below and above grade.
- ✔ Grounding to the residence's electric service-grounding electrode system.
- ✔ All of the conduit ends filled with a duct sealer.

The installation should look more like the diagram shown in Figure 6-4.

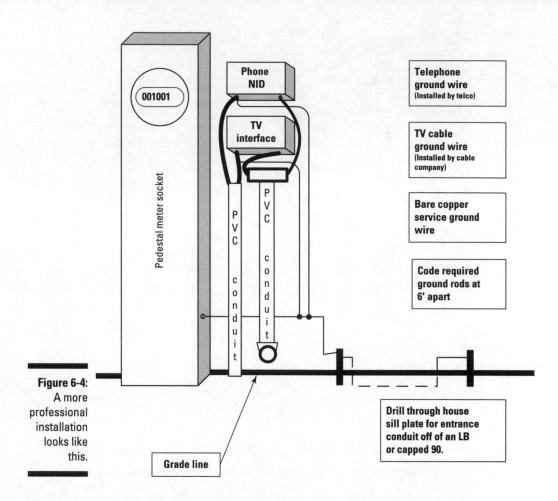

Telephone
ground wire
(Installed by telco)

TV cable
ground wire
(Installed by cable
company)

Bare copper
service ground
wire

Code required
ground rods at
6' apart

Phone
NID

TV
interface

Pedestal meter socket

001001

PVC conduit

PVC conduit

Grade line

Drill through house
sill plate for entrance
conduit off of an LB
or capped 90.

Figure 6-4:
A more
professional
installation
looks like
this.

Planning internal house wiring

The contractor or homeowner is typically responsible for all inside house
wiring leading from the customer side of the phone interface box to all the
phone jacks. Normally wires run from the utility interface box to some designated connection area in your home. This area could be a utility room, service closet, or basement area — any space large enough to hold punch-down
blocks and the equipment you want to install.

If every variety of communications service enters one designated area in the
house, integration between systems becomes far easier.

Some installers like to run serial wires directly from the NID to phone jacks, going from outlet to outlet inside the home. This method is common yet obsolete, because it severely limits your phone wiring options. Serial runs are also harder to troubleshoot and modify if needed. Making home runs from every outlet to a common location is a far better method.

The photos in Figure 6-5 show a mechanical room where the interface extension meets the rest of the house wiring. Note the following elements:

✔ A four-way TV cable splitter shares cable TV with the various rooms in the house. The cable company did a marginal job with this installation. The electrical contractor or homeowner will have to clean up this mess.

✔ A conduit through the wall brings both the TV cable and phone wire into the house.

✔ A phone junction block is mounted overhead. This is just a simple punch-down block connection. Three separate phone lines come in from the NID box, and this junction block divides those lines among eight rooms.

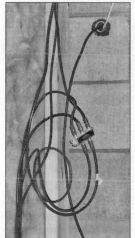

Figure 6-5: It looks like a mess, and yes, you can find a better method to the wiring madness!

The TV and Telco installations pictured in Figure 6-5 are functional, but unfortunately the sloppiness is also typical. The homeowner, builder, or architect hasn't defined a higher standard for the location, installation, and connection of communication equipment. When planning your installation, it should be

- ✔ Accessible
- ✔ At eye level
- ✔ Installed in a neat and orderly fashion

Also, follow the rough-in tips in Chapter 3 and trimming considerations in Chapter 4. The difference between installing a mess and installing orderly cables is often just a few extra minutes of work.

Wiring for Conventional Phones

Once the phone wire's in your home, usually it becomes your responsibility. Figure 6-6 show a wiring diagram for both phone and TV systems in a typical home. Most modern homes have more than one phone line, and each line can serve different locations.

Installing the wiring for your phone system is a big job, but you can take a logical approach. To install your phone system, follow these basic steps:

1. **Choose a central location for your communications equipment.**

   You can locate a wiring closet, basement, or other location for all your communications and security systems for when you're ready to integrate the systems. Co-locating equipment facilitates easier system management, aids in troubleshooting, and eases integration.

2. **Decide which rooms should have phone wiring.**

   At a minimum, we suggest lines in each habitable room and to any workshop areas in the garage or basement. Some people argue against a phone line in each room because of cordless phones, or because they don't believe that kids' rooms need phones. But keep in mind that cordless phones don't work when the power is out, and room uses can change over time. An up-to-date and versatile phone system will probably increase your home's resale value.

3. **Run the wiring using Cat 6 cable.**

Cat 6 cable has eight conductors, consisting of four twisted pairs of 22 or 24 AWG wire. The cable assembly measures about ³⁄₁₆" in diameter. If you want to have two separate lines in a room — for example, one line for phone and a second line for fax — you would use two of the four pairs.

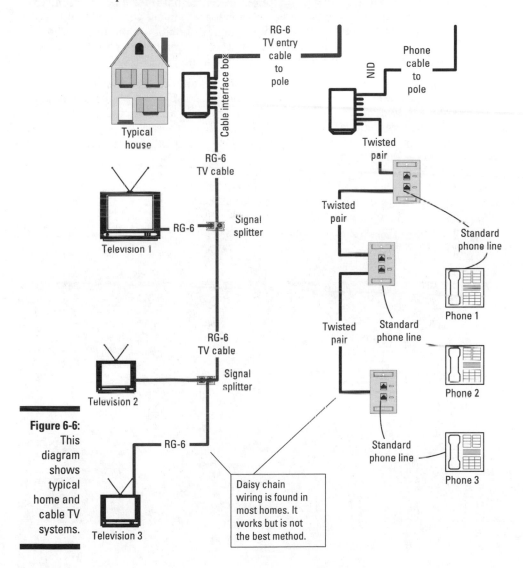

Figure 6-6: This diagram shows typical home and cable TV systems.

4. Terminate each line with an RJ-11 phone jack.

The RJ-11 standard defines a jack with six wire positions, although normally it's only wired with two wires to the center two pins to connect to single-line phones. Any single-line instrument or device plugged into the jack looks to pins three and four (the center pins) for a connection. To accommodate a phone and a fax on separate lines, you need two RJ-11 jacks. Two RJ-11 jacks and a four-space wall plate are pictured in Figure 6-7. Also in the picture is the RJ-45 Ethernet connector, and the F-style TV cable connector planned for this location.

If you connect a phone line pair to pins three and four, and then connect another line pair to pins two and five, you can supply two phone numbers to a standard two-line phone from the standard wall jack. When used in this configuration, the connection is defined as *RJ-14* instead of RJ-11. If you use all six connections, it's an *RJ-12 jack*. Ethernet connectors use eight-pin jacks and are called *RJ-45 jacks*.

If you use a two-line phone, you must use the correct type of extension cord between the phone and the wall jack. Most phone cords supplied with computers and faxes are single line. You can easily check a cord by looking at the plug end. If you only see two brass connections in the center two slots, it's a single-line cord.

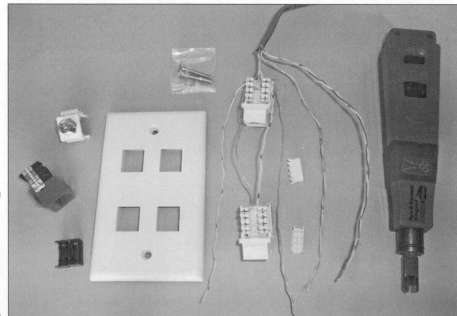

Figure 6-7:
RJ-11 jacks are available in multi-line configurations.

Installing a Home PBX System

A *Private Branch eXchange (PBX)* system is a phone network that shares one or more outside phone lines to make calls external to the PBX network. You're probably familiar with the PBX systems that many businesses use, but you may not know that homes can have them too.

A home PBX system can give you advanced control over your communications system and offers lots of features:

- Printer ready for generating call reports
- Ring all internal extensions
- Call pickup
- Call waiting
- Call ring back
- Do not disturb function
- Hold music
- In-home room-to-room calls
- Different ring tone patterns for in-home and incoming multi-line calls
- Auto-routing of incoming fax calls to a fax machine

A home PBX system is made up of several components:

- **Trunk lines:** The outside lines coming from the phone company.
- **Extensions:** The internal lines within the home.
- **Accessory systems:** Items such as voicemail, hold music, or an automated attendant.
- **Ports:** Each trunk line, extension, and accessory system.

A basic $300 home PBX system may use standard single-line phone sets and support two Telco trunk lines and seven internal extensions. Models to handle more lines and features are available for more money.

You have a few options for connecting the wires on a PBX system:

✔ Bring the home runs to a punch-down block near your PBX and then bring the wires from the PBX ports to the punch-down block.

✔ Bring the internal phone lines to a predesigned panel for residential PBX use, such as the Leviton 18 Port Structured Media Panel. From this panel, connect patch cords between jacks in the faceplate of the panel and the various network or phone devices.

When installing your internal home phone wiring, using Cat 6 wire is best. You only need one or two of the four pairs of wires for a PBX system, depending on which system you choose. If you have a two-line phone and fax at the same location, you could use up to three wire pairs in one cable. Many designers recommend either installing spare cables, or installing conduit to make future installs easier. These are good ideas if you wind up using them. If you never use them, they are just an additional cost, but Cat 6 cable is very cheap — usually less than $5 per run — and your house may be used in many different ways over the next few decades. An extra $5 spent now can save major rewiring expense and hassle later.

Integrating VoIP

Voice over Internet Protocol (VoIP) is an increasingly popular alternative to the conventional public switched phone network. With VoIP, you make your long-distance calls using *Internet protocols (IP)*. If you have (or plan to have) high-speed (DSL or cable) Internet access, you may want to consider VoIP for your long-distance phone calls, because many of the available plans offer highly competitive pricing.

Understanding how VoIP works

VoIP uses a device commonly referred to as a *phone adapter.* Some companies refer to this device as a *voice gateway.* The VoIP adapter converts the sound signal from a typical analog phone set to digital IP packets, and vice versa. The VoIP provider supplies you with this adapter, or you can purchase a compatible adapter from a list approved by the provider. If you use your VoIP system to call someone on a conventional analog phone system, the call goes to the supplier's nearest conversion point, which sends the call to a Telco in the call receiver's area. If both the caller and the receiver are on the same VoIP network, the call instead goes to their digital IP-connected phone.

Routing phone calls over the Internet is done through a *session initiation protocol (SIP)*. SIP initiates, alters, and terminates communications sessions between two or more participating devices over an IP network (the Internet) for telephony or for a multimedia presentation. To learn more about SIP, see RFC 2543 at `www.ietf.org/rfc/rfc2543.txt`.

On a VoIP system, the service provider assigns you a phone number. In some cases, you can choose the area code and phone number that your phone will use. Some providers allow you to invent a "virtual" number that rings to your present analog phone. That may be valuable to someone who often calls you long-distance, because the number is a local call for the other person.

Some VoIP suppliers have you make calls over local phone lines to their local or toll-free exchange equipment instead. Their equipment converts your voice to a digital signal and transmits it over the Internet. Check the details of any plan before deciding on one:

- ✔ Check the cost for making calls.
- ✔ Watch out for unexpected long-distance tolls your caller may be charged.

VoIP phone numbers aren't currently available in every area of the country.

If the only phone service you have is provided on VoIP, your phone may not work during a power outage. Directory and 911 services may be unreliable, too. Make sure you have some way to quickly reach emergency services if necessary.

Choosing a VoIP phone adapter

VoIP phone adapters are aimed at two different audiences:

- ✔ The home-user mass market with do-it-yourself installations.
- ✔ Small businesses, where the adapter is provided by a value-added reseller or partner of the hardware manufacturer or the VoIP provider.

We expect that with time some of the advanced features currently available to the small business market will trickle down to the mass market, allowing home offices and the digital homeowner to use and enjoy the advanced features and services. The following sections introduce you to consumer- and business-style VoIP adapters.

Consumer VoIP adapters

Consumer-style VoIP adapters typically have four or eight ports. The following list describes these ports so that you can recognize their purposes:

- ✓ **Power port:** The first port on a VoIP adapter is for power supply. It is usually low voltage DC from an adapter that plugs into your nearest power outlet.

- ✓ **Up-line Ethernet port (WAN):** One up-line Ethernet port is for connection to the line from your Internet modem, firewall, or router using an Ethernet cable. This port is often called the *wide-area network (WAN)* port. In Chapter 12, we recommend using a firewall or a router with built-in firewall on your broadband Internet connection. We also recommend using a multi-port Ethernet switch to distribute the network to the drops in your house. If you use an Ethernet switch, the up-line Ethernet jack on the VoIP adapter connects to the switch.

- ✓ **Down-line Ethernet ports (LAN):** The VoIP adapter may have one, four, or more down-line Ethernet ports (also referred to as the *local-area network (LAN)* ports). If the VoIP adapter has a built-in Ethernet switch, you could connect your computers or network drops to these LAN ports. However, if your network already has another Ethernet switch, then these ports on the VoIP adapter are unnecessary.

- ✓ **Down-line analog phone ports:** Usually the VoIP adapter provides two phone ports with standard RJ-11 jacks. They're labeled port one and port two, and connect to analog phones and options such as a fax or second phone line. Typically, port one must connect to the phone.

Most consumer-style VoIP adapters are designed on the assumption that homeowners are going to approach VoIP phone service as an either-or proposition. This means that many adapters don't include a port for connecting a conventional phone to the *Public Switched Telephone Network (PSTN)*. Because of the reliability issues surrounding VoIP, as well as the inability to call 911 emergency services, we view this lack of a PSTN connection as a disservice to the consumer. A notable exception is the OneFlex adapter (offered by QWEST), which has a port referred to as a Line (Failover) Port. This port connects to the PSTN for 911 calls over a normal phone line to the local phone company.

Figure 6-8 shows a diagram of the preferred method of installing a consumer-style VoIP adapter on your home network. Notice that the adapter is installed downstream of the router. You can install the VoIP adapter directly to the modem, but doing so reduces the control and level of security you can enforce on your data traffic. Keep in mind that these devices need electrical power, so if you lose power, you can't call 911 or make other calls. (See Chapter 15 for ways to add backup power to your critical digital systems.)

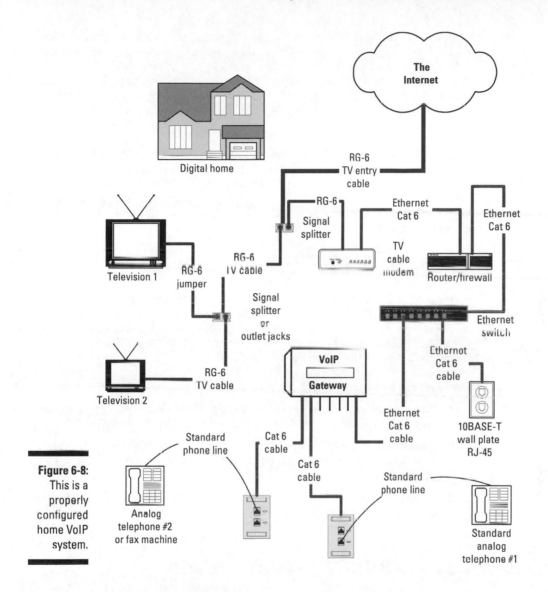

Figure 6-8:
This is a properly configured home VoIP system.

Business VoIP adapters

Business-style VoIP adapters differ from consumer adapters in that the phone sets are IP based; the signal conversion from analog to digital is performed within the phones. The phone sets connect to a multi-line-capable IP PBX using Ethernet connections. A typical IP PBX may handle up to 16 IP-based phone sets. The IP PBX may include two *Foreign eXchange Subscriber (FXS)* RJ-11 ports for connecting conventional analog phones or fax machines. The PBX gateway may also include a *Foreign eXchange Office (FX0)* RJ-11 port for connecting to the PSTN for handling calls when the Internet is down and for routing local calls to emergency 911. Business PBX equipment also usually includes features like voice mail, hold music, group calling, paging, and call forwarding.

IP PBXs usually require close integration by the VoIP provider or the value-added reseller to install and configure. Some of the tips we mention in Chapter 1 for selecting an electrical contractor also apply to selecting a VoIP provider or reseller. However, we expect that many of the advanced business VoIP features will trickle down to consumer-level VoIP in the near future.

Choosing a VoIP service provider

If you have a high-speed Internet connection through a cable or DSL modem, you are a candidate for VoIP services. Many providers have feature-rich service offerings and competitive prices. Geography isn't a huge limitation for deciding on a particular service provider, so compare plans and rates. Carefully consider the following points:

- **Price:** Consider monthly access fees as well as per-call fees.
- **Phone numbers:** Can you choose an area code and phone number, or are you locked into a specific number or range by the provider?
- **Equipment:** Which provider offers the best equipment for your home? Most VoIP service providers list which equipment is compatible with their service.
- **Technical support:** Does the provider offer good tech support both for your equipment and the service?

Videoconferencing from Home

If you work from home or want to keep in touch with distant family members, you could benefit from outfitting your digital home with videoconferencing capability beyond what's available on various picture phones. In the following sections, we show you how to keep in touch visually with family, friends, and business associates.

Equipping for videoconferencing

Due to the early adoption and acceptance of the *International Telecommunication Union (ITU)* H.323 family of standards, you can use a home computer equipped with a webcam, *network interface card (NIC),* and a high-speed Internet connection to conduct videoconferences with anyone on the Internet. A version of Microsoft NetMeeting — a popular videoconferencing application — is available for Windows 95 and higher. A videoconferencing application like NetMeeting can use one of two types of connections to place videoconferencing calls:

- ✔ **IP:** If you have a broadband Internet connection such as DSL or a cable modem, you can place conferencing calls over that connection.

- ✔ **Integrated Services Digital Network (ISDN):** If you have minimal need for an Internet connection, or if broadband Internet isn't available in your area, see if your phone company offers ISDN service. ISDN is typically slower and more expensive than DSL or cable, but is well suited to videoconferencing. Like DSL, ISDN allows voice and data to be transmitted simultaneously using end-to-end digital connectivity. This connectivity is achieved by sending signals at different frequencies on the same pair of wires.

Installing and using ISDN phone lines

ISDN lines use standard copper phone wires to transmit one channel of 64Kbps (kilobits per second) of data, or two channels totaling 128Kbps of data. Two-channel ISDN service is required for videoconferencing, and ISDN service must be installed and supported by your local Telco. Once ISDN service is installed to your home, connect an ISDN terminal adapter and modem to a phone jack. You can now perform point-to-point videoconferences to equally equipped locations.

The wiring for an ISDN phone jack isn't any different than wiring a standard phone line, except that the twisted-pair cable (Cat 3, Cat 5, or Cat 6) from the NID box to the phone jack where the ISDN modem is connected must be able to handle the 64Kbps speeds of each phone line channel.

Using ISDN is simple once you connect it and configure your application. Use the software to dial the recipient's ISDN number. Your call routes to the receiver's number over the PSTN. If he or she answers, you can begin conferencing.

Using IP-based videoconferencing

It isn't necessary to use ISDN and pay tolls for videoconferencing because the communication protocols, hardware, and applications that conform to the H.323 standard can also be used to connect point to point over the

Internet. If you plan to do a lot of videoconferencing, try to get two or more assigned static IP addresses from your Internet service provider. This makes conferencing easier because other parties can simply dial your conferencing IP address.

At this point you might ask, "Do I need VoIP service to do videoconferences over the Internet?" Thanks for asking! The answer is no; all you need is a decent upload and download speed with your ISP — any 256Kbps DSL or faster connection should suffice — and an IP address associated with your conferencing software. You can then place conferencing calls to other IP addresses or ISDN numbers.

Often, large companies with extensive WANs use private addresses within their own network for videoconferencing. If you work from home, you may be able to link to conferences via a secure company gateway, thereby minimizing office commutes.

Using gateways for multi-point conferencing

The videoconferencing standards for ISDN and IP conferencing also allow use of *multi-point control unit (MCU)* gateways — a device for controlling and broadcasting data packets to more than one end point. An H.323/H.320 gateway translates ISDN videoconferencing packets to IP connection points, allowing the dissimilar conferences standards (IP and ISDN) to communicate. This allows multiple participants into the videoconference at the same time. Gateways can be managed by a third party and scheduled for a particular user call time or unmanaged services operated on a first-come, first-served basis. Prices for multi-port MCUs are about $4,000.

Many third parties, such as Sprint Business Services, offer multi-point video-conferencing hubs for a fee. These virtual hubs can bridge between ISDN and IP connections as required. You could also install your own multi-point gate-way if your ISP has provided you with enough IP addresses. Most home users don't do enough multi-point conferences to justify the cost of a gateway.

Chapter 7

Installing a Public Address System

*O*ne of the things that really sets the modern digital home apart is an advanced communications system. Want to talk to someone on the other side of the house? This used to mean yelling or going to that room. A public address system eliminates that need, allowing instant and convenient communication with anyone in any room in your home.

Of course, public address and intercom systems are nothing new. But modern systems can do much more than simply allow you to talk. Other available features include

✔ Music, surveillance video, and weather alerts

✔ Doorbell notification

✔ Door lock control

✔ Outdoor and garage communication

✔ Baby monitors

✔ TV and entertainment system control

This chapter introduces you to the features available in a home public address system, and shows you how to plan for and install one in your digital home.

Planning a Home Communications System

As you plan your communications system, it makes sense to design it around your other multimedia systems. Can you incorporate the public address system into your speakers? Would you like to add video features or music to the intercom installations? These are just a couple of considerations.

Of course, planning the system also means choosing intercom components and mapping out wiring runs. Several kinds of systems are available, each with different advantages that may or may not mesh with your lifestyle. The following sections help you start planning.

Selecting locations

Deciding what you want included in an intercom system and then wiring the home to accommodate the system is a basic step-by-step process:

1. Decide which rooms will have intercoms.
2. Select intercom units with sufficient capabilities to meet your needs.
3. Draw a wiring map.
4. Wire the house per the intercom manufacturer's instructions.

You may decide to simply install an intercom in every room. But if you decide to place intercoms only in certain rooms, consider bringing wire to all the rooms so that they can be included later if desired. Cat 6 wire — the type used for most intercom systems — costs only pennies per foot. It only costs about $5 to pre-wire an average-sized room if you are providing the labor.

Keep in mind some basic rules and tips when wiring for intercom systems:

✔ You don't have to install an outlet box if you're only pre-wiring for a possible future expansion; simply get the wire in the wall cavity behind the drywall where you can later install a *low voltage (LV)* ring to accommodate the equipment.

✔ The rough in is generally done just inside the room next to the door. The installation height should be 5' above the finished floor.

✔ Don't run Cat 5 or 6 wires directly alongside wires for the electric power system. When two energized conductors are placed next to each other, a charge difference and electric field exists between them. The charge difference causes capacitance, which gives rise to noticeable interference. (*Capacitance* is electrical charge induced in one conductor by its proximity to the electromagnetic field of another when they're separated by electrical insulating material.) Normally the interference source is from a 60-cycle, 120- or 240-volt power line. These charge differences produce a 60-cycle audio tone called hum.

Ground loops can also cause interference with sound quality. All grounds should be connected to one grounding point. This ground point should be *common with* (meaning connected to) the electrical service ground. Once an item is grounded, it should not be grounded at another point or through another system.

Modern TVs don't come with grounded plugs. If they did, connecting an RG-6 coaxial from a cable company or satellite dish would ground the TV a second time and create a ground loop, thus leading to noticeable interference.

✔ If you want stereo sound in a room, run additional wires to the wall or ceiling speaker locations.

✔ An alternative to pre-wiring a house is to provide an easy method for getting wires to future installation areas. You have a couple of options:

- Run conduit to those areas. In the case of a first floor over a basement, install a short piece from an electrical box through the floor into the basement, if the basement is to remain unfinished.

- Run conduit to some other accessible location, such as the attic. Fasten the conduit to the stud and mark it on the blueprint. An LV ring can be cut in later. The conduit should end a few inches below or above the eventual LV ring installation. Use ¾" or 1" *Electrical Nonmetallic Conduit (ENT)*. A 1" conduit accommodates about six Cat 6 cables. If you need more capacity, install a second conduit.

  Installing ENT conduit is fairly easy. It is easily bent by hand and can be cut with a knife, but do not make sharp bends. Larger radius sweeps make it easier to pull wires though the conduit. Figure 7-1 shows two 4 × 4" boxes and plaster rings, as well as some ENT conduit and fittings.

When running conduit, you're limited to a total of 360° of bend in any run between pull points. Four 90° bends or any combination that add up to 360° is the maximum allowed. If more than 360° are needed, you must install a pull box. Each pull box starts the degree count over again. Not only is it a code violation to exceed 360° of bends between pull points, it is usually impossible to pull wires in a conduit that has more than 360° of bends. Resist any temptation to exceed the limit.

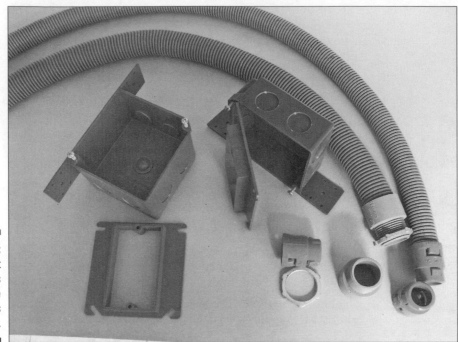

Figure 7-1:
Conduit
makes
future
installations
easier.

We assume in this chapter that the building finish is drywall. Your building finish could be something else, but the installation process is the same.

The diagram shown in Figure 7-2 is an example layout of a voice intercom system with auxiliary input and stereo sound. The manufacturer's recommended cable for wiring this system is Cat 5, and Cat 6 could be used as an upgrade.

Choosing wire

If you plan to pre-wire, how can you match the current carrying capacity of the wire to a future system? A number of intercom systems recommend using 16 or 18 AWG wire, but we believe that most future systems will use Cat 5 or Cat 6 wire. These systems send a higher voltage to the remote wall units; Cat 6 wire has about double the resistance of 18 AWG wire. You may have some line losses with Cat 6 wire on these systems, but they are generally insignificant.

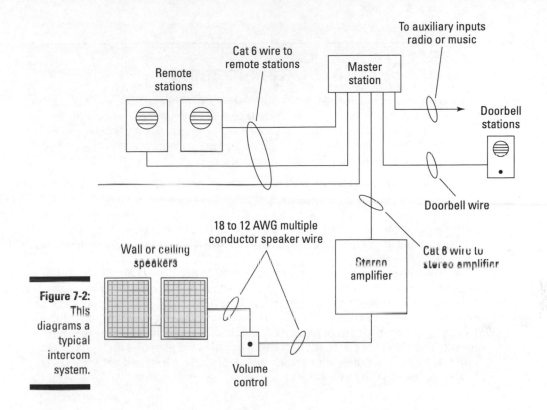

Figure 7-2:
This
diagrams a
typical
intercom
system.

Some home music systems use Cat 5 or 6 cable for external controllers, but they generally use heavier-gauge wire (usually 14–18 gauge) from the local amplifier to the speakers. The voltage required to make a lot of noise in a normal speaker is very low, but the advantage of high-current, low-voltage speaker wiring is that almost nothing interferes with the audio signal.

Selecting amplifiers and speakers

Amplifiers, or *amps,* help provide adequate power to speakers. Like speakers, amplifiers usually have a wattage rating, but about half of that wattage is lost inside the amp. This means that the amplifier capacity can be twice as large as the speaker loads connected to it. Despite the tendency to turn the volume up to 11 for our favorite tunes, the amp's purpose is to simply bring the volume up to the natural level of the instruments originally used to create the music, including the human voice. If the amp-and-speaker combination is too weak to reach equity, the instrument's full fidelity sound is impossible. Having to crank the controls to the max distorts the sound.

Step down, transformers

Commercial sound systems use 25- or 70-volt line output from the amplifier, which is then stepped down with a speaker-mounted transformer. Transformer step-down systems aren't considered suitable for re-creating high-fidelity music because of the nonlinear frequency response of any transformer. Some newer systems can drive 70 volts directly to the speakers, eliminating the transformer and thereby improving sound quality.

Selecting amps with a full frequency range of 20 to 20,000 cycles per second allows hearing of the harmonics and overtones of bells and stringed instruments.

In the future we expect to see more Cat 6 cable wiring local amplifier/speaker combination units, thus eliminating the need for heavy speaker wire. With this design, the speaker/amp unit needs four or six conductors depending on the volume-control scheme. Cat 5 and Cat 6 cable each contain eight conductors, which are made up of four twisted pairs arranged in a single sheathed jacket. The difference is that Cat 5 cable handles frequencies up to 100 MHz, and Cat 6 cable handles frequencies up to 250 MHz. Crosstalk between pairs is also reduced with Cat 6 cable.

Choosing intercom components

You have many intercom system and component brands from which to choose. A typical home intercom system can accommodate up to six remote speaker locations and chimes from three doors for about $250. At this price the units usually have built-in AM/FM radio receivers. As you move up, the units may have one or more auxiliary inputs that let you connect your own music system and distribute it to the connected speakers (in mono).

If you install an electric door strike on your front door, you can unlock the door for identified visitors from the master station and use the intercom to tell them to enter the house.

In addition to a voice intercom, you can have a video intercom. *Video intercom systems* use a small camera in the intercom unit to monitor any room on the system. They aren't complicated to wire: just four-conductor 18 AWG wire. You may find it advantageous to see who's ringing the doorbell before you remotely unlock it, or you may wish to see what the kids are up to. These video stations cost about $1,000 each. We cover other ways to do video monitoring throughout your home in Chapter 14.

Most intercom systems require a four-conductor cable run from the master location to each remote speaker location. You also need to supply 120-volt power at the master station.

Installing the Hardware

After you've planned out your home communications system, including planning the wiring and selecting components, it's time to actually install the components.

Installing LV rings

LV rings hold your intercom components to the wall. Figure 7-3 shows two single-gang LV rings. The LV ring on the left shows the drywall tabs folded back, which you do after inserting into the hole cut in the wall. The tabs provide a catch for the drywall screw and, when tightened, firmly mounts the ring to the wallboard. The ring on the right shows how they come in the package.

To install an LV ring, follow these steps:

1. **Cut a hole through the drywall the size of the raised, inner, open rectangle of the LV ring.**

   Notice the tabs across the opening of the LV ring. The tabs are part of the raised area away from what will be the frontal surface.

2. **Insert the LV ring in the hole and fold the tabs as shown on the left LV ring in Figure 7-3.**

3. **Install screws in the slots in each tab of the LV ring.**

   When the screws are tightened, the drywall is firmly sandwiched between the tabs and the frontal ring. The frontal flange keeps the ring from going into the wall, and the tabs and screws keep it from coming out.

You can mount LV rings anywhere in the drywall between studs. They don't have to be secured to a stud. The rings are available in one- and two-gang configurations, and are only approved for low-voltage wiring. Never use them for mounting a power switch or outlet.

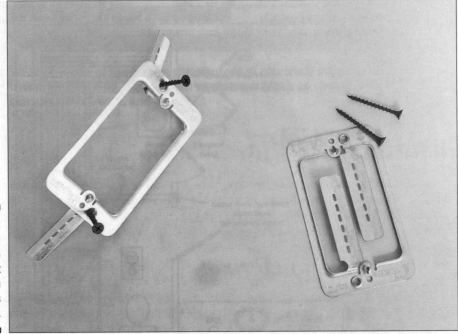

Figure 7-3:
LV rings are
used to
mount
intercom
components
to walls.

Installing a central control unit

Put the communications system's main console in a convenient, accessible
area. The main console has a few more features than the remote room units:

- Optional door release
- Talk switch
- Master volume control
- Status light-emitting diodes (LEDs) to show system activity

If the main console is the Great and Powerful Oz that gives you command of
your intercom system, the *central unit* is the man behind the curtain who
actually does all the work. The central control unit is usually located in a
basement or mechanical closet. This should be where all your phone, network, TV, and security system controls are located.

This central unit needs

- ✔ 120-volt power

- ✔ Two Cat 5 or Cat 6 runs to the main console unit

- ✔ One Cat 5 or Cat 6 run to all the room stations, including the door, garage, and patio units

Figure 7-4 shows modern intercom system wiring. This system uses Cat 5 or 6 cable to all stations. The main console requires two Cat 5 or 6 cables to the central control unit. The diagram doesn't show it, but the system also needs a 120-volt power supply.

Connecting radio antennas

If your intercom unit has an AM/FM radio, you probably need to include wiring for an external antenna, which goes to either the central console location or to the central control unit. When pre-wiring for broadcast radio (AM/FM) antennas, bring in two RG-6 cables from a high location on one of the gable ends of the house, down to outlets near the equipment.

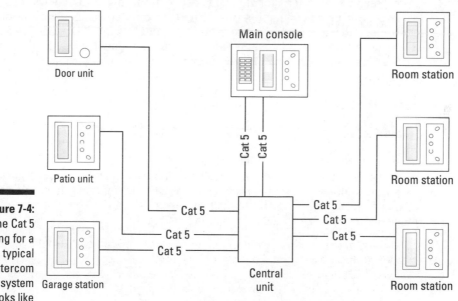

Figure 7-4: The Cat 5 wiring for a typical intercom system looks like this.

Need 120 volt AC power to central unit.
All other wiring is Category 5 or 6 wire

Feeling punchy

A *punch-down tool* presses the wires between two metal blades that cut through the insulation and hold the wires and create an electrical connection between the wires in that slot. When using a punch-down tool with a trimmer, make sure the tool is oriented so the trimmer cuts off the unneeded slack, as opposed to cutting the wire you're terminating.

Include a grounding block with a grounding strap before the cables enter the house. Antennas are attractive to lightning bolts, so properly grounding antenna cables is very important. Grounding must be to the electrical service grounding electrode system, as covered in Chapters 2 and 3. Grounding in two places can create ground loops and thus interference, so use a ground loop isolator when connecting the patch cable from the outlet box connector to the intercom/radio equipment.

Select the antennas for AM and FM radio based on the recommendations from the intercom manufacturer, and then follow all of the antenna manufacturer's recommendations for safe and secure mounting. You may want to install a waterproof connection box with RG-6 connectors near the antenna locations, and use a jumper cable from the outlet box, as shown in Figure 7-5. This eases future antenna maintenance or replacement. Always arrange the wires with a drip loop to minimize water buildup in the cable and corrosion at the connection points.

Installing and wiring remote locations

All remote stations for your intercom system are connected to the system using Cat 5 or Cat 6 cable. If you install an intercom in an unattached garage, gazebo, tree house, or some other remote location, you must use cable rated for direct burial. If part of the cable is exposed — as in the case of a tree house — the cable must also be sunlight resistant.

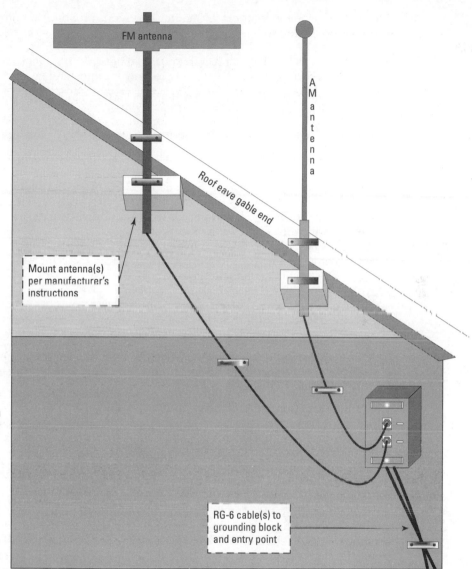

FM antenna

AM antenna

Roof eave gable end

Mount antenna(s) per manufacturer's instructions

RG-6 cable(s) to grounding block and entry point

Figure 7-5: Use a jumper between the antenna and the waterproof connection box.

Follow the recommendations in Chapter 3 for your roughing in your wires. Basically, you should

- ✓ Maintain as much separation as possible between parallel runs of electrical and communications wiring to prevent interference.

- ✓ Drill straight (*not* angled) holes in joists and framing, which makes for a cleaner installation and easier pulls.

- ✓ Drill holes far enough back that drywall screws won't contact the wires.

- ✓ Staple wires on vertical runs so they don't hang loose within the wall.

Again, these are just the basics. See Chapter 3 for more on running wires.

Unlike electrical wiring, all wiring runs from remote intercoms are home runs to the central control unit wiring location.

When making the wire runs to the control unit from the remotes, follow these tips to make the final connections easier:

- ✓ **Take advantage of color coding.** Cat 5 and Cat 6 cable are made up of color-coded pairs within the sheath, so simply use the same color wires on the same terminals from each remote intercom.

- ✓ **Label your cables.** Carefully label each cable as each home run is brought to the central location so that you know which room is served by each respective cable.

- ✓ **Block and jump.** If the units don't have spring-loaded push connections for the wires, you may want to use a *punch-down block* to terminate the remote runs and use *jumper wires* from the punch-down block to the screw terminals on the intercom equipment. This connection helps eliminate wire breakage and facilitates easier maintenance or replacement.

In some rooms, such as nurseries or children's playrooms, you may want to install intercoms lower than the standard 5' mounting height. An intercom at about 3' allows a small child to easily reach the intercom. Wire this station from above or, if fed from below, maintain sufficient slack in the cable during rough in; that way you can move the unit higher on the wall if the playroom later becomes a guest bedroom. Removing the LV ring, and then patching, plastering, and painting over the old opening on drywall board walls is easy.

Chapter 8

Installing Cable TV and Advanced Digital Services

The human body is made up of systems: the circulatory system, the nervous system, the digestive system, and a bunch of other systems we forgot to list on our seventh-grade biology test. Likewise, many systems work together in your modern digital home: electrical, telephone, security, intercom, and others.

Most modern homes also include a cable TV system, which is one of the systems we cover in this chapter. This may include conventional cable TV service using coaxial cable, or your area may be served by advanced new fiber optic systems. Fiber optics TV systems are gaining popularity because they offer data transmission speeds potentially far higher than any wired system in existence. In addition, fiber optics can supply many services simultaneously over one fiber cable pair. This chapter shows you how to plan your home's cable TV system, as well as how to plan for advanced fiber optics-based digital services.

Readying Your Home for Prime Time

As with any electrical system in your home, careful planning is critical.

1. **List the end-use equipment you intend to install and use in your home.**

   That list may include TV sets, DVD players, VCRs, and WebTV.

2. **Select the areas you want wired to TV jacks.**

At a minimum, these locations should generally include each bedroom, living room, and family room. The kitchen and dining room may seem optional to some folks, but we recommend wiring at least one TV jack to all habitable rooms. In larger rooms you may want to install more than one TV jack to accommodate alternative furniture arrangements.

Bringing TV service into your home

In most markets, the cable company's installer will make the service drop from the pole or underground service to an interface box on your house. For a fee, they're willing to install the in-house wiring to each TV in your home.

If you choose to have the cable company install the in-house wiring, you have little control over the quality of the installation. Cable company installers often run cable on the surface, and they like to drill holes in baseboards and hardwood flooring.

They can get away with this because TV cable installations usually aren't subject to the same level of critical inspection as home electrical wiring. Your best bet is to have the cable company stop at the interface box and handle the rest of it yourself. You can then either perform a clean installation or hire a reputable installer who will work within your guidelines.

Figure 8-1 shows a simple cable interface box. Besides the TV cables, the box also includes a ground wire that is connected to the grounding electrode system for your electrical service. A simple *splitter* is on the right side of the box in Figure 8-1; it splits the single incoming cable in two for the home. One supplies a cable TV signal and the other supplies broadband Internet to a cable modem. A single TV cable should run from the interface box to your internal distribution point where you would have distribution blocks. Cable companies in most markets don't allow the homeowner to make modifications within the interface box.

If the incoming cable TV signal isn't strong enough to supply all of your locations, install a *broad-spectrum amplifier* to strengthen the incoming signal.

Installing TV cable jacks

You should install cable TV jacks in much the same manner you do phone jacks. That is, each jack should be a direct home run to the distribution point served by the line coming into the house. Figure 6-6 in Chapter 6 shows a diagram of the ideal cable and telephone-line arrangement. When you decide the locations for TV jacks, mount the boxes or plaster rings to which the TV jacks will attach.

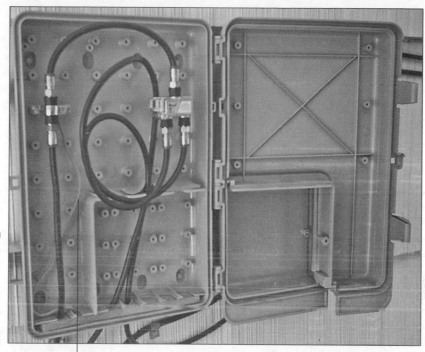

Figure 8-1:
A typical
cable TV
interface
box looks
like this.

Ground wire

Unless you have one of those special new TVs that runs on hamster wheels, you are going to need an electrical outlet near each cable TV jack. One of the neater ways to accomplish this is to use a combination outlet box like the one shown in Figure 8-2. This specialty box encloses all wiring as required by code, plus it has a companion open-back box for low-voltage wiring such as the TV cable connector. This combination makes for a neater appearance than separately spaced boxes, and it makes setting up your TVs more convenient.

You can split out lines from existing TV jacks using coaxial splitters (available at any electronics store), but the signal may have reduced quality. Each time the cable gets split, the signal gets weaker. We recommend that you only split TV lines from existing outlets during remodels where installing new home runs is difficult.

TV jacks are designed to mount to single-gang electrical boxes. Because there is no high voltage present in a TV cable line, a box isn't necessarily required. You can mount a 4" × 4" plaster ring, tile ring, or low-voltage (LV) ring to the stud (framing) and just bring the cable out through the ring opening. Plaster rings are available in plastic and metal. Choose a plaster ring that matches the building finish of the surrounding walls.

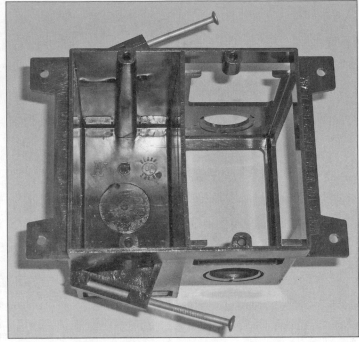

Figure 8-2:
This dual
outlet box
cleans
up your
cable and
electrical
installation.

Installing TV cable

When you install cable between your distribution point and the cable jacks, we recommend that you use RG-6 cable. This newer style is superior to older RG-59 TV cable, because you can run it near parallel power cables without any problem. RG-6 cable is shielded, thus protecting it from power line interference.

When you're installing TV cable, follow these general guidelines:

✔ The TV cable shield must be grounded at the customer interface by the cable company. If you're installing a dish system, ground the cable's shield to the service panel's grounding electrode before it enters the building. If the cable shield gets grounded a second time, it may cause an audio hum or a degraded picture due to ground loop interference.

✔ Terminate each RG-6 cable end using a good-quality F connector. Follow the manufacturer's instructions and use the crimping tool recommended by the F connector's supplier. F connectors aren't standardized, so make sure the crimper matches the connector style you're using.

Understanding decibels and signal loss

Each time a TV cable is connected to a device or to another cable, you lose about 8 dB (decibels) of signal strength. Some signal strength is also lost with each foot of cable. The loss on RG-6 cable can easily reach 6 dB over a 100-foot run. The video signal frequency also influences the amount of loss, with higher frequencies susceptible to higher loss rates. Thus, you can see why it's important to be as efficient as possible with your cable installations. Try to keep your cable runs short and connection numbers small.

Decibel measurements and what they mean are often hard to understand. *Decibels* measure the relative strength (plus or minus) of an electrical signal as an amount equal to ten times the common logarithm of the ratio of the two measurements. *Losses* are negative numbers and *gains* are positive. In the case of TV cable, at the source point from the interface box on your house the cable company supplies you with a certain signal strength; for reference purposes that becomes 0 dB in signal loss or gain. Each time the signal goes through a connector, the signal loss could be as high as –8 dB. For every 100' of cable the signal passes through, it loses –6 dB to the loss column. For example, if you have a cable run of 100' and two connectors, the signal loss would be about –22 dB (6 dB + –8 dB + –8 dB = –22 dB).

The frequency of the signal going through the cable also dramatically influences the loss, with higher frequencies susceptible to higher loss rates. Because this measurement is a log scale, the numbers appear to understate the actual loss. For example, the additional loss difference each time you go from –10 dB to –20 dB is not a linear 10; it is times 10. So a signal after a –20 dB loss is $\frac{1}{100}$ the strength of the reference signal.

Some cable companies supply free RG-6 cable with F connectors. The cable company may install the F connectors on your system even if they don't supply or run the RG-6 cable, thus saving you the cost of a crimping tool.

✔ The TV-set end of each cable connects to a cable TV wall jack. You will probably install the wall-jack faceplate after the building finish is in place.

✔ From the wall jack to the TV, use a flexible video jumper cable no longer than needed to easily reach from the jack to the television. Excessively long cables reduce signal strength.

Don't use heavy TV cable like that supplied by the cable company for the connection between the wall jack and the TV. These heavy, inflexible cables can break or damage the connector on the TV.

Connecting the common distribution point

The *common distribution point* is where TV cable home runs join the service wire from the cable company. To set up the distribution point, follow these steps:

1. **Install the lightning surge protection connector on the TV service cable to the grounding electrode *before* any splitters.**

   This provides lightning protection to your cable system. Some designers recommend that you connect the surge protection to a ground rod, but we strongly disagree. The lightning surge protection must be connected to the electrical service ground, as discussed in Chapter 3.

2. **If you have a cable Internet modem, install a two-way splitter on the service cable right as it comes into the house.**

   Connect one branch cable from the first splitter directly to your cable modem, and use as short a cable as possible. This ensures the best possible signal strength for your Internet connection. The other branch from the two-way splitter feeds your home's cable TV system common distribution block.

3. **At the common distribution point, install a splitter (like the one shown in Figure 8-3) with just enough connections to wire to each TV jack you will install.**

   If you have a cable Internet connection, you'll install a second splitter on the cable for the TV signal to feed a cable to each TV, as shown in Figure 8-4.

4. **Connect the cables that feed the home TV jacks to the splitter.**

   Only connect cables for the TV jacks actually being used. This ensures that you aren't wasting signal strength on unused cables.

5. **If you're using more than six jacks, install a wide-band amplifier to ensure adequate signal strength to each jack.**

   If you have a lot of long runs and many connections, choose an amplifier with frequency ranges that cover the channel frequencies you will be using. Also make sure that the amplifier at least equals your calculated dB losses. (See the previous section for more on dB loss.) Install the amplifier right before the TV splitter block, but after the splitter feeding your cable modem, if you have one.

6. **Connect a TV to a wall jack, pop some popcorn, grab the remote, and see how well the system works!**

Figure 8-4 shows a properly configured TV cabling system.

Figure 8-3:
Use a
splitter to
distribute
the cable
signal to all
the rooms in
your home.

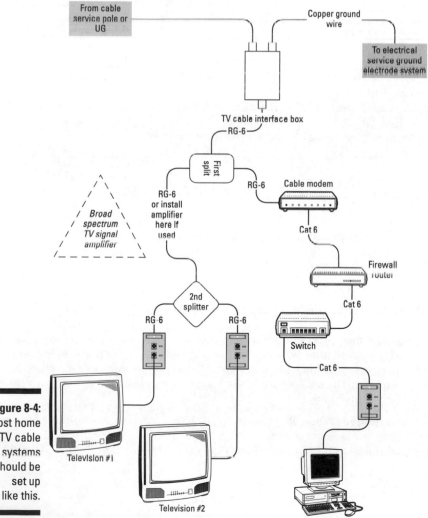

Figure 8-4:
Most home
TV cable
systems
should be
set up
like this.

Installing for a Fiber Optic Future

For more than a century, most communications cabling — be it for cable TV or telephone service — has been composed of copper wire. Signals are carried over these copper wires electrically. A few decades ago phone companies started installing fiber optic cable for long-distance voice and data connections. *Fiber optic cable* carries signals optically, making it far less susceptible to signal loss over long distances. Another advantage is that by using *Dense Wave Distribution Multiplexing (DWDM),* a fiber pair can be divided into dozens of channels, each supporting a different type of signal or protocol. (A *protocol* defines how data is coded and decoded on a transmission media such as copper or fiber.) For example, a fiber optic cable can carry Ethernet over one color of the DWDM; TV channels over another color; and standard phone, ATM, or ISDN data packets over another color. Over time this feature will allow advanced digital services to be provided directly to the devices in your home.

Most internal connections are still done with copper wire. Likewise, copper wire is used for most wiring between phone company switches and customer homes. But a few progressive companies like Verizon believe that fiber optic is the way of the future, and are offering fiber optic service directly to customers' homes in some major markets. The following sections show you how to prepare your digital home for the fiber optic future.

Understanding fiber optic cable

The *fiber* part of a fiber optic cable is actually made of glass. Data is carried by pulsing infrared light waves in the wavelength ranges of 850–1,550 nanometers. As the light waves emerge from the far end of the glass cable, the waves are converted back to electrical impulses by a light-sensitive receiver.

Fiber optic cables are divided into two categories:

- ✔ **Single-mode fiber:** Often referred to as *mono-mode* and *uni-mode cable,* single-mode fiber is very thin, usually only 8–10 μ (microns) in diameter. They conduct light impulses straight down the small center glass core of the fiber. The smaller size makes it more suitable to carry signals over longer distances.

- ✔ **Multi-mode fiber:** Ranging from 50–100 μ in diameter, multi-mode fiber carries data over shorter distances. Multi-mode is mostly cables within buildings and for on-campus connections between buildings. If used over long distances, the light waves attenuate against the outer shell in the larger fiber causing signal problems. The two most popular sizes are 50 μ and 62.5 μ. You could use either size when cabling your home, but the 62.5-μ cable is currently the most widely used.

A new plastic variant of fiber optic cable is called *POF,* or *plastic optical fiber.* POF is gaining popularity for connecting high-end audio equipment. However, you can't use POF interchangeably with multi-mode or single-mode fiber optic cable.

Consider your fiber optic strategy

How and whether you prepare your home for fiber optic services depends greatly on where you live and what services are currently available to you. Depending on where you live, you may approach fiber optic service using one of three strategies:

✔ **The "Be Ready" strategy:** If fiber optic service is already available in your area or you know it will be soon, this is your strategy.

1. Run a fiber optic pair to every box location to which you're installing Ethernet cable.

2. Terminate the box using a six-way faceplate like the one shown in Figure 8-5.

3. In the faceplate, install two RJ-45 Ethernet connectors, two RJ-11 phone connectors, one MT-RJ fiber (pair) workstation connector, and one RG-6 F-style video connector.

4. Take all home runs to your central distribution point.

✔ **The "May Need It Soon" strategy:** Follow this strategy if you think there's a good chance of fiber optic service coming to your neighborhood in the near future, but there are no immediate plans in place. In this case, pull a fiber optic pair to each Ethernet location, and simply leave the fiber pair un-terminated. It will be there if you ever need it.

✔ **The "Need It Someday" strategy:** If fiber optic service doesn't seem likely in your area anytime soon, but you want to make sure your home never becomes obsolete, install ½" or ¾" PVC conduit to all Ethernet locations. This allows fiber optic cable to be easily run in the future, if necessary.

When running conduit there should be no more than 360 degrees of bend between pull boxes, and keep the radius of bends to no fewer than 2".

Figure 8-5:
This six-way
faceplate
provides a
diverse
array
of connec-
tions.

Choosing home fiber optic service

If fiber optic phone, data, and video service is available in your area, we recommend that you move this option to the top of your list. This is especially
true if your service provider allows you to buy two or more static IP
addresses. As we mention in Chapter 12, if you only have a dynamically
assigned IP address, you are limited on some of the other cool communication stuff.

You don't absolutely have to get your phone, cable, and Internet services
from the same provider. In fact, having Internet service provided by both the
cable and phone companies may be a good idea, particularly if you rely on
Internet for your home office and one company won't give you two static IPs
or other premium services that you want. A static pair of IP addresses on a
slow service may be better than none at all.

When you order service, the phone company sends an installer to connect the
fiber cable to your home systems at some interface point, much as connections are made for phone or TV cable service. The trained installer runs the

fiber optic cable overhead or underground to a predetermined location at your home, terminating to the fiber cable connection at the *optical network terminal (ONT),* which in turn will feed to your home's common distribution point for the services provided, such as analog phone service or TV channels.

Connecting to fiber optic devices

If fiber optics have one downside, it's the nearly 100 styles of connectors used for terminations, cable-to-cable connections *(splices),* and jumpers. This variety can make connecting your devices to fiber optic services challenging, to say the least. But some connection types are more popular:

- **ST or straight connector:** This barrel-shaped connector looks like a BNC connector. The ST connector is used extensively.

- **SC or square snap-in connector:** A duplex arrangement normally sports these. Other duplex connectors include the MT-RJ and the MTP.

- **SFF or small form factor connector:** This connector allows two cables to connect into the same space as one SC connector. They're used in high-density installations where space is limited.

And the list goes on and on.

Jumpers can be purchased or made to connect between different styles of connectors. Keep in mind that the micron size of the fiber matters, so make sure to use the correct size cable for your equipment and cable system.

Even good splices and terminations in fiber cause some signal loss. When splices and terminations are done improperly, a very large amount of signal strength can be lost. Splice cables with the fiber nose-to-nose with the next fiber. Any offsets or angles cause major signal quality issues. You may want to hire an experienced fiber technician to do your terminations, and have the technician use test equipment to verify a quality installation.

Hooking up to the ONT

The *optical network terminal (ONT)* serves as a signal modulator/converter that changes light impulses from infrared light waves to the electrical impulses needed by your home electronic equipment. The ONT needs to be connected to house electrical power. If it loses power, you won't have phone service or access to 911 emergency services; when the ONT has lost its power, you lose your phone's dial tone. Most ONTs have built-in battery backups, and you may want to enhance this capability, as discussed in Chapter 15.

Although the phone company handles cabling to the ONT, wiring on the customer side of the ONT is typically the homeowner's responsibility. A typical ONT has connections for up to three service types:

- ✔ **Phone service:** A typical ONT has four voice ports for connecting up to four phone lines. If your home is already wired for phones, simply run jumper cables from these lines to your phone system's distribution point.

- ✔ **Video (TV) service:** The ONT also has a port for video signal output. Some fiber optic service providers offer video-on-demand, pay-per-view, and cable channels much like those offered by conventional TV cable companies. If you move your video services to fiber optics, simply connect a jumper cable from the ONT to your central cable distribution block.

- ✔ **Internet service:** If your fiber optic provider offers Internet service, the ONT will have an RJ-45 Ethernet jack to connect to the router or switch for your home network (or you can connect to a single computer, if you don't have a home network yet).

Checking availability

Information technology providers face a daunting task replacing existing copper wires with fiber optics. Replacing the so-called "last mile" of copper wire to all homes will likely take many years. Market forces will drive the availability of fiber optics, with the larger, denser market areas getting access first.

When can you expect to see fiber optic services at your front door? This will take some research on your part, and you might not get a straight answer from your phone company; they like to reserve their options and hold close their competitive plans. If you don't already have a press release or a commitment from a company in your area, expect to wait five years or more before it reaches your neighborhood. Regrettably, some rural areas may not see fiber optics for ten years or more.

Regardless of how long you have to wait, the well-wired digital home will be ready to adapt to fiber optics when they arrive. Once your home is wired or prepared for fiber optics, the waiting game begins. Fortunately, when that wait is over, you'll be ready!

Chapter 9

Adding Stereo and Surround Sound

. . . .

. . . .

*W*hen it comes to audio quality, there's nothing like being at a live concert (or having a troubadour and his troupe perform in your living room). The sounds of the live performance envelope the space around you, and you feel the performance as much as hear it.

You may not be able to exactly reproduce the live music experience at home, but bringing the best audio texture available into your house is simply a matter of selecting and properly installing quality audio components. There's more to setting up a high-quality audio system than connecting a couple of speakers to a receiver; this chapter takes the mystery out of home audio systems and shows you how to easily install quality audio in your home. We help you select, wire, and install basic audio components, and we discuss the various options for installing and enjoying stereo and surround sound in one or more rooms of your home.

Considering Whole-House Sound Systems

Have you ever said to yourself, "Self, I wish we could listen to classical violin music while we are dining?" With some careful planning and installation, you can. Your whole-house sound system may be comprised of a monophonic sound in some rooms, stereophonic sound in others, and full surround sound in special locations. (See the sidebar "The development of modern sound reproduction" for information about different sound types.)

The development of modern sound reproduction

In the early days soon after Thomas Edison developed audio recording, all sound reproduction was heard through a single speaker system. A single-speaker system — still common, particularly on small portable radios — is called *monophonic* sound.

The next major advancement in sound reproduction was *stereophonic* sound, which uses two speakers to provide two channel sound recordings. The first stereo recording was made in 1932. It provides a listening experience similar to a live band. With a stereophonic recording you may hear the violin coming from one side and the bass from the other. Stereophonic sound is recorded using two microphones. In the example here, the violin would be recorded near one of the microphones, and the bass near the other microphone. A singer may stand somewhere in the middle so that her voice is recorded on both audio tracks. By mixing the two audio tracks, the listener enjoys an audio experience more closely resembling a live performance.

In trying to improve on stereophonic sound, audio engineers created the next generation of sound recording, called *quadraphonic* sound. Quadraphonic sound offers four separate channels compared to stereo's measly two. This was an improvement, but quadraphonic playback equipment was expensive and cumbersome. Another drawback was that the listener had to be near the convergent center of the four-speaker axis to appreciate the effect.

Next came *Dolby Digital surround sound*. This innovative process imposed two coded signals on each of the two tracks in a stereophonic system. The signals are decoded by a sound processor and distributed to speakers on the listener's front right, front left, front center, rear left, and rear right. A low-frequency channel handles bass sounds. The main sounds are channeled to the right- and left-front speakers. A singer's voice or dialogue is heard from the center channel. Background sounds are sent to the rear channels. The benefits of surround sound include the ambiance and effects it produces when routed to properly located speakers. Surround systems produce a much more realistic feel, and a deeper connection with the music you hear and the video you watch. In high-action movies, for instance, surround sound puts the viewer right in the middle of the action.

As you decide what, if any, sound systems are appropriate for each room, you may be concerned about the cost of wiring. But whole home audio wiring is a far better investment than duplicating expensive equipment in many rooms. By putting your entire equipment budget towards a single system, your listening experience is less likely to be compromised from poor sound quality emanating from many pieces of cheap equipment. High-quality receivers and media players are expensive, but audio wire and quality speakers are relatively inexpensive. By wiring each room from a single high-end audio system, you can leverage the value and performance of your investments. This also streamlines your home because you don't need unsightly radios and audio equipment in every single room.

Using monophonic sound

Monophonic (single channel) sound is normally used by low-fidelity equipment like AM clock radios, low-end televisions, intercoms, weather alert radios, and telephones. These devices should be the only single-channel audio devices in the modern digital home. We'll make an exception for the old phonograph that played Uncle Benny's classical 78 rpm records, but beyond that, consider mono sound outdated. We cover phone wiring in Chapter 6 and intercoms in Chapter 7. Most of your other audio installations will be stereo or surround systems.

Enhancing audio with stereo sound

In Chapter 7 we show you how to integrate home audio systems into your intercom system. An integrated system provides a common distribution for multiple audio sources, but only if you select a multi-zone, multi-source amplifier system. You can't listen to a CD using the intercom speakers in one room while listening to an FM radio station over the intercom in another room if you have a single-channel (source) intercom system. To bring a mix of listening choices into a room you must install a multi-zone, multi-source sound system.

Selecting stereo speaker locations

With all this talk about surround sound, you might wonder why anyone would settle for plain old stereo sound. Stereo sound is still very pleasing to the ear, even if you have experienced surround sound. The separation of sounds is more pronounced in stereo than in surround, and stereo is much less expensive. While you may want to install surround sound in home theater rooms, most other locations inside and outside the house are good candidates for stereo.

To get good stereo sound, the speakers have to be widely separated. Follow these tips when installing stereo speakers:

✔ Place the speakers at least 6–8' apart.

✔ Avoid placing the sides or backs of speakers too close to walls.

✔ The speakers should be equidistant from the room's side walls.

✔ The speakers should be in front of you, and you should be on the center line between the two speakers.

Visualize an equilateral triangle with speakers at two of the corners and the listener at the third. This gives the listener the proper spatial awareness provided by the stereo sound tracks. Figure 9-1 shows how speaker separation and distance create a best listening zone for stereo sound.

Encompassing your listeners with surround sound

Surround sound re-creates a 360-degree field of sound by decoding audio signals recorded on two tracks. The system splits the sound to multiple speaker locations to coincide with the approximate locations of microphones (whether real or virtual) when the sound tracks were originally recorded. Table 9-1 lists the speakers included in the common types of surround sound systems.

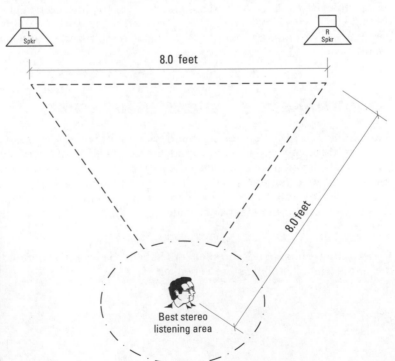

Figure 9-1: The oval identifies the best listening area for a stereo speaker layout.

Table 9-1	Surround Sound Speaker Output Channels	
Speaker	*Abbreviation*	*Frequency Response Range*
Speaker output channels in a 5.1 surround system		
Left front	L	3 Hz–20 kHz
Front center	C	3 Hz–20 kHz
Right front	R	3 Hz–20 kHz
Left surround	LS	3 Hz–20 kHz
Right surround	RS	3 Hz–20 kHz
Base, woofer (front & centered)	LFE	3 Hz–120 Hz
For 6.1 sound: The above 5.1 speakers, plus		
Center rear	CR	3 Hz–20 kHz
For 7.1 sound: The above 5.1 speakers, plus		
Left rear	LR	3 Hz–20 kHz
Right rear	RR	3 Hz–20 kHz

Choosing surround sound equipment

The surround sound equipment you get to pick out is listed here:

- Sound processor (also called the *receiver*)
- Front, side, and rear speakers with enclosures
- Bass woofer

Selecting surround sound equipment can be a challenge because of so many choices. We recommend not using price as your only measure of quality. Pay attention to basic features:

- Frequency range of the amplifiers and speakers
- Number of sound source input jacks available
- Power output in watts
- 5.1, 6.1, or 7.1 output options

A smaller room doesn't need 200 watts of power, but a larger room might. If you pay attention to your requirements and purchase a unit that matches your needs, it doesn't have to be expensive. If you have extra money in your budget, buy the best speakers you can afford because these components actually deliver the sound waves.

An easy way to choose surround sound equipment is to buy a prepackaged set of speakers and the processor from a single manufacturer — an *integrated system*. Most vendors call the surround processor a *receiver*. An integrated surround system costs from $200–$7,000. A sound-processor preamp with separate amplifiers costs about ten times as much as an integrated system. The more expensive equipment is *supposed* to be of higher quality, but this isn't always the case. The cost difference is mainly due to the fact that the integrated systems are mass produced. Whatever your budget, consider the following when choosing a surround sound processor:

✔ Your surround system should have at least 100 watts per channel of output power, even though you may only use half of those watts. A powerful amp means less distortion and better sound quality, even at lower volume settings.

✔ If you need a lot of power, a preamp system is required. Special effects sounds are richer and have a bigger impact if the preamp has the power to drive them through the speakers.

✔ If the processor you're looking at doesn't have Dolby Digital surround sound, consider another brand. Another, less common, surround processor format is *Digital Theater Systems (DTS)*. Some processors can handle both Dolby Digital and DTS.

✔ Some processors have built-in DVD players. This helps reduce wiring clutter and simplifies installation.

✔ Your processor should have these things:

  • Input jacks for every piece of electronic sound equipment you own or expect to own in the future.

  • At least six separate jack sets.

  • Analog sound channel inputs for CD, DVD, and VCR.

  • Digital sound inputs for CD and DVD.

✔ Select a processor with a remote that incorporates all the features you want. At a minimum, the surround processor's remote should include controls that allow you to adjust the various speaker levels while seated in typical listening locations. Some remotes can be programmed to control other devices such as DVD players and TVs.

✔ The processor must have standard output jacks for connecting the six speaker locations listed in Table 9-1 for full 5.1 sound. You have to compare what's available and what you want to pay for. Some units may have a special pair of jacks that allow you to connect only two speakers instead of six. The unit will mix all tracks on the sound to these two speakers and create the illusion that you have the full compliment of surround speakers. This isn't as good as real surround sound, but it's certainly a viable option if you have limited space or a limited budget.

You may want to match the type of jack used for wired-in speakers with the jack or connector on the sound processor. Both ends of your *patch cord* needn't be the same, but it usually makes installation easier. Matching or not, you can still make up your own patch cords, although buying pre-made patch cords is often easier and cheaper.

Arranging your surround sound speakers

Surround sound is recommended for places where you watch movies and TV. This may include a living room, family room, game or recreation room, home theater, master bedroom, or even some outdoor spaces.

Very small rooms aren't good candidates for surround sound because the walls reverberate the sound waves, thus detracting from the sound quality. The ideal room is fairly wide, because more of your audience is within the optimum listening zone. Drapes and carpeting can reduce echo and excessive vibration.

After deciding on rooms, it's time to lay out those rooms for the optimum listening experience. Choose from three different speaker layouts:

✔ **5.1 channel:** This layout includes right front, left front, center, right surround, left surround, and subwoofer speakers. Figures 9-2 and 9-3 in this chapter show a 5.1 channel arrangement. Figure 9-3 shows the proper angular arrangement.

✔ **6.1 channel:** This layout includes right front, left front, center, right surround, left surround, center rear, and subwoofer speakers.

✔ **7.1 channel:** This layout includes right front, left front, center, right surround, left surround, right rear, left rear, and subwoofer speakers. Figure 9-4 (later in this chapter) shows a 7.1 channel speaker arrangement. This is the ideal surround sound layout.

When shopping for speakers you can mix and match brands or enclosure styles to some degree as long as the opposing pairs are the same. *Don't* deviate from the minimum frequency response in Table 9-1 and *do* make sure the maximum wattage rating matches the rated capacity of your receiver (amplifier). Typical mass market sound processor/receivers will be within the ranges shown in the following list. If you aren't buying a prepackaged system, purchase the receiver first and, when equipped with the wattage rating, begin your quest for the perfect speakers and enclosure styles to match your décor.

- ✔ Left- and right-front channels may range in power from 40–130 watts.

- ✔ The center channel is typically 40–100 watts.

- ✔ The rears are 40–100 watts.

- ✔ The powered subwoofer is 50–250 watts.

Except for the subwoofer, each speaker should have exactly the same power rating, whatever wattage you choose. A speaker set like this typically costs between $700 and $1,500. We describe speakers and their proper layout in greater detail later in this chapter.

Figure 9-2 shows a basic 5.1 channel surround sound speaker layout that you might find in many homes, placed about without full regard to the proper angular placement for the maximum quality sound reproduction. When choosing the precise location for each speaker, follow the *International Telecommunication Union (ITU)* standard shown in Figure 9-3. Most recording engineers set up their recording microphones this way, so if your speakers follow the same layout you should be hearing the sound exactly as it was originally recorded. The ITU standard specifies angles for each surround speaker relative to the listener. The listener is directly in front of the center speaker, with the left and right front speakers 30 degrees to either side, and the surround speakers 110 degrees to either side.

If you have trouble measuring or calculating angles, place an enlarged photocopy of Figure 9-3 in the center of your room and pull strings tight over the lines to each speaker location.

Depending on the recording's mix, the center speaker can often be omitted. The voice coming from the left-front and right-front speakers can create a phantom center speaker just as in stereo, so long as you're centered between the speakers. If you're too close to the right or left speaker, the sound will seem to come from that source and not from the central video image, as it should. Some surround processors allow you to mix the front-center surround track to the left- and right-front speakers if necessary. You should also spend some time adjusting speaker levels to accommodate your room's shape and size. The processor's instruction manual should detail how to fine-tune speaker levels, as well as give recommendations for different room shapes and sizes.

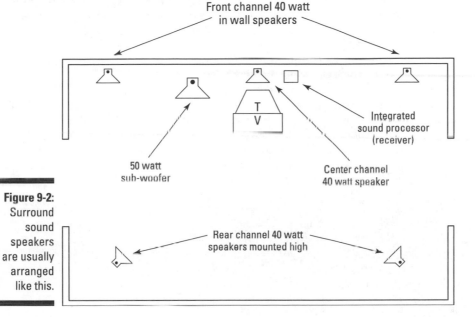

Front channel 40 watt
in wall speakers

T
V

Integrated
sound processor
(receiver)

50 watt
sub-woofer

Center channel
40 watt speaker

Rear channel 40 watt
speakers mounted high

Figure 9-2:
Surround
sound
speakers
are usually
arranged
like this.

Height is another important consideration when selecting speaker locations. The front speakers should be at sitting ear level or a little higher, which is usually about 4' above the finished floor. The surround speakers should be higher than the front speakers, usually 5'–7' above the floor. Mounting too high or too low interferes with how the sound waves travel within a room. The LFE or subwoofer can be mounted low or right at floor level.

If the speakers wind up in a walking area, watch out for knee-bump hazards. Also, items placed just above a person's eye level are in the head-clunk zone. Place a bookcase or other piece of furniture below the speaker, or hang decorative items near speakers at eye level to avoid collisions and headaches.

Configuring 7.1 channel surround speakers

Most surround sound systems are based on 5.1 channel technology. Newer systems are designed for 6.1 and 7.1 channels instead. Currently, most audio is recorded for 5.1 channel surround sound, although 5.1 recordings still sound great on 6.1 and 7.1 systems. 6.1 and 7.1 channel recordings are likely to become more common in the future.

Figure 9-4 shows a 7.1 channel speaker layout. The front speakers are in the same position as in a 5.1 channel system, but the left and right speakers are 100 degrees from the center, instead of 110 degrees. It may be difficult to position the speakers at exactly 100 degrees, so try for somewhere between 90 and 110 degrees. 7.1 channel surround adds two rear speakers, which are placed 130–150 degrees from the center speaker.

We recommend you wire for the 7.1 format with seven separate speaker locations, plus the subwoofer. Do this even if you're buying a 5.1 or 6.1 processor. You can omit the rear or side surround speakers on the 7.1 system to use a 5.1 layout, or you can use one or both rear speakers with a 6.1 processor. When you upgrade to a 7.1 processor, you'll have all the necessary wiring already in place.

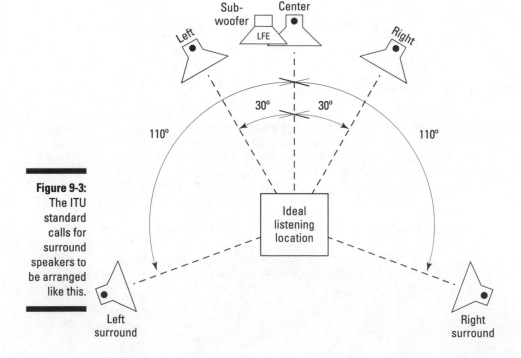

Figure 9-3:
The ITU standard calls for surround speakers to be arranged like this.

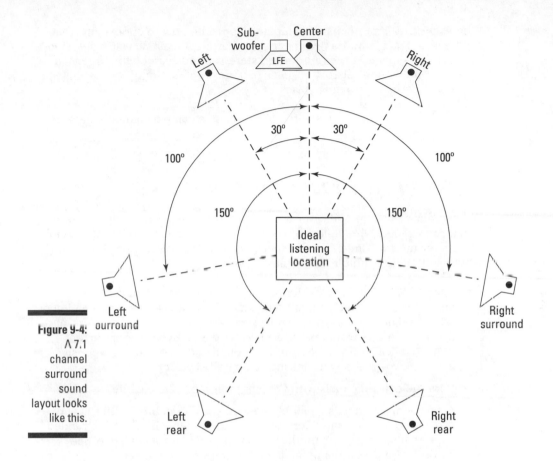

Sub-
woofer
Center
LFE
Left
Right
30°
30°
100°
100°
150°
150°
Ideal
listening
location
Left
surround
Right
surround
Left
rear
Right
rear

Figure 9-4:
A 7.1
channel
surround
sound
layout looks
like this.

Choosing and Installing Speakers

To enjoy stereo sound in more than one room, you should select a multi-
zone, multi-source, multi-room controller/amplifier such as those sold under
the SpeakerCraft label. The secret that makes these units work: multiple
amplifiers. Multi-room amplifiers that can distribute four input sources to any
of six rooms begin at about $1,000, and if you want support for more rooms
and sources, the cost can reach $5,000. Some systems include options such
as a communications interface to your home Ethernet network, allowing you
to control the system with computers.

When selecting a multi-channel amplifier/controller, try to choose one that produces at least 20 watts per channel (or better, at least 30 watts per channel). This ensures that the reproduced stereo sounds can be heard reasonably well and without distortion, even in larger rooms. Going way over 30 watts is unnecessary in most cases.

Listening to music or movies at too-high volumes can permanently damage your hearing.

Wiring multi-room systems

Wiring your rooms for audio speakers and controls is fairly straightforward. When running any wire, follow the basic rough-in tips we detail in Chapter 3. Of course, audio wiring has some special considerations, especially when you're setting up a multi-room, multi-source system:

- Install a two-gang box for the controls in each room. You *could* use a single-gang box, but we don't recommend it because the combination of advanced numeric keypad controls, *infrared (IR)* remote receivers, and manual controls would require a two-gang box. Even if your current plans only call for a single-gang control, blank covers are inexpensive and the two-gang box makes future upgrades easier.

- Wire the control panels with Cat 5 or preferably Cat 6 cable.

- Each room also needs a pair of two-wire speaker cables, with the wire sized to match the amplifier. Usually speaker cable is 12 AWG stranded wire or smaller. Make sure the wire is approved for in-wall use. See Table 9-2 for determining the minimum wire size you need.

- Select speakers that match your performance and design goals for the room. Speakers may be designed to mount on the ceiling or wall, or they may be in-wall or in-ceiling speakers.

- When using in-wall speakers on a wall shared with other living spaces, you may need to add sound insulation between the rooms. Otherwise, volume wars between the occupants may result.

Choose the correct speaker wire gauge from Table 9-2 based on the run distances you have to make. This table shows the maximum distance in feet to maintain <.5dB sound signal loss using AWG stranded copper wire for 8-ohm speakers and 4-ohm speakers. Measure the longest speaker run you will make and buy that wire size in bulk for all the runs to save money and simplify the installation.

Table 9-2	Speaker-Wire Size Selection Based on Run Length	
Using a Wire Size Equal to AWG	*Maximum Distance for 8-Ohm Speakers**	*Maximum Distance for 4-Ohm Speakers*
12	275'	130'
14	175'	85'
16	110'	55'
18	80'	40'
20	45'	22'
22	33'	14'
24	18'	9'

* For 70 volt speaker runs to speakers with transformers, multiply the distance in the 8-ohm column by 23.

Choosing speakers

If you're installing a 5.1 channel surround sound system, you need five regular speakers plus a subwoofer. If you're going to install 7.1 channel surround, add two more speakers to your shopping list.

All of the speakers you buy should have good frequency response. Some manufacturers give the numbers, and others just advertise full frequency range. Try to select speakers that have a frequency response ranging from three *cycles per second (CPS)* up to 20,000 CPS. This specification is also commonly stated as 3 Hz–20 KHz; it means the same thing.

You can do without the subwoofer until it fits within your budget. When you do buy a subwoofer, choose one with a 3–120-cycle frequency output rating for *low frequency effects (LFE)*. The lower frequencies just shake the house and the ground. The frequency at which a human can first perceive sound is usually more than 15–20 CPS. However, you can feel the vibrations from sounds as low as 3 CPS, even if you can't hear them.

Wiring in the speakers

Ideally, speakers should be hardwired into the walls. This is far less cluttered than running wires along the floor to freestanding portable speakers. When you put speaker wiring in the walls, install a separate run of 14 or 16 AWG speaker wire to each speaker location. The wire should be rated for in-wall use and have a UL rating of CL3. You can use this speaker wire for exposed wiring, but the wiring is unsightly.

To wire in the speakers, follow these steps:

1. **Determine the sound processor's (receiver's) location and install an electrical box to facilitate the wiring connections.**

   The speakers for your home theater system should be wired to an electrical box (usually a two-gang box) located behind the sound processor. The electrical box is covered with a home-theater wall plate, which allows easy connections to the sound processor and any freestanding speakers. Use patch cords between the wall plate and the sound processor. The patch cords may connect using banana jacks, binding posts with fork terminals, or spring clips and bare wires. All of your input sources — TVs, VCRs, DVD players, and so on — are also connected to the sound processor using jumper cords and RCA jacks.

2. **Run speaker wire from the processor or amplifier junction box to each speaker location.**

   Follow the general roughing-in tips described in Chapter 3. Remember, the speaker wire should be 12, 14, 16, or 18 AWG depending on the distance of the run.

3. **Install a single-gang junction box or LV ring at each speaker location.**

   If you wish, to get a neater installation you just bring the wire out through the wall and connect it directly to the speaker without using a box or LV ring. You can use an electrical crimp sleeve or some other flanged fitting as eyelets to trim out the wall. Make a hole in the wall finish with a tapered punch so that the sleeve fits tightly in the wall. Bring a few inches of wire out through the sleeve and tie it in a knot to prevent it from falling into the wall.

   Try to mount the speaker over the hole and bring the wire out through the speaker-mounting flange. If the mount provided with your speakers has no hole, carefully drill one yourself. During the rough in, leave two feet or more of slack in the wire to reach the speaker.

4. **If necessary, nail a block to the nearby studs to provide a backing behind the drywall to which the speaker is mounted.**

   This is necessary for any wall- or ceiling-mounted speakers that aren't mounted directly on a stud. Supporting speakers with only the strength of the drywall is not a good idea. The drywall can be torn if something hits the speakers and the speakers will vibrate if not mounted securely.

5. **Connect the speaker wires to the speakers.**

   Pay special attention to polarity when connecting speaker wires. The speaker diaphragm moves out as positive voltage is applied to the voice coil, and it moves in when negative voltage is applied. The polarity of the voltage determines which direction the diaphragm moves. For accurate sound reproduction, all speaker diaphragms must move in the same direction at the same time. The speakers will still produce sound if connected backwards, but the sound waves will not be properly synchronized with the other speakers.

6. **Turn your system on and play your favorite CD or DVD to test your installation.**

When connecting speakers, high-quality components are advantageous. Gold connectors are highly resistant to corrosion, for example. When wiring your surround sound room, if you can buy 12 AWG wire with gold connectors without breaking the bank, by all means use them; but don't feel like you have to beg your mother-in-law for a loan just to buy better speaker wires.

The DC resistance of 1,000' of 18, 16, 14, and 12 AWG wire is 8, 5, 3, and 2 ohms, respectively. You will probably use less than 100' for any single speaker run in your home, so the resistances at 100' are all less than 1 ohm. The DC resistance of an ordinary plated connector compared to a gold-plated connector is so insignificant as to be negligible. The resistance of copper is 1.7×10^{-8} (.000000017) ohms per meter, and gold is 2.24×10^{-8} ohms per meter. Before the connector is gold plated it usually is plated with nickel. Nickel has a resistance of 7×10^{-8} ohms per meter, which is about four times that of copper. We don't believe the human ear can tell the difference between a surround sound system wired with 16 AWG wire and plated connectors and that wired with 12 AWG wire and more expensive gold connectors.

Chapter 10

Wiring Family Rooms and Home Theaters

Your home isn't just a place to eat, bathe, and sleep. The modern digital home is also a place to entertain and be entertained, whether you're enjoying some time alone or with friends. Other chapters of this book focus on specific home systems like intercoms, electricity, cable TV, and computer networks. We show you how to select and install safe, correctly working components.

In this chapter we help you focus on the bigger design picture, bringing various elements and systems together to create the perfect entertainment space. Here we bring the basic building blocks together to create a multi-use family room, or a custom digital odeum of your own.

Designing for Adaptable Family Rooms

The definition of *family room* varies considerably from one family to the next, but they all have one thing in common: They're where family and friends come together, enjoy each others' company, play, and relax. This means that your family room should be versatile enough to adapt to a variety of uses, including

✔ **Play room,** where people of all ages play games.

✔ **Theater,** where you spend a night watching movies in your own high-tech theater.

✔ **Work place** for those family members with work-at-home jobs or home-work. Their work or school life all too often extends into the family room.

✔ **Meeting room,** a natural place to get together and discuss important topics.

✔ **Spillover space** for extra dining or sleeping space, or a special project room.

You can probably think of even more uses. Given the need for adaptability, you must carefully plan wiring and other digital systems in the family room.

Start simply:

1. **List all the activities you think will occur there, paying no attention to how often or how long the activity will occur.**

2. **Rank the items from most to least important.**

3. **Write down what systems are needed for each activity and the number of power outlets required for the activity.**

   For example, if you plan on having a computer in the family room, you need a communications jack (Ethernet if you have a home network and/or broadband Internet connection, or a telephone jack if you have a dial-up Internet connection). Regarding the outlets: In the activities listed in Table 10-1, sewing requires work-level lighting, while TV viewing needs low-level lighting, cable TV jacks, multiple electrical outlets, and possibly a surround sound system. (The following section explains lighting.) Your list should have as many items as needed to cover all of your family room activities.

4. **Plan your switch wiring, lighting, power outlets, and communications jacks.**

Table 10-1 Planning the Wiring for Your Family Room

Activity	Lighting Requirements	Wall Jack Requirements	Minimum Outlet Requirements
Watching TV	Low level	Cable TV	1
Playing movies on a DVD or VCR*	Low level	None*	2 (1 for TV, 1 for DVD/VCR/surround sound system)
Playing computer games	Low level	Ethernet for network/Internet connection	2 (1 for lamp, 1 for computer)
Homework	Work level	Ethernet for network/Internet connection	2 (1 for lamp, 1 for computer)

Activity	Lighting Requirements	Wall Jack Requirements	Minimum Outlet Requirements
Reading	Work level	None	1/reading lamp
Sewing	Work level	None	2 (1 for lamp, 1 for sewing machine)
Office work	Work level	Phone, Ethernet for network/Internet connection	2 (1 for lamp, 1 for computer)

* If you wired your family room for surround sound, you may have speaker wire preinstalled in the walls, emerging at the wall mounts for the speakers. See Chapter 9 for more about wiring for surround sound.

Lighting Your Family Room

Lighting levels and switch locations are important design considerations for any family room. Some types of lighting, such as fluorescent with plastic lenses, will reflect on TV or computer screens, creating unwanted glare. To prevent glare you must ensure that there is not a direct line of sight from a light to TV or computer screen.

To check your *lighting geometry* in relation to the TV screen when you're about to install the light fixtures, place a mirror where the TV screen will be. Position yourself in the viewing area. If you can see any lights in the mirror, they will cause glare on the screen. Move the light to change the angle. The same also goes for natural light sources that aren't covered by dark shades. Any natural light (doors or windows) you can see in the mirror will cause screen glare, and you can't move natural light sources. Drapes or shades come to the rescue if you can't move the TV to compensate for light entering windows.

Low-mounted wall lights are less likely to cause glare. These lights often have hoods or louvers to direct light down. When installing these fixtures, make sure they don't illuminate the wall below them so brightly that they cause reflections on the TV screen. Paradoxically, the closer you move a fixture to the TV screen, the less likely it is to cause reflection and glare. Of course, if the light is too far forward it will be more directly offensive to the viewer.

With a little planning, your family room lighting can be nearly perfect. To be totally perfect, light bulbs would need to replace themselves when they burn out. Maybe that level of perfection isn't possible, but you can come close. The following sections guide you through selecting some of the types of lighting systems you may use in your family room.

Measuring light levels

Different family room activities demand different levels of light. You may think of light in simple terms of dim, medium, and bright, but you can more precisely measure and express light levels. The four main units of measure used in home lighting are

- ✔ **Candle power:** Light intensity produced by one candle.

- ✔ **Footcandle:** Light intensity measured on a surface exactly 1' away from a burning candle.

- ✔ **Lumen:** 1 footcandle of light intensity on 1 square foot.

- ✔ **Lux:** Light's metric measure. A lux is equal to 1 lumen per square meter or 0.0929 footcandle.

The amount of light you need varies by task. (People who have a hard time seeing may need stronger lighting than given in the following table.)

Task	*Light Requirement (in footcandles)*
Cleaning a room	25–50
Close-up work	100–200
Lighting a hallway	5
Lighting the driveway	1

Lighting fixture manufacturers provide tables to help you calculate the light intensity you get by putting its fixtures in a given pattern (and at a determined mounting height with the recommended bulb or lamp). Light also can be measured with a light meter.

Figure 10-1 shows sample layouts of two 20' × 20' rooms.

- ✔ **The room on the left:** Four 2' × 4' fluorescent fixtures with parabolic lenses, as shown in Figure 10-2. These lights give the room 61 footcandles and use 1.5 watts per square foot — more than twice the lighting, while using a little less energy, than the recessed lights.

- ✔ **The room on the right:** Nine recessed lights with black baffles and 75-watt lamps. (The fixture shown on the left in Figure 10-3 has a white baffle.) This layout yields 25 footcandles of light and uses 1.69 watts per square foot.

We may call a fluorescent light component a *parabolic lens,* but it's not a lens in the usual sense — just a 1½" × 1½" array of squares. You can see the lamps if you look up from below the fixture, but the light seems to disappear as you move away. The silver or gold finished vertical grid hides the lamps when viewed at an angle and because they're at a right angle to the lamps, they pick up very little light unless the finish is degraded or dirty.

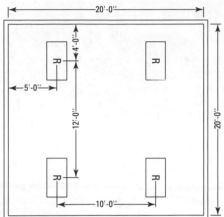

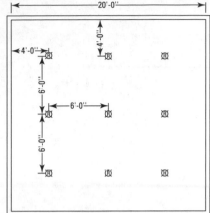

Figure 10-1:
Some lights shed more light on your family room than others.

Four 120 watt 2 x 4 foot recessed flourescent fixtures with parabolic lens on 10 x 12 foot centers illuminate this 20 x 20 foot room to a 61 footcandle level.

Nine 75 watt recessed flourescent fixtures installed on 6 foot centers illuminate this 20 x 20 foot room to a 25 footcandle level.

Selecting fluorescent fixtures

Some fluorescent fixtures work better than others in family rooms. As mentioned in the previous section, some fluorescent lights with lenses can cause glare on TVs and computer screens. However, 2' × 2' or 2' × 4' recessed fixtures with parabolic louver lenses like the one shown in Figure 10-2 cause little screen glare. Viewed from a short distance these fixtures just about disappear in the ceiling. You can certainly tell that the lights are on because the room is illuminated, but you can't see where the light is coming from.

Parabolic louvered lenses are made in various grid patterns. We recommend a 1½" square pattern that is 1" deep. The other patterns don't hide the light as well. Other advantages of fluorescent fixtures with parabolic louvered lenses include

- ✔ **Low maintenance:** Grid pattern lenses can't catch flies or other debris like ordinary fluorescent lenses.

- ✔ **Long service life:** Fluorescent lamps last 20,000 hours compared to incandescent lamps' 2,000 hours. The ballasts in fluorescent lamps fail sometimes, but typically last 15 years even with frequent use.

- ✔ **Low heat:** Fluorescent lamps use less electricity and produce less heat than incandescent lamps.

Figure 10-2:
Parabolic
louvered
lenses allow
you to use
fluorescent
lights in
many kinds
of rooms.

You can install parabolic lens fixtures in any area. Clean the lenses periodically. When installed in kitchens, you have to replace the lenses after about ten years because residue from cooking — maybe one too many burnt pizzas? — degrades the lens' silver finish.

Using recessed fixtures

Recessed fixtures are popular choices for family room lighting. As the name implies, *recessed lighting* fixtures are flush with the ceiling. Recessed fixtures are for general area lighting and their placement is important because you need to install enough fixtures to give adequate lighting. Some things to pay attention to when installing recessed fixtures include

- **TV screen and computer screen glare:** Move the lamp as high in the fixture as possible on adjustable fixtures.

- **Side reflection:** Choose fixture trims with black stepped baffles, or paint light-colored fixtures black.

- ✔ **Electrical connections:** Make sure they're good. It is a real inconvenience to have to access the junction boxes for recessed fixtures once the finish is in place.

- ✔ **Testing:** Install temporary lamps and test the fixtures after roughing them in to make sure everything works. Leave the temporary lamps in place for lighting during construction.

- ✔ **Fixtures:** Buy recessed fixtures (often called *cans*) with factory-installed junction boxes that are wired to the lamp holders with high temperature wire.

- ✔ **Lifetime:** Recessed fluorescent fixtures use less electricity and the bulbs last up to ten times longer than incandescent lamps, but recessed fluorescent fixtures are expensive.

- ✔ **IC rated:** If you're installing recessed lights in a ceiling that is to be insulated, make sure the fixtures are IC rated, meaning they're rated for direct contact with insulation.

Overhead lights are often controlled with dimmer switches. When dimmers are installed on incandescent fixtures, lamp life can be greatly extended, especially when the lamps are operated at low levels.

Figure 10-3 shows two IC-rated, recessed light fixture cans. Notice that the junction boxes are connected to the lamp holder housings with flexible conduit. Shown in the foreground on the left is the junction box's metal cover. In the flex conduit are the black and white wires that connect to the lamp holder. This wire is rated to withstand temperatures up to 150 degrees Celsius.

The trim on the right in Figure 10-3 is recessed light *eyeball trim.* The eyeball's *gimbal* allows you to aim the lamp, which is particularly handy for accenting a fireplace mantle or wall hanging. You also need the gimbal to properly aim the light when installing recessed fixtures on sloped ceilings. This trim takes an R-30 lamp. (The *R* stands for reflector and *30* is the diameter in ⅛"; the lamp is 3¾"). This ⅛" numbering system indicates the diameter of most lamps. The telescoping mounting straps are designed to be nailed to the framing or fastened to a suspended ceiling T-bar grill.

The wire running from the top of the recessed fixture can to the junction box must be 150 degrees Celsius-rated wire, not 90 degrees Celsius-rated Romex. The best way to ensure the right rating is to purchase and install a fixture that has the junction box and high temperature wire already in place. The junction box must be accessible by code. The box in Figure 10-3 is accessible after installation by removing three screws that hold the can to the mounting frame.

Figure 10-3: These two recessed light fixtures are IC rated.

Using track fixtures

Of the various lighting systems you can use in your family room, *track lighting* systems are among the most versatile: You can move the light fixtures along a track, and most can swivel to provide perfect aiming.

When you install a track, simply run a control wire to one end of the track location. You can install this wire in a box, or just bring it out through the wall or ceiling surface. Track lighting manufacturers make fittings to cover box openings. Other track-light system components, shown in Figure 10-4, include

- **Track connectors:** These link multiple tracks together. As you can see in Figure 10-4, these connectors may be straight, angled, or flexible.

- **Light fixtures:** These twist-lock into the track and can be aimed in almost any direction.

- **Power-feed connectors:** These feed power to the track. One of the connectors in Figure 10-4 is shown with the cover removed.

Track lighting track   Adjustable angle track connector   Cover for electric power feed connector

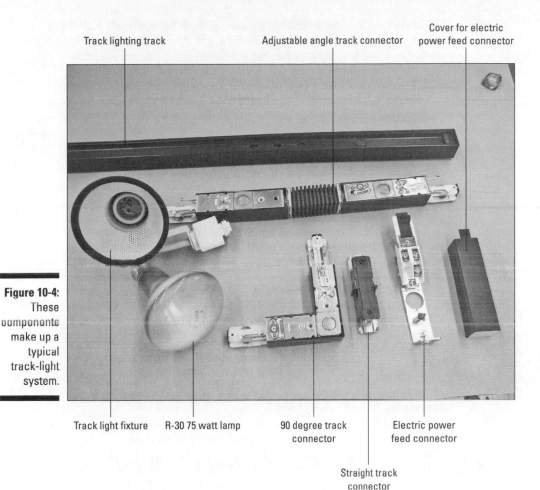

Figure 10-4:
These
components
make up a
typical
track-light
system.

Track light fixture   R-30 75 watt lamp   90 degree track connector   Electric power feed connector

Straight track connector

Supplementing with lamps and task lighting

You will probably want to augment your family room lighting with some floor lamps, table lamps, and other task lights in select areas. For example, a banker's lamp can help light up a desk, and a flexible-neck halogen light can illuminate a sewing table. Three-way switched lamps change lighting levels as needed next to an easy chair for reading, watching TV, or napping away the afternoon.

You can control most freestanding lamps locally using their built-in switches, or you can control them using switched outlets. When controlling lamps using switched outlets, remember

- ✔ X10 controls (see Chapters 4 and 5) can also be used to control lamps on switched outlets from anywhere.

- ✔ Touch-control lamps are handy in some situations, but you can't control them with switched outlets. To control touch lamps remotely you need a really long finger.

- ✔ We don't recommend that you control switched outlets using dimmers because the voltage from dimmer switches is DC. Home outlets usually supply AC voltage. Incandescent lamps handle DC voltage just fine, but sooner or later someone will plug in a piece of electronic equipment to the outlet. The result will be damage to both the equipment and the dimmer switch.

Lamps come equipped with 6' cords. These cords are normally 18 AWG wire. We recommend that lamps only be plugged into 15-amp circuits and not 20-amp circuits. If the cord becomes fouled or is chewed on (thanks to Fluffy), it's far more likely to burn if it's protected by a 20-amp circuit breaker. On a 15-amp circuit the breaker is more likely to trip.

Avoid using extension cords to plug in lamps; they tend to get left in place and become permanent wiring. If you can't avoid using extension cords, use 14 AWG heavy-duty cords to lessen the risk of a damaged cord, which can be dangerous.

Controlling your family room lights

The best lights in the world don't do much good if you can't turn them on. Because family room lighting must be adaptable to many uses, the switches must give you more control. The next couple of sections cover some of the ways to control the lighting in your family room. For additional information on roughing in and trimming out light controls, see Chapters 3 and 4, respectively.

Dimming light with dimmer switches

Dimmer switches are an excellent way to control light levels of incandescent lights. With a dimmer switch you can fine-tune light levels by simply moving the switch a little bit. Dimmer switches are described in greater detail in Chapter 4.

If you will be dimming more than 500 watts, use a single-gang box for the dimmer switch. High-capacity dimmer switches have cooling fins to dissipate heat, and finned dimmers don't fit well in multiple-gang boxes. Removing a cooling fin reduces the dimmer's wattage capacity. You can dim fluorescent lights with special dimmers and fixtures, but dimmers aren't generally a good option for fluorescent lights in home projects. Dimming fluorescent fixtures are very expensive.

Adjusting fluorescent levels with dual switching

Fluorescent lights can't be dimmed by traditional dimmer switches, but you can still adjust fluorescent light levels somewhat using *dual switching,* which controls a single or section of fixtures with more than one switch. Three-, four-, or six-lamp fluorescent fixtures can be purchased with one, two, or three *ballasts* (voltage converter). Each ballast controls one or two of the lamps, and each ballast is controlled by a separate light switch. Want a little light? Flip a switch to turn on one set of lamps. Want more light? Flip on another set of lamps.

Dual switching is inexpensive. In the case of a four-lamp fluorescent fixture with two ballasts, apply this switching to all of the fixtures in the room and you have two levels of lighting available:

1. **Wire the fixture to two light switches using three-conductor wire.**

2. **Connect one switch to the black conductor, and the other switch to the red conductor.**

3. **At the fixture, connect the black wire to one ballast, and the red wire to the other.**

   The white wire is the neutral for both ballasts.

Of course, dual switching is not an option for fixtures that have only one lamp or ballast. If you have a bunch of single lamp fixtures, connect every other fixture to one switch, and the remaining fixtures to the second switch.

Planning Family Room Outlets

In areas with a lot of electrical equipment, it's important to install a sufficient number of power outlets. That ensures that you can plug each piece of equipment, battery backup, and surge protector strip directly into a wall outlet. Install outlets in close proximity to where you expect to use electrical equipment.

We often install *quad outlets* (two duplex outlets) in the entertainment and computer areas.

In addition to good *outlet density,* you also want adequate *circuit density.* Run separate circuits to the areas that will have heavy use. This may mean separate circuits for the computer area, theater, wet bar, and others. Most of these uses have low power demands, with the possible exception of the bar. It may have a refrigerator, dishwasher, trash compactor, and a few plug-in items like blenders or ice crushers.

To give your family room the flexibility for periodic furniture rearrangements, install six jack plates (see Chapter 8) on two or three walls in the family room. These jacks provide connections for phone, Ethernet, RG-6, and fiber optics. At some point you may need to accommodate multiple computers and other devices in the family room.

Use a surge protector with your expensive electronic equipment. We recommend installing a whole-house surge protector in your home's electrical service panel. Redundant surge protection is perfectly okay. Often, the additional surge protectors or computer plug-in bars are necessary just to accommodate the various low-voltage transformer bricks a lot of devices use.

Designing Your Dedicated Home Theater

Once upon a time, the living room was the place where families got together to play games, visit with friends, read, listen to the radio, or watch TV. Then American homes started to sprout family rooms, which were used for most of the same things as living rooms, but in a more casual setting. Today, some upscale homes now include dedicated home theaters in addition to family and living rooms. Whether it's the rising cost of movie tickets, or the affordability of modern high-definition (HD) TVs and surround sound systems, the home theater is more common and important than ever.

The home theater differs from the multipurpose family room in that its only purpose is sound and video entertainment. From the room's overall design, to mood lighting and the 7.1 digital surround sound system, each element in a dedicated theater space must complement the others.

From an architectural perspective, the theater room should have six features:

 ✔ An unobstructed view of the video display. The video display, whether a large TV, a flat-panel plasma HDTV, or even a home theater projector, should be of significant size and scaled to match the room.

 ✔ A space 3–5' deep behind the video screen for wiring all the equipment and making the connections. Ideally, the wall behind the screen is a common wall with a mechanical room or dedicated closet. You can also use a shelf unit, but be sure that it's securely fastened to the wall behind it to prevent tipping.

✔ Overstuffed furniture on an angled floor. This allows unobstructed views for people seated in the second and subsequent rows. Instead of a sloped floor, you can mount a flat-panel TV high enough to view from a level floor.

✔ Very quiet and gentle air conditioning and heating systems with digital temperature controls.

✔ A command center for the video equipment, sound, lighting, and temperature.

✔ A small refrigerator if the bar or kitchen is far away. You can't forget those refreshments!

If your design includes all of these elements, not only will you have a home theater, but you'll have all the makings of a modern digital odeum.

Maintaining access to the equipment

One of the biggest mistakes in home theaters is setting up the equipment such that the connections can't be checked or changed without pulling out all the devices. A large closet or custom-built unit that divides the audio and video equipment and connections from the viewing area solves this problem. Figure 10-5 shows an ideal layout for a home theater setup. Custom cabinetry or custom shelving is a good idea, and can make the room more aesthetically pleasing. Locking pocket doors or other dividers can keep children away from the equipment.

Designing media rooms

The term *media room* is often used synonymously with *home theater*. That isn't wrong, but we think one essential ingredient separates a media room from a home theater: a computer. When we think of media room, we think of an area used for creatively working with various kinds of media. Therefore, the media room is as much a work space as an entertainment space. In a media room you might

✔ Burn custom CDs

✔ Make greeting cards

✔ Retouch and print pictures

✔ Make DVDs

When wiring a media room, form follows function. The room needs wiring for lights, power, and communications. Counter-height outlets may not be aesthetically pleasing in a living room, but in a media room they're task oriented and functional. Other helpful features include lots of storage, large and lengthy work surfaces, computer desks, and printer shelves.

Including a control center

If your budget and space allow, you may want to include a control center in your home theater. The control center's main feature is to provide extensions for all of the hardwired controls to a common location, including three-way switches for the lighting and a place for the remote controls for all the audio and video equipment. Put command center wiring at the end of a seating row (depending on whether you are right or left handed). The command center layout shown in Figure 10-5 requires a short wall or cabinetry with a custom-built control panel at a 45° angle to the person operating the controls.

The command center wiring plan should include

✔ Wires between the audio/video equipment and the control center

✔ Remote controls storage space

✔ An outlet for battery rechargers

✔ Three- or four-way switch runs to control lighting, or an X10 controller.

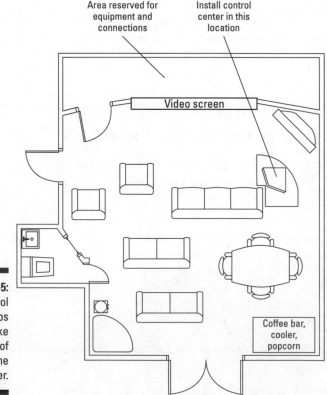

Figure 10-5:
A control center helps you take command of your home theater.

Maintaining clear sound zones

The most important feature of the home theater is the audio system. Video experts know that audiences are relatively forgiving of poor video quality, but notice even minor audio imperfections. Ideally, your home theater is wired for 7.1 channel surround sound as described in Chapter 9. When planning the sound space for your home theater, consider the following:

- **Furnishings:** Pay close attention to speaker mounting heights to avoid conflicting with the furniture. Make sure furniture doesn't block any speakers.

- **Telephone:** Do you need a telephone in the theater? Our feeling is that the theater is the last place you want a phone. However, you may want to watch a movie with the family while you're expecting a call from the boss. The nearly perfect solution is to use a little gadget called a phone flasher. A *phone flasher* plugs into a phone jack and an electrical outlet. You then plug a lamp — any lamp — into the phone flasher. When the phone rings, a relay in the phone flasher flashes the lamp on and off. This is much less disturbing than the ringer on the phone.

  However, you need to install at least one phone jack in your home the-ater if you're going to use pay-per-view or on-demand services that are initiated by telephone dial-up.

- **Wall thickness:** In a new construction, exterior walls are often made with 2" × 6" wall framing leaving a larger cavity for heat/cooling insula-tion. When designing your theater for new construction, consider using 2" × 6" interior walls (instead of a normal 2" × 4" interior wall) with sound-deadening insulation to minimize sound travel both into and out of the room. Remodeling projects are usually limited to having sound insulation blown into existing wall cavities and using heavier doors on the room entrance.

Chapter 11

Installing Video Systems and Cameras

Most homes built in the last 30-plus years had both electrical and telephone systems installed during construction. And in the last couple of decades, cable TV systems have become common. What sets a *digital* home apart from just a plain old home is that the former has modern systems like computer networks, multi-zone audio systems, and — you guessed it — advanced video surveillance systems.

Home video surveillance systems serve a variety of uses. They allow you to make sure that's Doug, not some stranger, in the big brown truck with a delivery. Cameras help you keep an eye on the kids' playroom, conduct videoconferencing over the Internet, and share views of your beautiful sunsets with distant friends. And of course, cameras are an integral part of a home security system. We describe security systems in greater detail in Chapter 14. Here we introduce you to the different types of available camera systems, including webcams and more traditional types. We show how to integrate video cameras into other home systems, and how to keep the cameras rolling even when the power goes out.

Selecting Video Components

A smart shopper — that's you — needs to carefully evaluate the different types of surveillance systems and cameras. Take the time to consider your needs before you begin shopping. Walk your home and property with a note pad, and assess areas where risks might be reduced by surveillance. Use your notes to help decide what to buy and install. Outdoor areas, for example, probably need weatherproof cameras with strong low-light performance. Indoor areas may call for smaller, more discrete cameras. The following sections help you evaluate the different features.

Reviewing camera features

If you want to install video surveillance, there's just no getting around the fact that you're going to have to buy some video cameras. Cameras range from very cheap with few features, to more expensive with better performance. Different areas of your home call for different types of cameras. Consider the following:

✔ **Size:** Size may be important, particularly when trying to hide a camera. So-called *bullet cameras* are intended to peer through small drilled holes, with the camera remaining hidden.

✔ **Camera resolution:** How crisp and clear do you need the picture to be? Higher-resolution cameras provide clearer pictures with sharper edges. They're always better — and almost always more expensive — than low-resolution cameras, but budget may limit your choices.

✔ **Operating temperature range:** Nearly all electronic devices can be damaged or temporarily fail when exposed to certain temperatures. Outdoor cameras can be exposed to high levels of heat, as well as freezing temperatures. Enclosures with heaters or fans can help keep cameras within operating temperature ranges.

✔ **Color or black and white:** Unless you're working with a very restricted budget, you should choose color cameras. They make it much easier to see what's happening on the screen.

✔ **Night vision:** You may need some cameras (especially outdoor cameras) to provide a visible image in the dark, without floodlights. If you're concerned about low-light operation, choose a camera with night vision.

✔ **Weatherproofing:** Cameras which will be fully exposed to the elements must be weatherproof. You can mount cameras behind glass and under porches to give the camera some protection from the weather and still get a view outside, but any camera installed outside should be a weatherproof model.

✔ **Sun shielding:** Cameras that will be mounted in locations that receive direct sunlight for any part of the day need sunshields, or else all the camera will record is a bright white spot.

✔ **Tamper-resistant housing:** Cameras in high-traffic areas, remote locations, or other unsecured spots may need a tamper-resistant housing. This feature doesn't stop someone who's truly determined to destroy the camera, but it prevents repair bills that come from foolish tampering.

- ✔ **Domes:** Protective domes can potentially protect your cameras from two things: bad weather and vandalism.

- ✔ **Motion sensors:** A camera equipped with a motion sensor turns on when someone comes into its field of view. The motion sensor can also trigger a local or general alarm, or trip a zone on the integrated security alarm.

- ✔ **Sound:** In addition to *seeing* video, you may want to *hear* what's happening. If so, select a camera with a built-in omnidirectional or directional microphone (mic). *Omnidirectional mics* pick up sound equally from all angles. *Directional mics* pick up sound within a defined cone-shaped area depending on what subtype you buy, the latter here picking up the narrowest area; see Figure 11-1:

  - Cardiod

  - Supercardiod

  - Hypercardioid

- ✔ **Dummy cameras:** A camera made for this book? No. A *dummy camera* is a fake you install simply to attract attention. Someone sees the dummy and thinks you have video surveillance, even if you don't. You also can install dummies to divert attention away from real cameras.

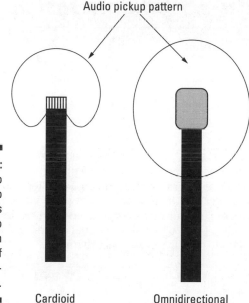

Audio pickup pattern

Cardioid   Omnidirectional

Figure 11-1:
The audio pickup patterns for two common types of microphones.

✔ **Power supply — AC, DC, or both:** Cameras need electricity to operate. If your cameras must operate even when the power goes out, you need a DC power source for backup power (probably a battery). Remote locations may be powered with 12-volt DC power and solar cells to keep the batteries charged. This application is great for solar cells because the cameras don't draw much current.

✔ **Remote rotation:** You may want to rotate a camera remotely or automatically. Some models let you tilt the camera vertically or pan horizontally. This may be a handy feature in some cases, but rotating cameras can be quite expensive and they need additional maintenance.

✔ **Zoom — optical or digital:** *Zoom* allows the camera to focus in close, in effect magnifying the subject. Digital cameras may offer both digital and optical zoom, although *optical zoom* is best because it maintains image quality. *Digital zoom* discards some image quality as it gets close to an image.

✔ **Auto iris:** The camera's auto iris causes the circular hole through which the camera sees to be larger or smaller, letting in exactly the right amount of light for a good picture. An auto iris automatically adjusts to constantly changing light conditions.

Choosing a video surveillance system

The simplest way to choose a surveillance system is to buy a kit containing all the necessary components:

✔ Cameras

✔ Monitor screens

✔ Video recorders

If you buy all the components in a kit, you greatly increase the chance that everything will work well together. Even when buying a startup kit you may have to buy additional wire, connectors, back-up power supplies, and other accessories. Typical prepackaged kits include four cameras, a video monitor that can display the inputs from all four cameras, and a recording device, along with the various controls. If you plan to install additional cameras, make sure your system's monitor and control unit can support them.

Surveillance systems — whether purchased in a kit or as separate components — usually come in one of two formats:

✔ **Closed-circuit TV (CCTV):** These usually include analog TV cameras and a monitor. Analog CCTV systems are less efficient because analog images are harder to store. You can connect CCTV systems to VCRs or *digital video recorders (DVRs)*.

✔ **Web-based cameras:** These cameras connect to your home network wirelessly or via Ethernet cables. The camera's internal circuitry generates a Web page containing the current camera image, and you can use any network computer to view the image using a Web browser. You may even be able to view the camera's image over the Internet if you have a static IP address, as described in Chapter 12. The camera's Web page can only show the current image, however; most cameras can't store images. You need a file server (usually a network drive) for storing video streams or pictures. For more on using webcams with a home network, see Chapter 12.

For the modern digital home we believe that Web-based cameras are the way to go. Setting them up is easy and increasingly affordable. The biggest advantage to Web-based cameras is that you can connect up to 254 different devices on one network, each with its own IP address. If the network includes a file server, a router/gateway, and a PC that uses an IP address, that leaves you with the potential to install up to 251 cameras. It is hard to imagine that the average home would need more than 200 cameras, but it's good to know that you probably won't run up against a limit.

Installing Your Video System

How you install your surveillance system depends mainly on your purpose for installing cameras in the first place. Two primary yet potentially complementary reasons exist for installing cameras: security or convenience. You needn't hide cameras installed primarily for convenience, although you can anyway. If a security camera is visible, it may deter an intruder. On the other hand, hiding cameras reduces the possibility of tampering or vandalism. Consider using the previously mentioned dummy camera left in plain sight and a hidden camera at the same time.

Positioning cameras

You determine camera placement and aim by carefully analyzing the areas you want to keep an electronic eye on. Common camera locations include

✔ Front and back doors

✔ Walkways

✔ Porches

✔ Driveways

✔ Remote buildings

✔ Children's playroom

Once you've listed general locations, choose specific locations for physical mounting of the cameras. Each location is unique, but here are some mounting tips:

- ✔ **Under eaves:** Eaves provide some weather protection, and you can usually mount the cameras on framing members. You may be able to locate this 2' × 2' lumber by looking where the siding is nailed. Keep in mind, however, that although eaves provide *some* weather protection, you should install weatherproof cameras in outdoor locations.

- ✔ **Suspended ceilings:** To install a camera that peers through a hole or dome in a suspended ceiling, install a mounting frame above the ceiling tile. The mounting could be a manufacturer-supplied item available with the camera or just some lumber that spans and is attached to the ceiling framing.

- ✔ **Above eye level:** Mounting cameras above a pedestrian's normal range of sight usually provides the camera a better view and enhances its security. Sometimes the field of view you want requires a lower mounting location. In such cases, try to mount the camera in something or otherwise hide it so only the lens end is exposed. You can put a bullet camera in your mailbox or house number plaque.

- ✔ **Hidden in plain sight:** You can hide a camera by making it look like something else. For example, you could place a camera inside a thick, hollowed-out book on a shelf.

- ✔ **Strong mounting:** Make sure the mounting bracket is strong enough to support the camera. For outdoor cameras, keep in mind that wind and ice may add extra stress to the mounting.

If your area is prone to burglary and vandalism, install a dummy camera in an obvious, prominent location. A highly visible camera may discourage theft or vandalism, and even if someone vandalizes or steals it, you won't lose an expensive piece of equipment.

Supplying power to your cameras

Unless you install solar-powered cameras, you need a power source at each location. Most cameras run from power supplies plugged into conventional 120-volt AC power. Most units are equipped with a weatherproof cord that you plug into a standard receptacle. If the receptacle isn't accessible from *grade level* (or ground level), you don't need a *Ground Fault Interrupter (GFI)*, but you probably need an in-use weatherproof cover. By code, if the receptacle can only be reached via ladder, it isn't accessible. See Figure 16-1 for an in-use receptacle cover.

You may want to have your security system on its own circuit. Keep in mind, however, that having the security system on a separate circuit is a potential problem: Unless the system has a battery-powered alarm that sounds when the power is out, the system can be shut off without you being aware of it.

Connecting cameras to the network

Cameras connect to your home network or surveillance system using a variety of methods. They may be wireless or use Cat 5, Cat 6, RG-6, or RG-59 cable.

Regardless of the connection type, follow the general rules of wiring when installing your cameras:

- ✔ Any wiring you install must be listed for the environment in which you install it. For example, wiring for outdoor cameras should be sunlight resistant, waterproof, and rated for direct burial if necessary.

- ✔ Outdoor power receptacles accessible from grade must be GFI protected and have in-use covers on the boxes.

- ✔ Webcams normally use Cat 6 cable to send data to the network server for your surveillance system. Take extra care to protect the Ethernet jacks from weather, including using the weather- and water-resistant connectors discussed in Chapter 17.

Part III
Installing Home Networks and Advanced Technology

The 5th Wave   By Rich Tennant

© RICHTENNANT

"Roger! Check the sewing machine's connection to the PC. I'm getting e-mails stitched across my curtains again."

In this part . . .

Not long ago computer networks were the exclusive domain of the government, universities, phone companies, and large corporations, but now anyone can install and collect the multiple benefits of home computer networks and computer-automated controls.

The chapters in this part show you the right ways to wire networks within your home. You also see how to get help from a little digenie code-named Hal (*dij'- en- e:* anthropomorphized digital software that does one's bidding when summoned by voice commands or the clock), who lives in one or more of your home's computers and does whatever it can to help run the house.

Chapter 12

Home Networks and Internet Connections

*I*f you don't connect your home to the Internet, your home network is like an island, helplessly isolated from the online world. That online world includes a wealth of information, entertainment, online classes, and efficient means of communication by e-mail or instant messaging. An Internet connection also allows you to control the devices in your home, communicate with people in your home, or monitor things when you're away. Imagine knowing the thermostat setting or checking the status of sump pumps, heating equipment, and alarm systems in your home from anywhere in the world. Would you like to be able to turn on a crock pot from the office before you begin your commute home? All of these things and much more become possible with a speedy and reliable Internet connection. Once you're connected to the Internet, "Get the most from that connection," should be your mantra.

This chapter provides an overview of home networks and Internet connections. It shows how to install the modems, network wiring, routers, firewalls, network hubs, and switches used to connect your computers and other devices to the Web, and it shows how to select protective devices used for controlling the family's browsing experience. We also compare the alternative connection methods and various features of typical Internet connection service plans.

What in the world is the Internet, anyway?

The Internet is a worldwide data communications network that grew out of an earlier network called *ARPANET (Advanced Research Projects Agency Network)*. This network connected agencies of the United States Department of Defense with contractors, educational institutions, and research centers. This early network facilitated rapid communications between computers using different operating systems.

The ARPANET (and later the Internet) moved large amounts of data from different computer hosts by breaking the data into small packets of data, and then routing those packets over interconnected devices. The data was reassembled on the distant end, regardless of which path the data packets followed to get there. This communications scheme of using any available pathway provided reliability because it allowed connections even when some links were down. The interconnections looked like a spider's web, leading to the nickname *World Wide Web.* As more alternative pathways were added, the network's reliability increased, making it a great means of communication.

Understanding Internet Terminology: Stirring the Alphabet Soup

A lot of different technologies work together to connect your digital home to the Internet. These technologies are commonly known by acronyms that may be new to you. In this section, we decrypt some of these acronyms and the technologies they represent.

POTS (Plain Old Telephone System)

Preceding the Internet's development was a worldwide analog communications system called *POTS*. This system allowed — still allows, actually — someone in San Francisco to place a phone call to someone in London simply by dialing the correct number sequence. The number sequence is an international phone number composed of numbers conforming to the following format:

[international access code] + [country code] + [city code] + [area code] + [phone number]

To call the British Broadcasting Corporation in London from the U.S., you would dial 011-44-08700-100-212. The voice call would be routed using this number over local and long-distance communications lines and switching devices to find just the right phone at the London, England-based international news and broadcasting service.

IP (Internet Protocol) addresses

Just like a phone number finds a phone or fax machine, the Internet uses numbers called *IP addresses* to find other computers or devices connected to the Web. IP addresses use the pattern *n.n.n.n,* where *n* is a number between 0 and 256. A typical IP address might look like 10.245.10.1.

The numbers used in IP addresses are interpreted by computers in binary format. The largest possible number in an IP address is 2^8, but they are always expressed as base-10 numbers in conversation and writing.

Each interconnecting device and computer on the Internet is assigned a unique IP address. To connect the computers and devices in your home to the Internet, you must have at least one IP address to handle Internet communications. Usually, your ISP automatically assigns it.

Each computer and device on your home network also has a unique local IP address. Usually, a device called a *router* stores the IP addresses of the devices connected to your home network and facilitates communication between those devices. We describe routers in greater detail later in this chapter in the "Installing and configuring a router" section.

DNS (Domain Name Services)

If you need to find someone's phone number, you can dial directory assistance or open a phone book. The Internet has its own directory assistance called *DNS.* This service provides IP addresses to your computer for computer hosts on the Internet. For example, the IP address associated with the domain name Novell.com is 130.57.4.27.

The beauty of DNS is that it works in the background. When you enter a *uniform resource locator (URL)* such as www.dummies.com into your computer's browser, DNS looks up the proper IP address automatically. Your Internet-connected computer queries the nearest DNS host, and the IP address associated with the URL is returned to your computer so your request is routed to the right place.

DHCP (Dynamic Host Configuration Protocol)

DHCP is a tool networked computers use to automatically assign IP addresses to each computer on the network. On a DHCP-enabled network, a DHCP service automatically assigns unique IP addresses to each computer on the network as it boots up and connects. This is sometimes called *dynamic assignment* of IP addresses.

Alternatively, you can manually enter and configure the IP address on each computer (otherwise known as *hard coding* or assigning a *static IP address*). ISPs sometimes offer a choice of connecting your home computers to the Internet though DHCP dynamic assignment, or by manual assignment of a static IP address.

The permanent manual assignment of an IP address is more useful because it also facilitates easy communication to your home devices from external locations across the Web. When you select an ISP, try to choose one that allows manually assigned (also called *static*) IP addresses.

Reviewing Your Internet Connection Options

An Internet connection not only provides you with access to e-mail, movies, music, news, and the world's largest library of information, it also lets you access the computers and devices in your home from any computer that's connected to the Internet. You could be in a coffee shop in Paris, log into a webcam aimed at your front door, and see who's come by to visit (or solicit).

But before you can perform any online magic, you need a connection to the Internet. Start by finding out which communications companies in your area offer Internet services. These companies are called *Internet Service Providers (ISPs)*. People living in cities and major metropolitan areas often have many companies and service plans to choose from. If you live in a more rural area, your options may be a bit more limited. Not all services are alike in terms of speed, cost, and quality, so it pays to do some research and find the best value in your area — compare the features that each service offers and compare the costs. You may find that a faster cable or *digital subscriber line (DSL)* service costs only slightly more per month than a slow, obsolete dial-up service.

The following sections detail all of the possible connection types, some of which may not be available in your area. Table 12-1 lists the typical service-plan options. Research which options are available in your area, and then fill in the prices in Table 12-1 to help find the best value.

Table 12-1	Internet Service-Plan Comparison			
Typical Service Option	*IP Address(es) Assigned*	*Upload Speed **	*Download Speed **	*Price*
DSL Home User				
A	1 Dynamic	128 Kbps to 384 Kbps	384 Kbps to 1.5 Mbps	$
B	1 Dynamic	384 Kbps to 512 Kbps	1.5 Mbps to 3.0 Mbps	$
C	1 Dynamic	384 Kbps to 608 Kbps	1.5 Mbps to 6.0 Mbps	$
DSL Professional User				
D	1 to 5 Static	128 Kbps to 384 Kbps	384 Kbps to 1.5 Mbps	$
E	1 to 5 Static	384 Kbps to 512 Kbps	1.5 Mbps to 3.0 Mbps	$
F	1 to 5 Static	384 Kbps to 608 Kbps	1.5 Mbps to 6.0 Mbps	$
TV Cable Modem Connection				
G	1 Dynamic	Up to 384 Kbps	4.0 Mbps	$
H	1 to 5 Static	Up to 768 Kbps	8.0 Mbps	$
Fiber Optic Connection				
I	1 Dynamic	2.0 Mbps	5 Mbps	$
J	1 Dynamic	2.0 Mbps	15 Mbps	$
K	1 Dynamic	5.0 Mbps	30 Mbps	$
Other Internet Connection				
L (fill in)				$
M (fill in)				$

* Speeds expressed are between the modem device in the home and the next upstream device in the provider's point of service location. Actual connection speeds to Internet hosts and sites may vary.

Dial-up service

Rural areas are often limited to *dial-up connections* over POTS lines. The disadvantage to dial-up connections is that they don't provide an always-on connection. To use the connection, your computer must first dial the ISP and sign in, often a clucky process. Also, and more importantly, dial-up connections are the slowest of all the Internet connection methods.

ISDN (Integrated Services Digital Network)

ISDN service provides you with a faster way to connect to other digital services over phone lines. ISDN connections consist of either of these 64 Kbps (kilobits per second) communications links, both of which are sometimes called *B channels:*

- One (single channel)
- Two (dual channel)

To connect your computer to ISDN, an ISDN terminal adapter is installed between the phone line and the computer. Because ISDN can also handle analog phone calls, the terminal adapter may include an outlet to plug in a standard analog phone. You can also connect a fax machine to your ISDN service. An advantage to ISDN is that it's faster than dial-up.

T-1 lines

Major telecommunications companies sometimes offer high-speed Internet connections over *T-1 lines,* which provide connection speeds at 1.544 Mbps (megabits per second). T-1 connections are fast and always on, but they also tend to be very expensive.

Fractional T-1

Sometimes you can buy fractional T-1 Internet service in 64-Kbps increments, with an *overhead,* or loss, of 8 Kbps per each 64KB channel for maintaining the control signaling between the two devices. A full T-1 data connection can be divided into 24 channels. (A *channel* can move 64KB of data per second across the lines.) You could, for example, contract for fractional T-1 service at 384 Kbps.

Broadband cable

Cable modems connect computers to the Internet over TV cable. Cable TV companies that provide Internet connections may offer speeds as high as 6 Mbps for downloads and 768 Kbps for uploads. Cable modems comply with a standard called *Data Over Cable Service Interface Specification (DOCSIS)*. Broadband cable connections are always on, and are usually cost effective, especially for people who already have cable TV service.

DSL (Digital Subscriber Line) or ADSL (Asymmetric Digital Subscriber Line)

DSL is a very popular Internet connection method. *DSL* data signals travel over POTS and provide an always-on connection. *ADSL* provides connection speeds that differ between downloading data and uploading data to the Internet. DSL works by imposing a signal on the phone wire that differs in frequency from standard analog voice signals. A filter is installed on each phone in the home or office to help keep data signal noise from being heard on the analog voice channel.

One major advantage of DSL over dial-up is that you can use your phone or fax machine while online. Because DSL runs over POTS, any necessary repairs are likely to happen rapidly. Phone service is usually a state-regulated utility and time-to-repair statistics receive some attention from state regulators. This adds to the overall value proposition of using DSL if it is available to your home.

Fiber optic service

In a few very fortunate areas, some telecommunications companies are offering fiber optic data and voice services directly to residences. *Fiber optic* cable carries signals using light waves instead of electricity. These light waves can reach very high data-transfer rates and are unaffected by magnetism, *line attenuation* (reduced signal strength), noise from power lines, or electrical storms. Fiber-to-home services are usually more expensive than copper wires, but the higher speeds compensate for the cost and are hard to resist if available in your neighborhood.

Options for fiber Internet service speeds can reach 30 Mbps when downloading from the telecommunications company's central office with upload speeds of up to 5 Mbps. Of course, the connection to your phone company is probably a lot faster than the rest of the Internet, but at least the connection within the last mile to your house won't be the slowest link.

BPL (Broadband Over Power Lines)

BPL — or *Power Line Communications* — technology is slowly moving beyond the testing environment, but because it imposes modulated radio waves into unshielded electric power lines, it may not take off like some other technologies previously mentioned in this chapter. There are data security risks and the potential for interference with other radio receiving and transmitting devices that plug into the power lines. The best advice is to watch this one and carefully compare this to other options in your neighborhood as this type of service evolves.

Amateur HAM radio operators and those providing emergency services are concerned about the potential for radio frequencies to cause unmanageable interference with their radio communications. Nearby two-way radio traffic from those same sources may cause packet losses to occur on the power line data traffic.

Area wireless services

Wireless Internet services come in two flavors:

- ✔ One is transmitted and received over cell phone towers to either a cell phone or a special wireless modem card on a computer.

- ✔ One uses equipment that conforms to the 802.11 wireless networking standards developed by the IEEE (Institute of Electrical & Electronics Engineers).

This gear is mainly used for home and business wireless networks, as well as at Internet hotspots, but some communities are now set up to provide free or low-cost wireless access, turning whole towns into giant cyber cafés. Using 802.11 wireless Internet access presents some security and service-level challenges both for the provider and the end user.

Area wireless services may play a role in your digital home design for supporting backup communications to alarms and providing communications in the event of a catastrophic failure of your primary connection (sometimes caused by yellow-bellied fiber-seeking backhoes).

Connecting Your Home Network to the Internet

After you've reviewed the different options available in your area and have chosen your ISP, you need to get your home connected to the Internet. Your

ISP will guide you through the steps necessary to get connected. The following sections help you set up your computer or home network to take advantage of your new Internet connection.

Installing a DSL or cable modem

Internet service providers do their best to make installing DSL or cable modems as simple as possible — if you're only connecting a single computer. Most ISPs send you an automatic setup disc and basic instructions. If you have more than one computer or device to connect to the Internet — and we assume you do since you're reading this book — you need to connect the cable or DSL modem to a router or switch as described in the following sections.

If you get DSL, follow these basic steps, which should also be supplied with the modem:

1. **Install a phone line filter in every phone line in your home, and then connect your analog telephones to the Phone port on each filter.**

   The ISP should provide phone line filters with the DSL modem, and you can also buy them at many electronics stores. Every phone line must have a filter — even lines not used by the DSL modem.

2. **Connect the supplied DSL cable between a phone line filter and the DSL port on your DSL modem, as shown in Figure 12-1.**

3. **Connect an Ethernet cable between the RJ-45 port on the DSL modem to your computer's *network interface card (NIC)* or to your router/firewall device.**

   The ISP probably supplied an Ethernet cable with the modem.

4. **Connect the power cord to the DSL modem and plug it into a surge-protected power source.**

   Ideally, you should connect the DSL modem to an *uninterruptible power supply (UPS)*. This prevents connection troubles in the event of a power surge and brief power outages.

5. **Turn on your computer, insert the setup disc, and follow the instructions provided by the ISP to configure your DSL account.**

After your DSL account is configured, disconnect the DSL modem from your computer and plug the Ethernet cable into a router or switch, as described in the next section.

Figure 12-1:
View of
typical DSL
modem
connection
ports.

Installing and configuring a router

The first device between the Internet and your home's computing devices is the modem, often provided by the ISP. The second device to install is a router. A *router* allows your connection to appear to the ISP as one IP address, while at the same time connecting up to 254 computers and devices in your home to the Internet. The router uses DHCP to assign unique, local IP addresses to each connected device.

When a computer on your home network connects to the Internet, the router acts as a proxy for the computer's upstream requests and downstream data. The router uses a process called *network address translation (NAT)* to keep track of the requests and downstream data traffic for each private IP address on the network.

Most consumer routers also include a firewall. A *firewall* allows the device to block (deny) or pass (allow) data packets that meet certain criteria, thereby protecting your network from unauthorized access. Your Windows computer operating system has firewall settings built in, and you can load third-party firewall software to enhance security. Use the firewall setting in the router and computer to complement each other and increase security by setting them up to work together. The connecting interface of a router/firewall device is illustrated in Figure 12-2. The router in Figure 12-2 has one uplink port to connect to the DSL or cable modem via an Ethernet patch cable with RJ-45 connectors. Additional Ethernet ports are for connecting computers or additional switches or hubs to the router. (Switches and hubs are described in the next section.)

After you have successfully configured your first computer to work with your cable or DSL Internet service, take these steps:

1. Disconnect the Ethernet cable between the modem and your computer.

2. Connect the modem directly to the router's upstream port.

3. Connect your computer to the router.

Usually, the router manufacturer includes a CD ROM that walks you through the installation and configuration process. After the router is installed, you can manage the router from your computer's Web browser.

Your first goal is to get reliable high-speed connectivity. You can configure and refine firewall rules based on your security requirements later.

Figure 12-2:
A router allows many devices in your home to share a single Internet connection.

Using firewalls

Most consumer-oriented routers also include built-in firewalls. The firewall provides a barrier between the devices connected to the network in your home
and the rogue devices and hackers on the Internet intent on harming your systems. The firewall uses rules that allow or deny network traffic to pass through
based on specific security criteria. The rules generally start with the concept of
"deny all," and then a list of exceptions is created to allow trusted traffic to
pass through. Having this level of control is particularly valuable when you
want to control children's access to Internet sites, as discussed in the sidebar,
"Controlling your child's Internet access," elsewhere in this chapter.

The fine details of blocking access to the Internet, dangerous e-mail messages,
or specific Web sites are beyond the scope of this book. The instructions and
documentation provided with the router/firewall you choose should provide
further information so you can design custom filters and rules.

Understanding hubs and switches

Ethernet *hubs* and *switches* work much like routers in that they store or forward network data traffic from one device or computer to another. But that is
where the similarity ends. If you use a hub to connect your network devices
together, every port on the hub sees all the network data traffic on every
other port. For example, if you have a four-port hub, the signals sent from
your computer are transmitted to each of the three other ports. If the signal
only needs to go to one other computer, broadcasting the signal to all ports
is not a very efficient use of network bandwidth.

Unlike a hub, a switch (shown in Figure 12-3) is intelligent enough to only pass
data to a specific port. Switches also allow additional controls over the network traffic on a per-port basis, and these are referred to as *managed ports*.
Most consumer routers have built-in unmanaged switches for connecting at
least four computers. Hubs are useful for temporarily connecting more than
one nearby computer to a single network drop. Switches are preferable when
you need dedicated bandwidth for your permanent network.

Figure 12-3:
Switches
make more
efficient use
of network
bandwidth
than hubs.

Preparing to Wire Your Digital Home for Networking

You can do a lot of cool things with home networks today, and the possibilities for tomorrow are even greater. To take advantage of these possibilities, you need to wire your home with network outlets, often called *network drops*. Figure 12-4 shows the devices, box, and cover needed for a network drop in any room. Installing network drops in every room may not seem necessary right now, but doing it now makes your home ready for whatever tomorrow's home networking opportunities may bring.

Our wire-it-now bias may show when we suggest that every room in new construction should have at least two each of the following:

- ✔ Phone jacks
- ✔ Ethernet network outlets
- ✔ Two-pair fiber cables
- ✔ TV cable jacks

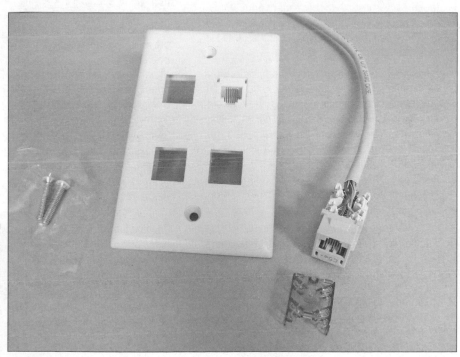

Figure 12-4:
Network drops connect each room to your network.

Wire the elements into electrical boxes or LV rings and connect them to a central wiring closet, which should be a dedicated space in the basement, a warm wall in the attached garage (for homes without basements), or other dedicated space. In addition to these elements, consider whether to run three additional Cat 5 or 6 cables to each room for audio/sound channels and intercom systems. The central wiring area should have

- Electrical power outlets that are served by at least two different circuit breakers in the service panel.

- The same height, access, and clearance requirements spelled out for the electrical service panel in Chapter 2. Larger rooms (such as a big family room) or special use areas like home offices may warrant additional network drops.

TIP

Controlling your child's Internet access

One way to think of the Internet is as a library. While a wealth of information is available, not all of this information is appropriate for children. On the other hand, access to information and technology is critical to the modern educational process. This dichotomy often finds parents and guardians conflicted about the best course for their children.

Remember: Rather than think of an Internet connection as an all-or-nothing choice, realize that you can likely couple control technology with an appropriate measure of adult supervision to satisfy your concerns. The technology alone or supervision alone is probably not enough to thwart the determined and curious child. Using both — together — in a thoughtful manner is the best approach. Several tools are at your disposal:

- **Firewall access-time controls:** You can configure your firewall to create rules that limit the time of day computers in the home can access the Internet. For example, you can limit access to the times on weekday evenings and weekend days when you expect to be present.

- **Firewall URL filtering:** Another simple approach is to create a rule that allows access only to parent-approved Web sites. If any other URL is entered in the Web browser, the firewall blocks the data traffic, preventing that site from being viewed. Building specific access lists may be time-consuming, but it provides the level of control many parents desire. As your child earns trust and develops maturity, you can add sites to the access list.

- **Content-filtering software:** You can filter specific kinds of content with products such as SurfControl or Cyber Patrol. This approach costs money, but some parents may consider the undertaking worthwhile. Content filtering and blocking products can also protect computers from spyware, viruses, and worms.

One of the most annoying things we have found in many recently constructed homes is a wanton disregard for orderly arrangement of services and utilities. A typical new home basement may have the electrical service coming in on the northeast corner, the TV cables on the southwest corner, the phone line in the middle of the north side, the natural gas lines entering from the southwest corner, the basement sump pump in the southeast corner, the water pressure tank in the center of the south elevation, the water heater in the northwest corner, and the furnace in the middle of the basement. All this disarray adds up to only about 40 square feet of usable floor space remaining in the basement. Perhaps we exaggerate a bit, but all of these elements should be organized by design, not by each trade doing its own thing. When designing a new home or remodeling, pay attention to the big picture and try to enforce some logic, order, and discipline to the placement of services and utilities.

Of course, you need some way to organize and connect all the cables running into your wiring closet or area. The best way is to invest in a 19" rack and mount all of the cable runs to patch panels in the rack. Wall mounted racks with swing away hinges make accessing the back punch-down blocks easier. One layout that's particularly useful has a hinged patch-panel rack that swings away from the wall to the left, and an equipment rack or shelf that swings away to the right, with cable sling hooks on the back wall between them. It is important to bring all of the cables to the closet, referred to as *home runs*. When all the communication cables from every room are brought to a central point and properly labeled, it adds a professional look to the project and makes future changes and expansions easier.

Understanding Wireless "Wiring"

Wireless home networks use radio waves to transmit data, usually over short distances. In-home wireless devices often connect wireless network interface cards on computers to wireless-equipped broadband Internet modems. The advantage of wireless networking equipment is that not every room must be wired with Ethernet cable to connect to the home network.

Wireless networking devices conform to IEEE standards for wireless devices. The most popular standards are 802.11b and 802.11g. The main difference between these two is the speed at which data is transmitted between devices. The newer standard is 802.11g, and it can transmit data at speeds up to 54 Mbps. Older, slower 802.11b devices transmit at up to 11 Mbps. Most 802.11g devices are compatible with 802.11b networks.

Someone listening or hacking into your network is the major security risk involved with any wireless device. Do not deploy wireless network equipment without using all the available security features. Read the manuals for the wireless equipment and take the time to fully implement the manufacturer's security recommendations. Also, we recommend that you only enable wireless network devices when needed. An easy way to do this is to plug the wireless access point into a switched power outlet and flip the switch off when you are done.

Setting Up Your Home Network

After you have purchased all your networking equipment and wired in your network drops, it is time to connect everything and turn your home Ethernet network into a working system complete with Internet access. The best way to show the whole system is with a big picture diagram. This section will present two high-level designs for home networks.

The first design — shown in Figure 12-5 — assumes that the residence only requires access to Internet services. The second design — Figure 12-7 — shows a slightly more complex implementation where two-way Internet access is needed. The latter design is ultimately more useful for the digital home. As features are added to the home network over time, these basic network diagrams increase in scope and complexity.

Once you sketch out your plan, keep your diagram up to date. Good documentation is a great aid when it comes to adding, changing, or troubleshooting.

The basic DSL Internet connection diagram in Figure 12-5 shows a single computer connected to the Internet with the aid of a router/firewall. In this example, the DSL modem is connected to a standard phone jack using a line filter; see Figure 12-6. One side of each line filter has one jack connecting a standard telephone line plug, and a second jack for connecting Cat 3 cable to the DSL modem; see Figure 12-1. We recommend that you wire in a jack in your central closet and plug in one or more DSL filters as needed. This keeps the living-space wall jacks in a neater condition. The DSL side of the first filter goes into the input jack on the DSL modem, also in the central closet area.

When first connecting the service, it may be necessary to connect the Cat 5 or Cat 6 Ethernet cable directly to the computer to sign up with the ISP before inserting the router/firewall and switch between the modem and the computer(s). With this type of service, the analog phone signals and the DSL signals travel along the same twisted-pair copper wire back to the phone company's central office. Because each signal is carried on different frequencies, you can use the phone at the same time you use the Internet.

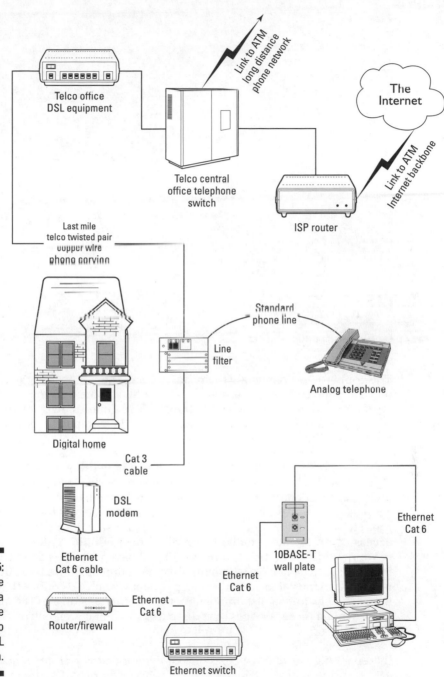

Figure 12-5: This home connects a single computer to a DSL modem.

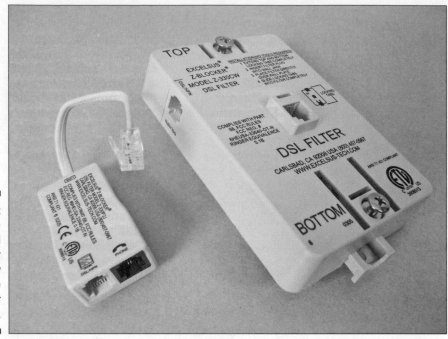

The copper wire connecting the residence and the phone company's central office is referred to as the *last mile*. To get DSL service, the copper line serving your residence must be within the distance limits allowed by the provider. These distances vary depending on the equipment used and usually range from 2 to 3 miles, or sometimes more.

The ideal home network design for the digital home should look more like Figure 12-7. The major difference between the designs in Figures 12-5 and 12-7 is that an additional firewall/router has been added to open access to Web servers and devices like webcams used for surveillance. The use of a second firewall device helps protect the computers and simplifies the rules for your access control strategy on both firewalls. These additional devices use some of your additional static IP addresses, if you have any. The added cost of an Internet service package with more than one static IP address facilitates including all the value-added services you may want. To control these additional devices from a distant point on the Internet, install a VPN concentrator for providing these services over a secure communication link on this side of your network.

By separating the different parts of your network into discrete branches, you gain security control and increase utility with fewer risks. Of course, these diagrams are only a starting point. Adding devices to your network and adding allowed Web sites and Web servers to your firewall rules can easily become a recurring hobby for the whole family. The possibilities are only limited by your imagination as new networking technologies open up more possibilities every day. So don't delay — get started on your home networking and Internet connection project today.

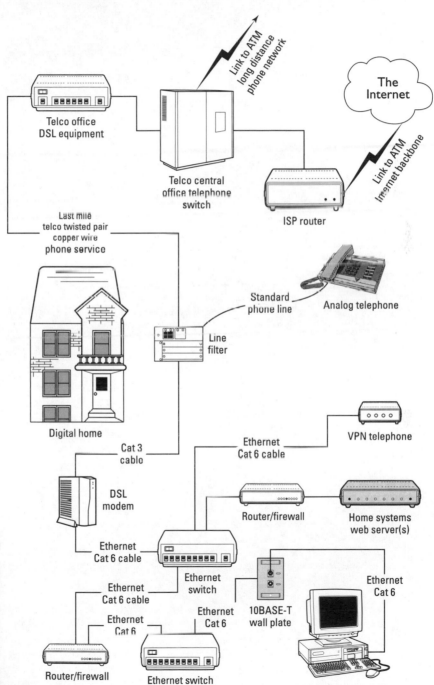

Figure 12-7:
The ideal
digital home
uses
multiple
router/
firewall
devices.

Chapter 13

Integrating Computer Controls and Voice Technology

Some people are control enthusiasts (okay, control freaks) and have a hard time giving over the reins. If you're an enthusiast, you may wish you could control everything remotely. Oh sure, in Chapter 5 we show you how to install remote controls for lights and other home features. But now imagine controlling your home with your voice. This may sound like science fiction (or something that requires an expensive butler), but this type of control is possible right now.

In spite of your enthusiasm for control, you may harbor a disdain for repetitive or annoying tasks, such as turning off the outdoor garage lights, shutting the garage door, or activating the lawn sprinklers. The home automation software and hardware described in this chapter can take care of such repetitive tasks. You don't have to be a card-carrying computer geek to reap the benefits of home automation. Some technically proficient do-it-yourselfers may have led the way, but anyone can install automation components. After attentive installation, the care and feeding of said systems may require no more maintenance than a refrigerator. This chapter describes some of the advanced automation controls you can integrate into your home.

Selecting Home Automation Components

If you want to bring electrical systems under voice command, as if your home were a starship zooming to distant galaxies, you're going to need some specialized equipment. Don't worry — you don't need hyperdrive modulators or dilithium crystals. All you need is the right software and hardware. The following sections introduce you to those things — all of them available right now — to make your home ready for the 21st century and beyond.

Choosing automation software

The best way to automate your home is to use a software program that runs on your personal computer. Many home automation programs are commercially available. We recommend HAL, which is short for *Home Automated Living,* the name of the company that produces several versions of home automation software (www.automatedliving.com). The HAL software runs on any computer running recent versions of Microsoft Windows.

Home Automated Living currently offers three versions of the HAL software:

- ✔ **HALbasic:** If you're on a budget, HALbasic gets you going with a limited feature set.

- ✔ **HALdeluxe:** Once HALbasic is up and running, upgrading to HALdeluxe is easy. It has all the basic features, plus things such as caller ID.

- ✔ **HAL2000:** Version 3.5.0 (or greater) provides the richest feature set, with an extensive laundry list of control devices that will work well with the software. With a list price of only $369, HAL2000 should be on your purchase list (or at least be an upgrade goal).

Several add-on programs are available for the HAL programs:

- ✔ **HALvoices:** These add-ons are available for all versions of HAL and provide a more human voice for command responses (as opposed to the standard robotic voice). Two versions of the add-on are available:

  - • U.S. English with a male voice (Michael) and a female voice (Michelle).

  - • U.K. English with a male voice (Charles) and a female voice (Audrey).

  We like the voice named Audrey the best, but if you have youngsters in the house they may prefer the standard robotic voice. The HAL Web site has samples of the voices.

- ✔ **HALdmc:** Think of HALdmc as your personal digital disc jockey. This add-on allows you to control music playback via voice commands, and you can bring up particular songs when you issue certain commands. For example, you can program a tune to play when you give a command to dim the lights.

In Chapter 9, we discuss room-to-room stereo systems and multi-zone, multi-source controller-amplifiers. There we recommend systems with multiple inputs. If you have such a system, one of the inputs can connect to a computer running HALdmc. Using the computer and the HAL software, you can play CDs, MP3 files, and WMA files anywhere in the house. When used in conjunction with HAL, you can easily control music, audio books, or learning and motivational CDs. Also, if you would only like to control music, you can deploy the HALdmc digital disk jockey software without using X10 light switches or the other appliance-control features provided by the HAL control programs.

✔ **HALdvc:** This add-on integrates HAL with your home surveillance recording system. It allows you to control recording and playback by voice or to automate recording tasks. HALdvc works with IP webcams, closed-circuit TV, and other surveillance cameras like those described in Chapter 11. See Chapter 14 for more on security zones and alarm systems.

Selecting a computer to run HAL

The system requirements for HAL software are modest by most current PC standards, but we recommend going beyond the minimum requirements.

The computer that runs your HAL software should have

✔ Plenty of Random Access Memory (RAM)

✔ A big hard drive for plenty of storage space

✔ A fast processor.

Although powerful computers are attractively priced today, this isn't the best place to squeeze the budget for your automated home. Purchase modern, reliable computer equipment under extended warranty, so it can serve you reliably for many years.

To run HAL now and in the future, we recommend that your computer should meet these requirements:

✔ **Case:** Tower case with at least a 400-watt power supply and four drive bays

✔ **System board (also called the *motherboard*):**

- PCI Express slot

- Three PCI slots

- Built-in network interface card (NIC)

- Sound card

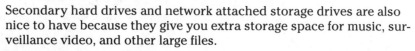

✔ **Operating system:** We recommend Windows XP Professional with current service packs installed. (HAL will run on Windows 98, Windows Me, Windows XP, and Windows 2000, but the higher level of security features available in Windows XP Home Edition and Windows XP Professional make these versions a better choice. Also, Windows 98 will no longer be supported in any appreciable way by Microsoft.)

✔ **Processor:** Any Intel Pentium or equal processor running at 2.66 GHz

✔ **RAM:** At least 1 gigabyte (and 2GB or more isn't a bad idea)

✔ **Storage and drives:**

- 250GB; 7,200RPM hard drive

- CD-RW/DVD-ROM removable media drive

Secondary hard drives and network attached storage drives are also nice to have because they give you extra storage space for music, surveillance video, and other large files.

✔ **PCI card:** HAL Voice Portal card

✔ **Interfaces:**

- Serial com ports 1, 2, 3, and 4

(You may need to install an additional card in an available PCI or ISA slot in your PC to gain serial com ports 3 and 4.)

- 9-in-1 card reader

- Three or more USB ports

- Parallel port

✔ **Network interface:**

- 10/100 Mbps built-in or PCI NIC

- A second 1,000 Mbps NIC

If you're using your PC to play a lot of music, we recommend that you install a high-quality sound card such as Creative Labs' Sound Blaster card. You can't use your high-quality amplifiers and speakers to their full potential if they're attached to an inferior sound card.

A natural human voice is typically in the range of 200 Hz to 7 kHz. This range is well within the capabilities of even basic sound cards, so the recommendation for a high-quality sound card is only for music playback. For HAL voice synthesis, the system board's built-in sound card should be adequate.

Wiring Your Home Automation Computer

The computer controlling your home automation system may seem to take on a personality of its own after a while. This is especially true if you regularly communicate with the computer using voice commands. You may come to think of the computer as your own personal protocol droid — kind of like C-3PO. In the next few sections we introduce the most important pieces of equipment, connections, and wiring you need to make the communications system work.

Connecting HAL to the telephone

A good way to control your home automation computer is by using the *plain old telephone system (POTS)*. When HAL software connects to the phone system, you can send commands to HAL from a phone within your home, as well as from a phone that's halfway around the world. Actually, controlling HAL from phones outside your house may be easier: To control HAL from inside phones, your phone system must be wired so that all phones used to control HAL are connected to the POTS's NID through the HAL computer's HAL Internal PCI Voice Portal.

In Chapter 6, we describe the *Network Interface Device (NID),* which is provided by the phone company in most markets. If you only have one phone line coming into your house, you must route it through the HAL Voice Portal and then out to the other extensions. Install two phone jacks near the HAL computer, as shown in the upper left of Figure 13-1. The phone line should be routed from the first jack directly to the NID. The second jack feeds a punch-down block where other home phone extensions are connected.

Installing voice-command stations

To control your HAL system using voice commands, you should install voice-command stations at strategic locations throughout your home. Each command station consists of

- A microphone, which allows HAL to receive your commands — "HAL, dim the lights," "HAL, pause the music," "HAL, open the pod bay doors."

- Speakers, which allow HAL to provide audible feedback and play music.

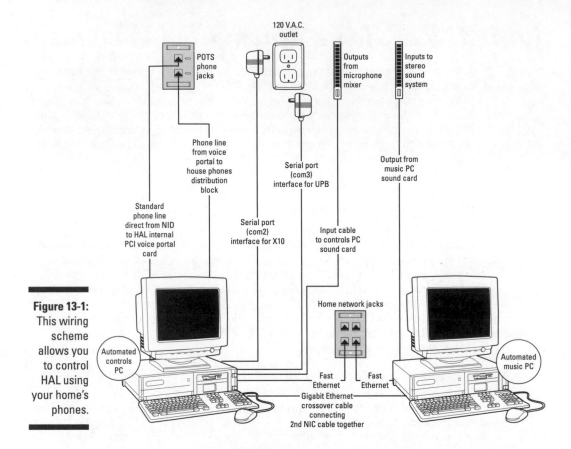

120 V.A.C. outlet

POTS phone jacks

Outputs from microphone mixer

Inputs to stereo sound system

Phone line from voice portal to house phones distribution block

Serial port (com3) interface for UPB

Output from music PC sound card

Standard phone line direct from NID to HAL internal PCI voice portal card

Serial port (com2) interface for X10

Input cable to controls PC sound card

Figure 13-1: This wiring scheme allows you to control HAL using your home's phones.

Home network jacks

Automated controls PC

Automated music PC

Fast Ethernet

Fast Ethernet

Gigabit Ethernet crossover cable connecting 2nd NIC cable together

Connecting a microphone to the sound card on the PC that runs HAL software provides another way to give voice commands. But most folks want more than one microphone (and more than one place in the house to interact with the control software).

To give voice commands from multiple places in the house, you can install a microphone mixer to feed the voice commands spoken throughout the house to the computer's sound card. A *microphone mixer* is a device that takes the input from two or more microphones and combines them so that you only need to use a single input jack to plug into the sound card. A microphone mixer also controls the strength (or volume) of the input signal supplied to the amplifier from the various microphones, and it compensates for the length of the microphone wires and the differences in the acoustics and background noises in the various locations where you installed the microphones. Mixers with automatic volume controls are available, but tend to be expensive. Consider installing a mixer with slide controls that enable you to adjust each microphone's volume manually. Also consider the location of the microphones, and how far your voice will travel before the microphone picks it up. Ideally, you want to have the microphones located where you spend the most time in each room. This way, you don't have to get up from your recliner to have HALdmc play "I Walk The Line" by Johnny Cash.

The speakers in each voice-command station can provide voice feedback after executing commands. However, you should consider when you do and when you don't need this feedback. If feedback for every mundane task is piped through the speakers in every room, your family may start to feel like they're living on a Navy ship where every five minutes the boatswains mate pipes, "Sweepers, sweepers, man your brooms."

Now that you know what the voice-command stations do, you're probably wondering what they look like. As far as we know, voice-command stations don't come in simple off-the-shelf solutions, so we recommend using slightly modified intercom station faceplates over two-gang boxes. This do-it-yourself project is fairly simple.

To create your command stations, follow these general steps:

1. **Buy a faceplate for an intercom system like those described in Chapter 7.**

   If you can't buy just the faceplate, start with a regular intercom station and remove the original speaker.

2. **Replace the faceplate's single original speaker with two small speakers.**

   You can find speakers at electronics stores like RadioShack. You want to install two speakers because your sound card output is in stereo.

   The voice-command station and your home intercom system can share speakers. Keep in mind, however, that if you wire the synthesized voice output from HAL into the regular intercom system, voice feedback from HAL will be piped all over the house, Navy style.

3. **If the faceplate doesn't already have a Push to Talk button, install one.**

4. **Drill a hole in the faceplate to accommodate a two-pole three-position (DPDT with OFF) slide or push switch.**

5. **Drill a second hole to accommodate the face of a small microphone below the speaker grill.**

   For best results, choose an omnidirectional microphone in the voice-command station. Ideally, the station unit is mounted about 4' above the floor. Connect the microphone to the mic input on the control computer's sound card; if you'll have more than one voice-command station, the microphone for each unit needs to connect to a microphone mixer.

Wireless microphones are available for your voice-command station. A wireless mic may come in handy if you have a physical limitation that makes using a wall-mounted microphone difficult.

6. **Use the existing volume control or install one in the blank faceplate.**

7. **Run Cat 6 cable from the voice-command station to the mixer.**

   If you haven't done so already, connect the mixer and computer sound card with Cat 6 cable or shielded audio cable.

8. **Wire the three-position switch so you can turn off the unit entirely, transfer control to the Push to Talk button, or leave the microphone on all the time.**

   To do this, wire the center (common) connections on the switch to the lines leading to the microphone mixer or input into the sound card. Use the contacts that connect to the center pins when the switch is moved to the first On position to wire to the first connection on the Push to Talk button. From the other side of the Push to Talk button, connect to the microphone. (Then when you press the Push to Talk button, the microphone is connected to the sound input on the computer.) From the second On position, the contacts of the three-position switch are wired to bypass the Push to Talk button right to the microphone. (Then when the three-position switch is in the second On position, the microphone is on all the time.) When the three-position switch is in the middle, the microphone is off and pushing the Push to Talk button does nothing.

   Figure 13-2 shows how your completed voice-command center might look.

You can also make a movable remote control for your voice-command station. Mount the intercom faceplate and other hardware in an attractive box, and then connect it to the Cat 6 cable via an RJ-45 jack. Now you can set the control next to the easy chair and play Mozart on command.

Fancy voice-command stations like the one described here aren't absolutely mandatory. If you wish to just keep things simple, connect the synthesized voice output to an amplifier and bullhorn-style speakers centrally located in the house. This solution may not seem ideal, but it is definitely simple.

Interfacing with the home's electrical system

To actually control your home's lights and stereos, the computer running HAL must be able to interface with the home's electrical systems. Interface control and automation is easiest if you have already installed an advanced control system such as X10 or *Universal Powerline Bus (UPB)*. See Chapter 5 for more on X10 and UPB devices.

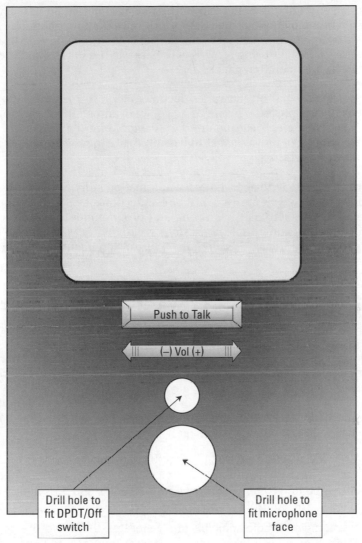

Figure 13-2:
The voice-command station should look something like this.

Push to Talk

(–) Vol (+)

Drill hole to fit DPDT/Off switch

Drill hole to fit microphone face

Automation software can control many proprietary and open-standard devices. (X10 is an example of an open standard where devices are made by more than one company and are designed to be compatible with the X10 standard.) These devices simply plug into a power outlet and into the computer using either a serial or USB port. The signals injected into the control module by the computer travel to the X10 switches, dimmers, and receptacles over your home's wiring. When you issue commands, the computer sends an address-coded signal through the power lines to do as you commanded. For example, the signal may turn on the coffee pot, dim the lights, or open a door lock.

Although any 120-volt outlet will work as an automation interface, we strongly recommend that the outlet for the automation computer be on a separate circuit from the rest of the house. It should be on a dedicated 15-amp circuit breaker using 14 AWG wire between the outlets and the home's main power distribution panel.

Review the automation software's documentation to see what interface devices are supported. This helps as you plan and shop for controls. Where possible, select electrical and interface devices offering USB connectivity. Some devices can only connect to a computer using the computer's traditional serial ports.

If you have special devices that your automation software doesn't support, you may have to wait until a control for it becomes available or consult with a professional electrician and a computer programmer to make everything work. You may even be able to do some creative daisy chaining so that a supported interface triggers a switch that controls an unsupported device.

Providing backup power to the automation system

In Chapter 15, we discuss backup power systems and note that part of installing backup power is deciding which home systems are critical. Your home automation system may or may not meet your personal checklist as a critical item, but we recommend that you at least install a *UPS (uninterruptible power supply)* for the automation computer, which provides backup power for a few minutes.

This UPS provides several important advantages:

- A UPS compensates for short duration spikes and dips in the power supplied to the control system's computer.

- If you have a whole-home backup generator, the UPS protects the PC for the few seconds it takes for your backup generator to come online.

- If power is lost, the UPS triggers a gentle shutdown process for the computer. For this to work, the UPS must be connected to the computer using either a USB or serial cable, and special control software must be installed on the computer. Initializing a proper shutdown when battery power is low protects your computer from damage and data loss.

- You can use a networked version of the UPS software to send signals over the network to shut down other computers and servers on UPS devices.

Several companies offer UPS devices, and they're available in any office supply or home electronics store. We like the products and software made by American Power Conversion (www.apcc.com).

Networking your automation system

The value of home automation software doesn't have to end at the walls. If the automation control computer is connected to the Internet, you can view the latest video from webcam at the front door to see who stopped by while you're on assignment elsewhere.

An Internet connection is necessary to reap the full benefits of automation software. You should also install a network drop near the automation computer and connect the computer to the rest of your home network. (We describe networking and Internet connections in Chapter 12.) With providers offering DSL Internet service in some markets for as little as $15 per month, having Internet access is no longer a luxury. You may even be able to recoup some or all of that cost by using *Voice over Internet Protocol (VoIP)* phone services as discussed in Chapter 6.

As you go beyond the automated control system basics mentioned in this chapter, you may need additional cables and connections. Install your home automation computer and connections in a space that will accommodate future additions to your system. Also, always maintain some clear space around the equipment and connections for future maintenance and modification.

Programming the automation interfaces

After all of your hardware is installed and properly connected, it's time to configure the HAL software to interface with the devices in your home. If you have ever used a Windows program before, you will find the HAL software easy to use. All you need to know to program your home automation controls is how to make selections from drop-down menus and text boxes. The manuals provided with the software are great both for reference and training as they take you though the initial configuration steps and into advanced customization.

The HAL software provides a wizard to guide you through the steps to interface with the devices in your home. The following steps take you through a common interface setup with the HAL software — configuring an automated X10 switch:

1. **Launch the HAL software by choosing Start⇨All Programs⇨HAL.**

   The HAL system screen appears.

2. **Select the Devices tab and click the Add button.**

   The Device Wizard screen appears, as shown in Figure 13-3.

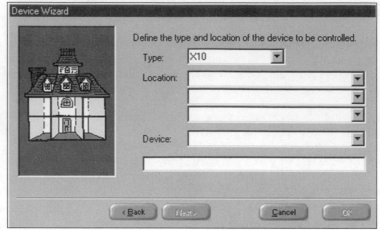

Figure 13-3:
The Device
Wizard
walks you
through
setup.

3. **From the Type drop-down menu, select the kind of device to configure.**

Figure 13-3 shows X10 chosen (because we're configuring an X10 device for this example).

4. **From the Location drop-down menus, select the appropriate room.**

See Figure 13-4.

5. **From Device drop-down menu, select the appropriate device.**

As you choose from the Location and Device drop-down menus, a name for the device appears in the long text field at the bottom, as shown in Figure 13-4. Each device must have a unique name in this field. The device name is important because this is how the HAL software identifies the device when you issue a voice command. For example, we're setting up for the living room lights in this example, and so we gave it the name Living Room Light. If you name your HAL software Gertrude during installation, you issue a command by saying, "Gertrude, please turn on the living room light."

Name your devices so that each name is distinct. Try to avoid using device names that sound too similar — for example, Bedroom Lights and Bathroom Lights. You might want to use Kathy's Room Lights instead of Bedroom Lights, so that the device name is easy to remember but still unique.

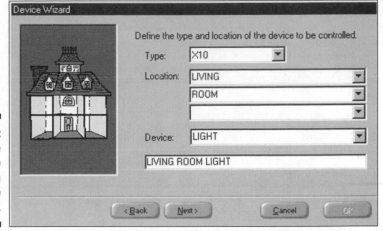

Figure 13-4:
Make sure
each device
has a
unique
name.

6. **Click Next to reveal the screen shown in Figure 13-5.**

7. **Specify the house code and unit address.**

   Each X10 device has a unique house code and unit address. See Chapter 5 for more on setting and obtaining codes and addresses for X10 devices.

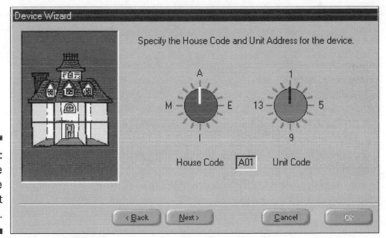

Figure 13-5:
Specify the
house code
and unit
address.

8. **Click Next, and set options unique to the device.**

As you can see in Figure 13-6, this screen is where you set each device's behavior. Some devices can simply turn on and off, while others are dimmable or have other options.

9. **Test the device by clicking one of the test buttons shown in Figure 13-6.**

The test buttons include On, Off, and Dim. To turn off a device that's currently on, click the Off button.

10. **Click Next to finish setting up that one device.**

The Assigning Groups window appears, enabling you to assign the device to a group. If you do so, you can control every device in that group with a single command. For example, you can assign every light in the house to a group called House Lights, and then turn on or off all the lights with a single command.

11. **If you want to, assign the device to a group.**

12. **When you're finished, click the OK button.**

Okay, it is time to ready, set, program your own Gertrude or Gilbert. Setting up home automation controls can be fun and certainly provides some extra freedom.

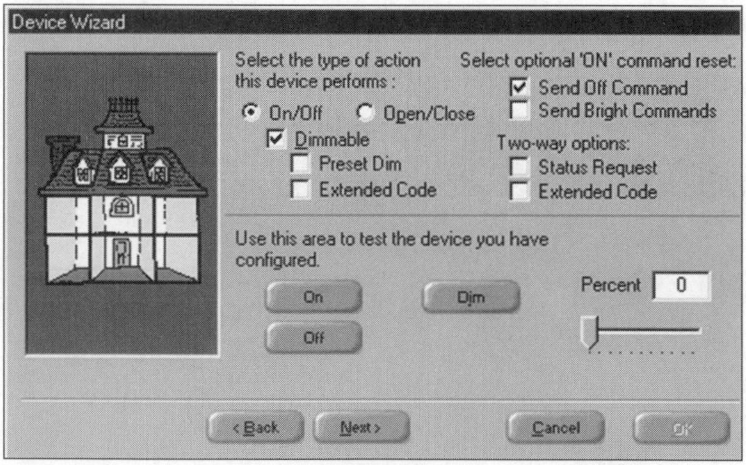

Figure 13-6:
Set device
options
here.

Part IV
Security and
Safety Systems

The 5th Wave   By Rich Tennant

" A centralized security management system
sounds fine, but then what would we do
with all the dogs?"

In this part . . .

The chapters in this part show you how to wire alarms with features that enhance your home's security and take proactive measures to protect your belongings while you're away. This part also tells you some of the ways you can wire backup power-generation equipment to keep your critical circuits and equipment working when the hamster wheel at the power company stops turning.

Color Plate 1: This photo shows a closet light switch controlled by a pilot switch. The pilot light in the switch illuminates so that you can tell that the closet light is on, even if the door is closed. The closet is well lit with a 32-watt, four-foot florescent strip fixture. See Chapters 3 and 4 for many good tips on wiring for lighting.

Color Plate 2: A variety of Decora devices, ranging from combination devices where two switches are installed in a single space, to dimmer switches that you simply touch to operate. To find out how to add the finishing touches to your wiring project like the pros, see Chapter 4.

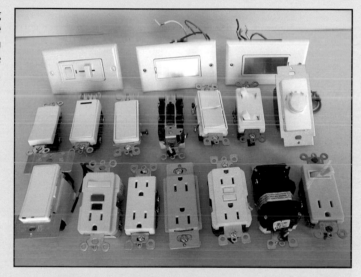

Color Plate 3: Using X10 controls made it easy to control the lighting fixture and fan in this room without needing to rewire (and possibly damaging the expensive oak wall panels in the process). Chapter 5 tells you more about using X10 remote controls.

Color Plate 4: This is a color photo of a three-way switch showing the proper connections. It illustrates a switch wired in accordance with the diagram shown in Figure 4-5 (see Chapter 4). In this photo, you can see the ground wires that were omitted for simplicity's sake from Figure 4-5. For more about connecting three-way and four-way switches, turn to Chapter 4.

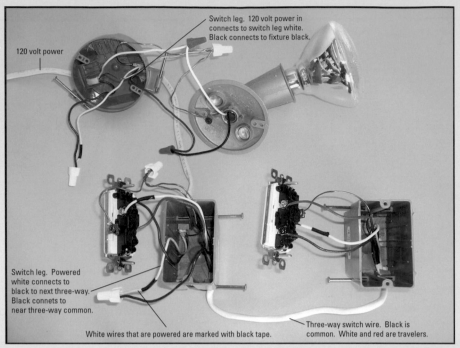

120 volt power

Switch leg. 120 volt power in connects to switch leg white. Black connects to fixture black.

Switch leg. Powered white connects to black to next three-way. Black connets to near three-way common.

White wires that are powered are marked with black tape.

Three-way switch wire. Black is common. White and red are travelers.

Color Plate 5: The connection view of a surround sound processor, with numerous jacks for connecting the processor to other devices and speakers. See Chapter 9 for more about surround sound and for diagrams that show the correct angular layout for surround sound speakers.

Color Plate 6: This table shows the electrical symbols used on digrams throughout this book. Use this table to interpret the kitchen and whole house wiring diagrams shown in Color Plates 7 and 8, respectively.

Symbol	Description
⊃⊙	Duplex receptacle
⊖	Single-pole switch
⊖³	Switch w/ superscript # 3 or 4 way
⊖ᴸ	Lighted switch superscript L & superscript F
▷▣ ⊙	Light fixtures wall ceiling
⊒⊜	230 volt receptacle
GFCI ⊃⊙	Ground fault receptacle
◁	Telephone receptacle (wired with Category 5 four pair cable)
─▽	Television receptacle
⊗	Recessed fixture
⊛	Smoke detector w/ battery backup
◇⊗	Fan-light combination fixture
DM ⊖	Dimmer switch
─⊡	Door bell
⊡	Central vacuum outlet
▭	One tube fluorescent strip
▭	Four tube fluorescent wraparound
✕	Paddle fan (requires special electrical fan hanger box)
☐	Recessed fixture

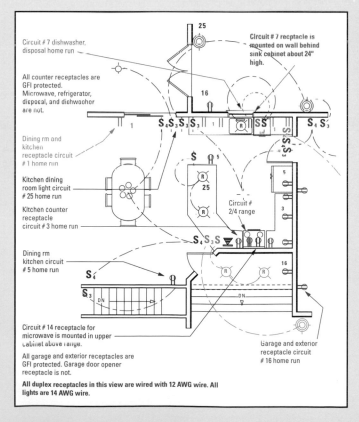

Circuit # 7 dishwasher, disposal home run

All counter receptacles are GFI protected. Microwave, refrigerator, disposal, and dishwasher are not.

25

Circuit # 7 recptacle is mounted on wall behind sink cabinet about 24" high.

16

Dining rm and kitchen receptacle circuit # 1 home run

Kitchen dining room light circuit # 25 home run

Kitchen counter receptacle circuit # 3 home run

Circuit # 2/4 range

Dining rm kitchen circuit # 5 home run

Circuit # 14 receptacle for microwave is mounted in upper cabinet above range.

All garage and exterior receptacles are GFI protected. Garage door opener receptacle is not.

Garage and exterior receptacle circuit # 16 home run

All duplex receptacles in this view are wired with 12 AWG wire. All lights are 14 AWG wire.

Color Plate 7: This is a closer view of the wiring in the kitchen area (see Color Plate 8 for the wiring diagram of the entire house). The kitchen is the busiest area for electric circuits. This diagram includes some details that had to be omitted on the whole house diagram, such as the light over the sink and its switch. For more information on accommodating the electrical needs in the kitchen, refer to Chapter 3.

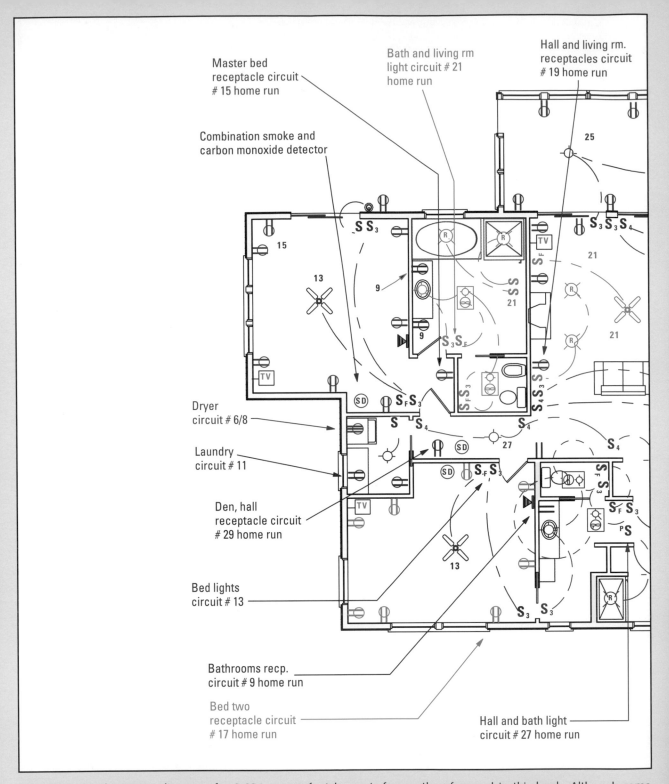

Master bed
receptacle circuit
15 home run

Combination smoke and
carbon monoxide detector

Bath and living rm
light circuit # 21
home run

Hall and living rm.
receptacles circuit
19 home run

Dryer
circuit # 6/8

Laundry
circuit # 11

Den, hall
receptacle circuit
29 home run

Bed lights
circuit # 13

Bathrooms recp.
circuit # 9 home run

Bed two
receptacle circuit
17 home run

Hall and bath light
circuit # 27 home run

Color Plate 8: This wiring diagram of a 2,031 square foot house is frequently referenced in this book. Although some circuit numbers are present, rather than placing a circuit number next to each usage, we color-coded the various circuit devices to make it easier to see how the wiring circuits should be run. In each instance, we indicate where the circuit from the panel is run, and each one is marked as a home run with the circuit number. Notice that all the receptacle circuits are separate from the lighting circuits.

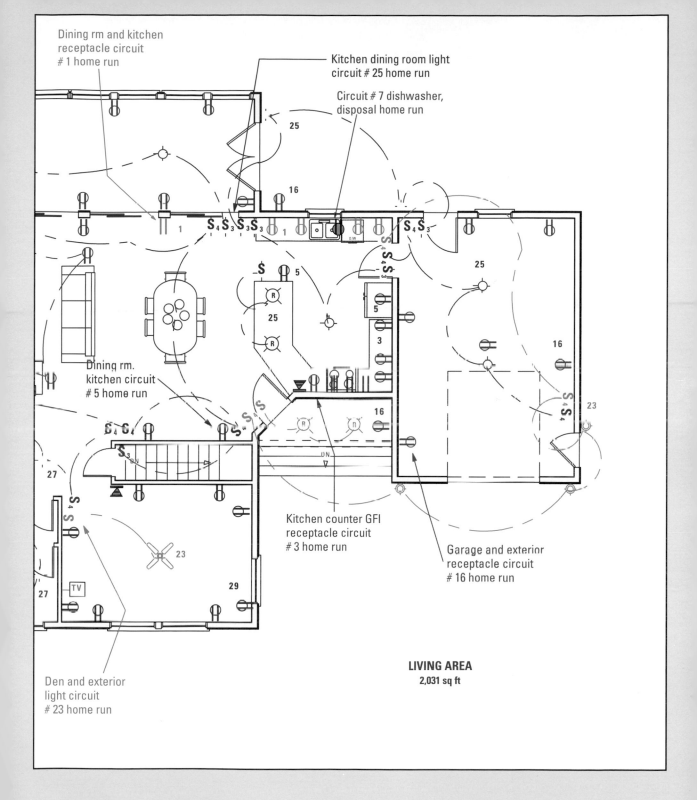

Dining rm and kitchen receptacle circuit # 1 home run

Kitchen dining room light circuit # 25 home run

Circuit # 7 dishwasher, disposal home run

Dining rm. kitchen circuit # 5 home run

Kitchen counter GFI receptacle circuit # 3 home run

Garage and exterior receptacle circuit # 16 home run

Den and exterior light circuit # 23 home run

LIVING AREA
2,031 sq ft

Color Plate 9: This photo shows an inverter-battery power system for a very remote camp. With solar power and a backup generator supplying power for the inverter batteries, the owners enjoy the convenience of round-the-clock power when they visit their tranquil hideaway. To discover more about backup power systems, see Chapter 15.

Color Plate 10: A Katolight backup power generator is shown in this photo. Katolight offers generators powered by engines made by a variety of manufacturers. This generator is powered by a GMC V-8 engine that is fueled with natural gas. Installing a backup generator can keep your home's circuits working during an extended power outage. See Chapter 15 for more about backup power.

Color Plate 11: This photo shows the transfer switch for the Katolight generator presented in Color Plate 10. The conductors are phase identified by applying colored tape. The red tape identifies phase A, the blue tape identifies phase B, the plain black wire indicates phase C, and the white wires are the neutral conductors. The backup generator phase wires must be installed to match the power company's phase rotation. This 400-amp capacity generator uses two conductors for each phase (parallel conductors) to accommodate the high-current loads.

Color Plate 12: The antique stop light in this photo was installed for the homeowner's amusement (and maybe because it's something the neighbors don't have). Visitors probably guess there is no valid reason to stop when the light is red, but they usually stop anyway. Chapter 17 provides the instructions to build and install a stop light of your own.

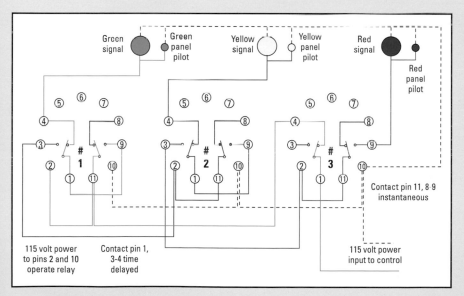

Green signal · Green panel pilot · Yellow signal · Yellow panel pilot · Red signal · Red panel pilot

⑤ ⑥ ⑦ · ④ ⑧ · ③ ⑨ · #1 · ② ⑩ · ① ⑪

⑤ ⑥ ⑦ · ④ ⑧ · ③ ⑨ · #2 · ② ⑩ · ① ⑪

⑤ ⑥ ⑦ · ④ ⑧ · ③ ⑨ · #3 · ② ⑩ · ① ⑪

Contact pin 11, 8-9 instantaneous

115 volt power to pins 2 and 10 operate relay

Contact pin 1, 3-4 time delayed

115 volt power input to control

Color Plate 13: This wiring diagram illustrates the control that operates the stop light. By tracing the colored circuits from green to yellow to red, you can follow the operational sequence of the time delay relays that make this control work. See Chapter 17 for more information on how this control works.

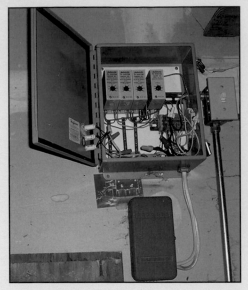

Color Plate 14: The finished control panel operates the antique stop signal shown in Color Plate 12. If you wire a controller for a traffic signal (covered in the "Just for fun: Wiring a traffic signal in your driveway" sidebar in Chapter 17), it may look very similar to this one.

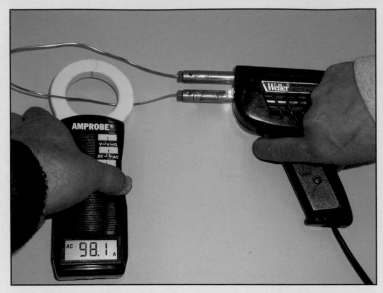

Color Plate 15: When a #12 AWG wire is loaded at 100 amps by the high-current transformer in this soldering gun (even momentarily), it heats up very quickly, as you can see. At 98.1 amps, the wire starts to turn color from the heat after only a few seconds. Chapter 16 provides more information about calculating current loads for branch circuits.

Color Plate 16: This photo is an example of measuring the power factor with a power factor meter. The power factor meter needs to sample the voltage cycle and current cycle evident on a line at the same time so it can compare them. The meter reports the phase angle difference (power factor) as a cosine. When the voltage cycle and current cycle are exactly in sync, the power factor is 1. See Appendix B for more information about understanding the power factor.

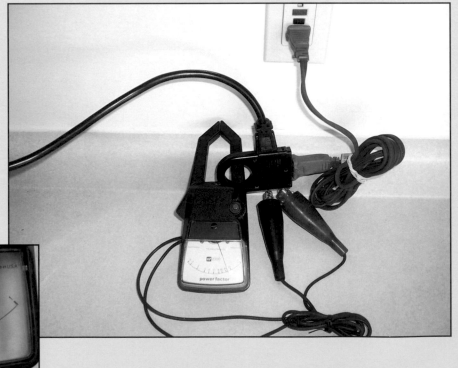

Chapter 14

Working with Security Zones and Alarm Systems

Home alarm systems aren't a modern invention. "Burglar alarms" are now more commonly called *intrusion detection and control systems* Along with intrusion detection (in layman's terms, that's "knowing when someone's breaking in"), modern alarm systems can detect fire, carbon monoxide, temperature, and water. They may also provide remote monitoring so you can keep an eye on your home even when you're not there.

In this chapter, we show how to wire and install various alarm systems and devices, including surveillance. We also show how to integrate these systems into your communications systems. Finally, we help you assess the risks in and around your home, and introduce you to common-sense steps that make your home safer. If you feel your home is your castle but don't want to dig a moat or hire a fire-breathing dragon, this chapter helps.

Protecting Your Home with Alarms

The alarms available today offer a lot of options while also being relatively inexpensive. In our view, even a system with modest features is better than none at all. Many of the individual alarm components discussed in this section are available in many building- and home-improvement supply stores. You can get some of the specialty items at electrical-supply stores or from alarm installation contractors.

Your alarm system can begin as a basic control unit, and you can add features as your needs require and budget allows. Our recommendation is to include alarm wiring to every location where an alarm may be needed during initial construction or during any major remodeling project. The wire itself is inexpensive and much easier to include before the drywall is in place.

Comparing intrusion alarms

Your alarm has parts just like you do:

- **The dukes: alarm company sign.** The most important part is the alarm company sign in your yard, which can deter an intruder.

- **The heart: intrusion alarm panel.** This is preferably located out of sight. All of the sensors and control keypads are wired to this panel.

- **The brain: operations center.** This keypad should be in a convenient location. The monitor and control keypad is located near the door you most often use to leave the house. This operations center allows you to arm the system as you leave and set a time delay to disarm the system when you get back (but you can add keypads to other locations). You indicate that you're not an intruder by entering a security code. Some controls also have one-button access to emergency numbers, while others allow you to arm and disarm with a key chain remote, or by using the Internet or a touch-tone phone.

- **The nerves: control panel.** The center is wired to door, window, and motion sensors and is usually in the basement or a mechanical equipment area. If any of the sensors signals the system, it activates a signal to alert you of the findings. The signal can be audio, visual, or both, and it can be in one or multiple locations. The center can also automatically make phone calls for help. The central control panel should be out of sight and locked. A metal mounting box with a hinged, locking, plain-metal cover recessed into a wall can also provide protection for the control panel.

Some alarm systems incorporate the control panel into the convenient access pad. These systems are often used in smaller spaces and apartments and have the siren, phone dialer, and battery backup all in one location. When an experienced intruder hears the siren and recognizes this type of unit, he can simply smash it, putting the alarm system out of operation before it can dial the monitoring company or the police. For best security we recommend that you avoid such systems.

Intrusion-detection systems can be divided into two basic types:

- **Single zone:** A typical intruder alarm system consists of one central control unit. These systems usually have a 120-volt power unit and include a battery backup to ensure operation when the power goes out (whether due to natural causes or intruder disconnection). The central unit is wired to sensor switches at doors and windows using two-conductor cable. A single-zone system drawback is that the whole shebang is either enabled or disabled.

- **Multiple zone:** A *security zone* is an area you've defined. Larger homes may have six or more unique security zones. You can control each zone independently, depending on its use or need. Turn off the kitchen monitoring if you plan to be in there for a while, but leave the other zones fully armed. We recommend multiple-zone systems.

Understanding sensors

Your alarm's control system needs something to monitor, and that something is *sensors* — the devices that tell the central control system when a door or window has been opened, or when motion has been detected.

Magnetic

Alarm systems use one of two types of magnetic sensors for doors and windows:

- **Closed-circuit:** Closed-circuit door and window sensors are two-part magnetic switches. The magnet is mounted securely to the window frame or door, which is the moving item. The on/off switch is mounted to the stationary door or window casing. When you open the door or window, the switch opens (breaks contact) and opens a circuit to the central control. This initiates the alarm process, which may include a local alarm, phone dialing, and other actions. Figure 14-1 shows a typical magnetic window switch. Notice that the actuator magnet is separate from the wired half of the sensor. The *actuator magnet* is mounted to the door, so it makes more sense to make this the moving part. Failed wires on an closed-circuit system make themselves immediately known. A broken wire sends an alarm just as a sensor switching to open would. We believe closed-circuit systems are more reliable because they constantly monitor themselves.

- **Open-circuit:** These systems also use magnetic sensors at doors and windows, but the circuit closes instead of opening when the door or window opens. If a wire or connection fails on a open-circuit system, you've no way to detect it without testing.

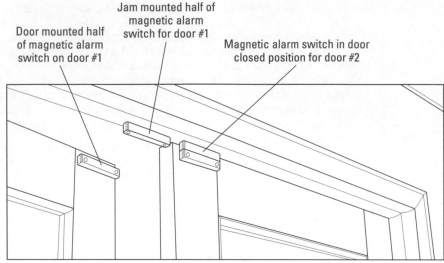

Door mounted half of magnetic alarm switch on door #1

Jam mounted half of magnetic alarm switch for door #1

Magnetic alarm switch in door closed position for door #2

Figure 14-1: Most window sensors are magnetic.

Nonmagnetic

Alarm systems use one of two types of nonmagnetic sensors for doors and windows:

- ✓ **Button switches:** These magnetic switch alternatives are recessed into the doorframe. A ball or probe on the switch face moves back and forth to operate when the door is opened or closed. Button switches are available to match open- or closed-circuit systems with switch types that are normally open (off) or normally closed (on).

- ✓ **Motion:** Detectors for motion come in two flavors:

    - **Passive Infrared (PIR):** You may get a false alarm from this heat detector if you aim it toward heat sources such as ducts or sunlit windows.

    - **Dual Technology (DT):** This type emits high-frequency sound waves that bounce back to the sensor. With those waves it can detect heat and disturbances. Both elements — fluctuating heat and disrupted sound reflection — must be present to trip this alarm. DT sensors usually detect pets, although some are sophisticated enough to ignore small ones.

Wiring and installing sensors

Unless your control-equipment manufacturer recommends otherwise, all of the alarm sensors will be wired using a four-conductor, 22 AWG or heavier, unshielded cable with solid or twisted-copper conductors. The cable should also have a UL Class-2 rating.

Cable from each switch location is a home run directly to the master control unit location. Follow the manufacturer's recommendations for pre-planning, drilling, and installing the wiring. Also, check out Chapter 3 for additional home wiring tips and guidelines. Try to keep the wiring and the switch sensors hidden and protected to increase the alarm's security and reliability. As with other low-voltage, communication, or control wiring, maintain sufficient separation from home power wiring. We recommend at least 4" to 6" or more of separation on parallel runs.

When installing alarm trip switches on doors or windows, drill for (and perhaps install) the switches in the door and window casements prior to them being installed in the house framing. Of course this only applies to new construction or major remodels. Having nearly unobstructed access to door and window casements makes the installation and wiring job far easier. If you're going to equip many windows of similar construction with switches, use a drill or routing template. Also keep in mind that switches may fail and need replacement, so leave some hidden slack in the wires. Many spring or ball switches have metal cover plates screwed into the wood that you can remove for switch replacement.

When using DT or PIR motion sensors, follow the manufacturer's recommendations for wiring. Motion sensors often require two sets of unshielded twisted-pair cable. One twisted pair carries the alarm trip signal to the control unit, and the other pair brings low-voltage DC power to the sensor device. Some sensors may need to plug into a 120-volt power outlet instead.

Increasing safety with supplemental alarms

Intruders aren't the only potential hazard. You can install many other types of detectors: smoke alarms, carbon monoxide, high water, low temperature, and propane or natural gas detectors. The following sections introduce you to some common supplemental alarms that you should use in your home.

Smoke alarms

Smoke alarms are a must in every residence and are required by building codes in new construction. As a starting point, building codes require at least one 120 volt interconnected smoke detector with battery backup in each of the following locations:

- ✔ On every floor, including the basement.
- ✔ In every bedroom hallway, within 6' bedroom doors (unless local codes require an alternative placement); the hallway detector counts for that floor.
- ✔ In every bedroom.

Code also now requires smoke detection alarms to be interconnected. The interconnection causes every alarm to sound when only one of them detects smoke. The interconnect wiring is three-conductor cable; one power, one neutral, and one interconnection conductor.

The *National Electrical Code (NEC)* requires that bedroom power circuits be arc-fault protected, so smoke alarms are often supplied with power on the bedroom lighting circuit. Frequently, local building codes require additional smoke alarms, both in terms of numbers and locations. Modern smoke alarms are typically wired with 120-volt power during the electrical rough in. See Chapter 3 for additional rough-in wiring information.

Three additional wiring types for smoke and fire alarms include *NPLFA (non-power limited fire alarm), PLFA (power limited fire alarm),* and *CI (circuit integrity).* CI cable provides circuit integrity under fire conditions for a specified time period. See Article 760 of the 2002 NEC for more information about fire alarm wiring.

Most new smoke alarms, like the one in Figure 14-2, include an on-board 9-volt backup battery. When the battery's failing, many models let you know with a mild (yet annoying) ping. Change the batteries periodically. Without power outages, the batteries may last four years or more. You hear folks saying "Replace the batteries when you change the clock back to standard time." Whether they know it or not, they're talking about battery-powered smoke alarms, not 120-volt smoke alarms with battery backup. In the former, the battery is only used when the power is out.

Keep spare batteries on hand, just in case at 2 a.m. the battery monitor lets you know about the impending battery change. Like most batteries, if you keep spares in the freezer they stay fresh. As soon as they are room temperature, they can deliver power.

Smoke alarms can stand alone, or they can be tied into the detection control center to broadcast a warning of any alarm or to dial emergency phone numbers. The local alarm is fine if you're home, but when you're away you may want extra protection for pets or people who cannot hear an alarm. An integrated central alarm-control unit can be programmed to call 911, your monitoring services contractor, and your cell phone or pager.

Heat detectors

Heat detectors are a good choice for supplementing the smoke alarms in your home. Put them in mechanical rooms, laundry rooms, attics, storage rooms, basements, and in the kitchen. Heat detectors are either

- Triggered at a specific temperature
- Triggered by a rise in temperature
- A combination of both

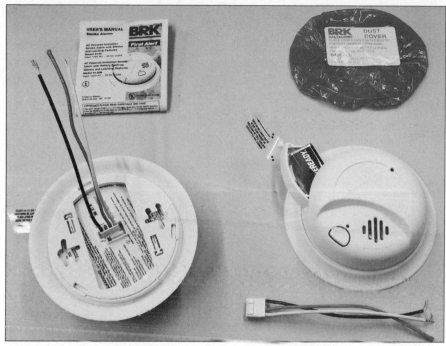

Figure 14-2:
Smoke
alarms
usually
include a
battery
backup.

Often, smoke detectors trip false alarms in kitchens or vented attic areas, so including a heat detector provides added protection. Like smoke detectors, heat detectors can be wired into your home's master alarm-control unit.

Carbon monoxide detectors

Carbon monoxide (CO) is referred to as the "silent killer" because the gas is odorless and tasteless. Your home should have CO monitors if it:

✔ Has enclosed parking, such as an attached garage.

✔ Uses any fossil fuel heating or refrigeration source.

✔ Has a fossil fuel electrical generator within close proximity.

Although not required in every state, CO detectors can help prevent death or serious injury if any of the fossil fuel-burning appliances, furnaces, refrigerators, or combustion engines cause a harmful buildup of CO. Figure 14-3 shows one of the many styles of CO detectors available at building-supply stores.

Just like smoke alarms, CO detectors can be hardwired in and interconnected, and you can link them to the central alarm control unit. CO detectors use the same three-wire cable smoke detectors use. Rather than using CO detectors in the following areas, it may be better to use smoke-CO–combination detectors.

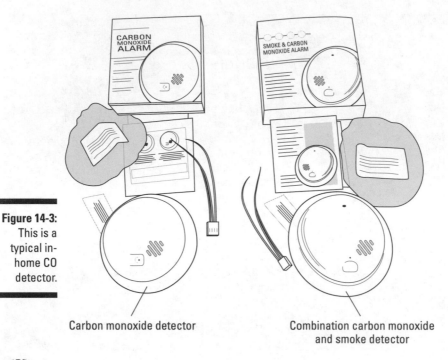

Carbon monoxide detector

Combination carbon monoxide and smoke detector

CO detectors should be installed in all habitable and enclosed areas of your home. Like smoke alarms, this means one

✔ On every floor, including the basement

✔ In every bedroom hallway

✔ In every bedroom

Check with your local building code officials for specific requirements in your area. If you don't have CO detectors and you do have fossil fuel appliances or an attached garage, get some immediate protection from CO detectors that plug into your electrical outlets. If you buy a battery-powered detector, select one with battery-charge monitors, and remember to change the batteries at least twice yearly.

CO detectors are likely to become a code requirement for all homes, apartments, and work areas. If you're building a home, protect your family by installing smoke-CO–combination detectors even if your local codes don't currently require them.

Radon detectors

Radon (Rn) is a radioactive gas that emits metallic particles, as well as cancer-causing alpha, beta, and gamma radiation. Radon is odorless and invisible.

According to the United States' Surgeon General, radon is second only to smoking in causing lung cancer deaths. The U.S. Environmental Protection Agency publishes comparative maps of areas prone to moderate or high levels of radon in the soil, water, and rock. The maps are at www.epa.gov/radon/zonemap.html.

Radon levels can be tested using a one-time test kit, or with a constant air monitor. Radon is measured in pCi/L (pico-Curies per liter) of air. In the U.S., the EPA says that any level over 4 requires corrective action. Other countries have set a lower threshold for concern, and some states (like New Jersey) are trying to lower their standard to 2 pCi/L. For more information on radon and its dangers see www.epa.gov/iaq/radon/pubs/citguide.html, or contact the EPA or your state's radon office.

Consumer Rn detectors typically only have a local alarm and LED. Select an evaluated Rn detector accepted by the U.S. EPA. Wiring for an Rn detector simply requires a well-placed outlet, and the detectors should be on every floor, including the basement and attic, away from doors, windows, and air ducts. Placing Rn detectors away from well-ventilated areas ensures effectiveness.

The display readings can be periodically evaluated using a professional monitoring service or by sending in a test kit once or twice per year. Plug-in Rn detectors cost about $150 to $200. If you detect radon, you can lower the risk by installing vent pipes and ventilation equipment at a typical cost of $800 to $1,200.

Flood or high water alarms

More than one homeowner has had the unpleasant surprise of a burst water pipe or overflowed plumbing. A flood or high-water alarm usually detects elevated moisture levels or small water leaks. Others may include float switches that detect the presence of high water. The devices can sound alarms, or they can be set up to turn off the water supply to a specific appliance such as a clothes washer, water heater, refrigerator, water/ice dispenser, or even the whole home. Some systems detect a very thin layer of water, call a programmed phone number, and describe the flooding based on which sensors are tripped. Sensors may also monitor sump pumps to make sure they're working correctly.

Freezing or overheating alarms

Heating and cooling system alarms can detect falling or rising temperatures. When a potentially hazardous fluctuation is detected, they can trigger an alarm and notify you, a neighbor, or an alarm-monitoring company before any major damage occurs. Freeze alarms are an important consideration in northern climates, because water heating systems and pipes can freeze and burst, causing flooding that can destroy a home.

The simplest freeze alarm is a thermostat that turns on a colored light in a window (so a neighbor can see potential freezing while you're away). You can set the light to illuminate at a specific temperature, such as 40 degrees Fahrenheit. With a master alarm-control unit, you can preset high or low temperatures for alarm tripping.

Personal medical event alarms

You can add medical-alert services to some alarm systems, and standalone medical alarms are also available. With these services, an alarm alerts the medical-alert monitoring company; it can call emergency help for you. You may want to consider whether someone in your family needs medical-alert services when you select a master control unit. Also make sure that emergency backup power (described in Chapter 15) is available for critical medical equipment.

Alarm systems may make you eligible for discounts on your homeowner's insurance premium. Check with your agent to see if your system qualifies for discounts. In some states, alarms must be installed by contractors specifically licensed to do alarm systems, so check with your local building code-enforcement office to see if you can install them yourself. See Chapter 1 for tips on selecting electrical contractors; these same tips apply to alarm contractors as well.

Wireless sensors

Many, if not all, of the sensors mentioned in this chapter are available in wireless versions. Wireless sensors may seem like an attractive option, especially if you're retrofitting an alarm system in an older home or have to wire remote areas.

However, wireless sensors

 ✔ May not be as easy to assemble into one integrated system because wireless sensors are usually brand sensitive. Sensors from one manufacturer may not work with control units from another manufacturer. This isn't usually a problem with hardwired sensors.

 ✔ Are usually considered less reliable because they're prone to radio interference. Interference can cause false alarms or disrupted monitoring.

 ✔ Have batteries that need to be replaced or charged.

The copper wire for alarm systems can be solid or multi-stranded. On *stranded wire,* one *whisker* (strand) can make a connection that tests okay but fails to carry enough current to trigger during an alarm. Our advice is to test all On/Off switch circuits with the switch in the On condition. Perform the test using an ohmmeter and test for a low-resistance reading before connecting the circuits to the control module. Keep a log of your test readings. Should you need to troubleshoot the circuits later, these readings will be valuable. Chapter 20 covers some popular troubleshooting tips.

A cell phone is another wireless element you may want to add to your alarm system. A more sophisticated and determined intruder may know that if he cuts your telephone line he can put your security system out of order. He may also be smart enough to do this at the utility pole before entering your property. A cell phone acts as a backup. In this case, a wireless notification system can be harder to defeat than a wired system, so long as cellular service is available and reliable. One risk with cell-phone notification is potentially delayed call setup time: If many people are using the closest cell tower, there may be a significant time delay before your call is initiated.

Surveilling Your Surroundings

Even if you have eyes in the back of your head, you won't be able to watch every part of your home all the time. This means that surveillance must be a key consideration as you plan your home's security system. Surveillance equipment can vary from a simple digital camera to a complete *closed-circuit TV (CCTV)* system. Most systems also incorporate infrared sensing so that they only photograph or monitor areas of your home when people are in a camera's field of view. You could even use a webcam to monitor areas of your home and provide a view of your property over the Internet or on a Web-capable cellular phone. The following sections introduce you to the most common types of cameras used in a home surveillance system.

Digital cameras

A digital camera wired to a monitoring switch can give you a record of who has been on your property. Some models can store up to 50,000 images on a time-lapse basis. You can operate most digital cameras by remote signal from a door opener or a manually given command. A drawback to remote digital surveillance cameras is that you have to charge the camera's battery frequently.

Closed-circuit television (CCTV)

A CCTV system generally consists of a camera that is activated by an infrared sensor, a VCR, and a video monitor. A system that has to monitor a large area may incorporate several cameras.

Traditional CCTV monitoring systems are less popular and less efficient than modern digital systems, and CCTV systems are destined to continue that decline, if not become altogether obsolete. Some specialized equipment can use the analog cameras and convert their images to digital signals, which can then be stored on a computer.

If you're buying a new surveillance system, we recommend avoiding CCTV systems, even if they use a *digital video recorder (DVR)*. Some manufacturers market such systems as if they were all-digital. When buying a system, make sure the cameras are digital as well as the recorder. There's nothing wrong with using analog equipment that Uncle Bob gives you. It's just that analog CCTV quality doesn't compare to digital.

The wiring install for a CCTV remote camera is a 120-volt power circuit to provide camera power, plus an RG-6 coaxial cable to carry the video signal. Some equipment requires a third wire to allow the camera to communicate with your home's alarm system.

Webcams

An *Internet protocol (IP)* webcam may be the best modern option for video surveillance. *Webcams* are similar to a digital PC camera, except that the webcam also processes the digital signal on board and transmits the information in data packets. Webcams can be linked to a file server or Web server that can store still images or full-motion video. From the server, the images can later be archived onto CDs or DVDs. You can easily configure and manage IP cameras using Web browsers. See more on IP and wiring for home networks in Chapter 12.

The webcam pictures are far superior to analog images. Once recorded, the data doesn't degrade like analog CCTV/VCR recordings do. The data can be shared over an Ethernet wired or wireless network, and even over the Internet. The IP-based information is highly compressed and far less bulky to archive than VCR tapes. Webcams don't necessarily need a computer to operate, although if you want to record video rather than just monitor it, you need a computer, file server, or *Network Attached Storage (NAS)* device. You can control some webcams remotely to rotate 360 degrees, tilt, and zoom. Some high-end cameras cost more than $2,900, but decent IP cameras can be purchased for about $200 or less.

Part of the appeal of IP-based webcams is that they let you watch your home from far away using the Internet. As we discuss in Chapter 12, if you have an always-on Internet connection and two or more permanently assigned IP addresses, you can access your IP cameras directly from almost any computer. You could mount up to 254 (the limit for one network) webcams around your premises. That's a lot of monitoring! You can set up a *virtual private network (VPN)* with authentication and passwords so that only authorized users can view the server that hosts and manages the cameras.

Webcams require the same wiring as other computer network equipment. Each camera requires a network service drop with Cat 6 cable and a home run to the central wiring closest switch for the network. The major difference between camera and computer network wiring is that the boxes with the RJ-45 connectors are usually mounted higher on the wall (or even in the ceiling) for cameras. You can recess and cover with an access plate any camera-mounting locations that a vandal or intruder can get to.

Integrating Alarm and Communication Systems

The most basic type of alarm system simply makes a sound. For this to be effective, an audible alarm requires three things:

- ✓ A person must be home.
- ✓ The person must be able to hear the alarm.
- ✓ The person must be able to react to the alarm appropriately. During a fire, someone who's bedridden wouldn't be able to leave the house without help. A person who's deaf may not hear an alarm.

Take away any one or all three of these elements and the audible system fails. Thus, it makes sense to interface your alarm system with your communication system, because then the system is effective even if one of the elements is missing.

Earlier in this chapter, we mention alarm system auto dialers. Twenty years ago, most auto dialers called police or sheriff offices, but recently private alarm monitoring and security companies have taken over most home alarm monitoring. You can pay a monitoring company, which calls you when an alarm is detected. If you don't respond, the company can call the police or other outside help. Other systems dial a list of preprogrammed phone numbers. To head off false calls, generally the 911 administrator doesn't want 911 on an auto dialer. The list of numbers may include your work or cell phone, a neighbor's house, or a relative's home.

The heart of an *auto dialer* system is the auto dialer. This device connects to a standard phone line, and when triggered, dials the monitoring company.

If you have only one phone line to your home and you're using *digital subscriber line (DSL)* to connect to the Internet over your copper phone line, be sure the installation to your dial-tone auto dialer is downstream of a DSL filter. This provides the dialer with a clean, clear dial tone. Also follow the alarm manufacturer's instructions to properly install an RJ-31X jack ahead of the house phones to give the auto dialer priority for use of the phone line. If your budget allows, use a dedicated line and phone number for your alarm system's auto dialer.

You can connect an auto dialer to a cell phone as a backup, or use it as the primary dialer in areas with no landline service. If the alarm control unit is in a concrete wall or basement, use a cell phone auto dialer that can connect to an external antenna, and then

1. **Run a cable to an antenna mounted in the attic or on the roof.**

2. **Use RG-58 or RG-6 cable with the appropriate adapters for this antenna run.**

3. **Aim a directional-gain antenna, such as a Yagi, right at the cell tower serving your phone.**

   A Yagi-style antenna is designed to be highly directional. The design is named after a Japanese electrical engineer, Dr. Hidetsugu Yagi, who invented the concept.

4. **If your system uses an external antenna, make sure the cable is properly grounded and high enough to prevent tampering.**

5. **Thoroughly test the equipment after installation.**

A computer can also interface with the alarm to provide the ability to send a tripped alarm notice. Once the computer knows the alarm has been tripped, it can

- ✔ Use a modem to dial your pager and send a canned message.

- ✔ Send text messages to your cell phone or send a priority e-mail at your work.

- ✔ Notify many phone numbers, in different ways, about any of the alarm conditions.

Improving Your Home's Safety

Alarms are just one component in an effective security system. You can take many steps to improve your safety in and around your home. In the following sections we tell you how to expand and leverage the value from your alarm.

Get the facts for your area

In some areas folks don't lock the doors; in others, locks aren't enough to keep out unwanted guests. If you're in an unfamiliar area, you may want to check with neighbors or the police to assess your risks.

Electronic control

If a jingling set of keys seems too old fashioned for your modern digital home, you may want to consider controlling access electronically. *Card readers* are one possibility. Some card readers work from a distance, such as a driveway gate opener, so you can simply leave a card on your car's dashboard. You may have to wave other cards directly in front of a reader or pass it through a slot, like a credit card. Various card sizes are available, ranging from credit card-size to smaller key-chain tags.

Other options include numeric keypads or biometric devices. You can integrate keypads with a card reader so the card holder must enter a password as well as present the card. Using two components together is called *two-factor security,* and it affords additional security should you lose the card or have it stolen. Biometric access controls include devices that scan your finger or the palm of your hand.

No matter how secure you make your home, you may need to allow someone in when you aren't there. Your house sitter can enter a password, enter your house, check on your pets, and water the plants. Then, when you get home, you can change the password.

Although your home's safety and security should be a concern no matter where you live, it's important to know the crime picture in your area. For current crime statistics from the FBI, visit www.fbi.gov/ucr/ucr.htm. This information will help you more accurately evaluate the major risks in your area.

Screen visitors

Any contractor you hire should be licensed. He should be stable enough to belong to some trade associations. One such association is the *Home Builders Association (HBA),* which screens business owners and requires that all applicants be licensed. Contractors who've been in business for a long time are usually more dependable. The employer's and his employees' appearances are an indicator of their character and work. Someone who comes to work groomed and in clean clothes shows concern about his appearance. There's a good chance he'll also care about his quality of work.

Be careful who you let into your house. Anyone who becomes familiar with the premises may put you at risk. A policeman needs a search warrant to access your home. Don't let some unknown person in your home that you didn't invite. Often, wrongdoers say they're from the company that installed your pump last year, or pose as building inspectors or utility workers. An intercom system coupled with a video camera is valuable for this reason. When someone rings the doorbell, reply over the intercom and ask the visitor to please look into the security camera so her face can be recorded and identification can be verified; if necessary, you can then call the company the person says she works for.

Make some security elements visible

You should advertise the security measures used in and around your home. You may even want to exaggerate this advertisement. If a potential intruder thinks he's being recorded on video, that may serve as a powerful deterrent. Most intruders won't enter a house if they think it has an alarm system. You can advertise your security system in a variety of ways:

- Post warnings at doors and windows that say, "This house is protected by brand X security system," or "Alarms present." These signs should be obvious to the most casual observer. You may also want to install signs on the lawn.

- Install motion-sensitive lights and position them so they show off your security warning signs.

- Make one or more cameras noticeable from the outside of your home.

- Include loud alarms that sound when intrusions are detected, and provide a prerecorded notification over loudspeakers.

Secure your home

Installing an alarm system isn't going to make your home safe all by itself. You can and should do many other things to truly secure your home.

Some home security tips include

- When your family is going on vacation, have the post office hold your mail and subscriptions or have a trusted friend or relative pick them up.

- Don't leave the lights on all day and night while you're away. Your lights should turn off in daylight. Lights on in the daytime are an invitation to thieves — most burglaries actually occur during daytime — and so is only one light on at night. Use timers connected to lamps throughout the house to turn some house lights on and off at different times. You can even install timers to turn on radios or TVs.

- Locate the security system's central control unit in an area both out of sight and under lock and key.

- If you have bushes under the windows, consider installing trip wires or ground-pressure switches near each window to set off alarms.

- Connect your alarm system to X10 controls, if you use them. Intruders don't like bright lights, so discourage them by causing most or all of the lights in and around your home to turn on when an intrusion alarm is tripped. See Chapter 5 for more on X10 controls.

✔ Flatten and hide boxes from newly purchased electronics and other valuable items. They advertise that you have new stuff worth stealing.

✔ Beef up door-entry hardware and installation. Unless you've left windows open, the easiest place to break into a modern house is the front door. Most intruders know they can open modern doors with one hard blow near the doorknob. To block this easy entry, install four-screw strike plates on your door, as shown in Figure 14-4. The stronger four-screw plates only cost about $6, so they're cheap insurance. You should also put one long screw on each of the three door hinges.

Strike plates should be attached with 3" screws instead of the ¾" screws that come with standard lockset strike plates. The longer screws go into the door's rough framing, not just into the trim like a standard attachment. However, if you have a window next to the door, you may have to use shorter screws. When you install a four-screw strike plate, you have to enlarge any existing mortise to accommodate the larger strike plate. The *mortise* is wood removed to allow the strike plate to flush with the doorframe. The mortise depth is about ⅛" deep and is shaped to accommodate the strike plate. The screws should be angled slightly back to catch the door framing.

✔ Install shock-detection switches on entry doors in addition to the standard open-condition sensor switches. Shock-detection switches activate your alarm when someone *tries* to force entry into your home, not just when they actually enter it.

Figure 14-4:
Four-screw
strike plates
are much
stronger
than
standard
two-screw
plates.

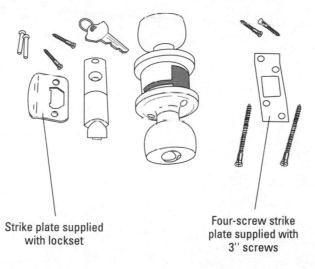

Strike plate supplied
with lockset

Four-screw strike
plate supplied with
3'' screws

Chapter 15

Backup and Alternative Power

- -

- -

*W*hat if the power goes out? Some convenience items — like the toaster and maybe the coffee maker — you can probably do without for a while. Other things are essential — like the refrigerator, medical support equipment, and the fish tank — and will create expensive and heartbreaking problems if they don't have backup power. This chapter introduces you to the different types backup power systems available, and shows what you need to install one in your home.

We also introduce you to alternative power sources. Sources like solar and wind help you reduce your energy bills, and they may serve as emergency backups if your electrical service goes offline. Some alternative systems may even allow you to live entirely *off the grid,* which means your home isn't even connected to an electrical utility at all.

Identifying Your Home's Critical Systems

Be selective about what you need to keep energized during a power outage. This is especially true if your home is connected to the power grid, which it is if you pay an electric bill. You may decide that during a utility outage you only want to energize things such as:

✔ A few important lights

✔ Refrigerator

For alternative power systems, you can purchase refrigerators that run under their own power, which is supplied by a built-in propane or kerosene generator.

✔ Furnace

✔ Smoke, security, carbon monoxide, and radon alarms

✔ Medical devices

✔ Sump pump; fresh water pumps

Of course, you could install a system that powers the entire home. Just keep in mind that the larger the usage list, the more expensive the backup power equipment will be.

Before you can figure out how much backup system you need, you must measure how much power the critical devices use and add up the wattages. Table 15-1 lists typical electricity use for common household appliances and systems.

 Power loads for things like lighting and coffee makers are fairly steady, but some appliances and pumps with motors create additional load — many times that of the running load — during startup. Your design must account for the current used to start the motor, especially for devices such as water pumps and saws. (The motors in clothes dryers and refrigerators do not have significant starting currents.)

Table 15-1	Typical Appliance Electrical Load		
Appliance or Device	*Amps*	*Volts*	*Watts*
Coffee maker	7.5	120	900
Computer	1.2	120	140
Dishwasher	11.7	120	1,400
Electric dryer	17.5	240	4,200
Electric stove	33.3	240	8,000
Electric stove burner	3.8	240	900
Hair dryer	8.3	120	1,000
Microwave	8.3	120	1,000
Fresh water or sump pump	7.5	120	900
Refrigerator	4.6	120	550
TV	1.3	120	150
Toaster	7.5	120	900
Washer	4.2	120	500
100-watt lamp	0.8	120	100

Tallying electric usage

A moderately equipped home uses about 1 kilowatt (kW) of electricity per hour for convenience use. *Convenience use* means lights, TVs, coffee makers, toasters, and the like. This estimate doesn't include using high-wattage appliances such as the air conditioner, oven, water heater, and electric clothes dryer. A family of four that uses 24 kW per day probably has an electric stove, water heater, and clothes dryer, along with the normal convenience appliances. Using 24 kW per day at a rate of 10 cents per kW equates to a monthly electric bill of about $72.00.

Besides deciding which systems are critical and which aren't, try to anticipate future needs. It isn't uncommon for people to spend a couple hundred dollars on a cheap generator, only to wear it out quickly because it didn't have enough capacity. Often, spending a little more money up front results in savings over the long term.

Comparing Types of Backup Power

Power outages can happen anywhere and anytime, and it seems to us that power companies are less concerned these days about preventing those outages. Include your power-outage exposure risk as you plan your home, considering both the likelihood of an outage and the loss you will experience during an extended outage. This will help you decide how much backup you need, as well as the best type for you. The following sections describe the most common types of backup power.

Uninterruptible power supplies

The smallest backup power supply normally used in homes is an *uninterruptible power supply (UPS)*. A UPS is basically a battery unit that charges itself when you plug it into wall power, and then provides backup power during an outage. A UPS most often powers a computer. The battery in a UPS lasts a finite amount of time. If the power outage is long, you may only have time to save your computer data before the UPS runs out of power. Most UPS units used with computers are supplied with a cable and interface software to shut down the computer before the UPS battery runs out of power.

Many commercial-grade UPS units have been taken out of service because the internal batteries are old and no longer hold a charge. These heavy-duty units were often designed to provide 1 kW to 3 kW of power. You can get these units cheaply if the batteries are no good, and in most cases you can replace the batteries.

Inverter systems

If a computer-style UPS isn't quite powerful enough to suit your needs, consider stepping up to an inverter system. A UPS is a self-contained system. It stores *direct current (DC)* power in internally housed batteries, and then a component called the *inverter* converts that to the *alternating current (AC)* power most household electrical devices use. The inverter is a component of an inverter system. It uses the same technology as the UPS, but the external battery banks are much larger than those inside a UPS. They both convert battery power into *alternating current (AC)* when needed. Figure 15-1 shows a typical inverter.

Most UPS units don't deliver enough current to power refrigerators and other big-load systems, but you can install a battery bank and use an inverter to connect those batteries to your electrical system when necessary. A *battery bank and inverter* are basically just a large-scale UPS for your home. A few hundred dollars' worth of batteries could power a house on limited use for several days without a recharge. And like a UPS, the battery bank provides instant power when an outage occurs; you don't have to wait for a generator to start up. When the outage ends, the inverter turns into a battery charger and recharges the batteries.

In addition to instant startup, a battery bank and inverter make for a very low-maintenance system. The disadvantage is that you only have power for the length of time that the batteries' charges last. For this reason you may want to add a generator for periodically recharging the batteries during longer power outages. You can buy an inverter that automatically starts the generator when the batteries are discharged.

Inverter systems vary enough in size and are uniquely integrated into the wiring system to handle all or part of the home's electrical load. As such, they aren't normally available in big-box stores. Once you decide on size and features, you buy from an electrical supplier, regional distributor, or manufacturer.

Batteries are designed for two primary types of service:

- ✔ **Lead-acid batteries:** Batteries such as the one in your car supply a large amount of current over a very short time for powering the starter motor. Once the car starts, the alternator handles the loads.

- ✔ **Deep-cycle batteries:** Batteries such as the one used for a boat's electric trolling motors or in electric golf carts supply a steady amount of current over a long period of time.

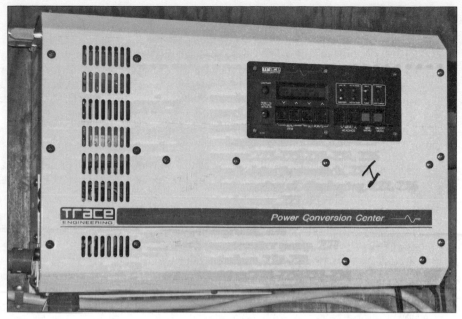

Figure 15-1:
Inverters
allow you to
power your
home using
batteries.

Batteries are constructed three ways.

- Gelled cell
- Wet cell
- Absorbed glass mat (AGM)

Lead-acid batteries are either gelled or wet. Of the three listed here, AGM most resists freezing, produces less gas when charging, and maintains a charge in storage for longer periods. The drawback is that AGM batteries are more expensive than standard lead-acid batteries of equal capacity.

To compare batteries' ampere-hour capacity, always compare against the 20-hour rating. The higher the ampere-hour rating, the longer the battery supplies a given load. A 12-volt battery is considered *fully discharged* when its produced voltage dips to 10½ volts, which is 1¾ volts per cell.

Green power systems

No, this section isn't about the engines in John Deere tractors. They're called *green* because they don't cause conventional pollution. Wind and water systems use their respective mechanical forces to spin generators and generate DC voltage to charge batteries or use directly.

So-called *green power systems* include

- **Wind:** The cost of wind power blows us away (pun intended). A unit that produces 1 kW costs about $3,000. Older systems with batteries used DC wiring systems within the home. But with the development of high-efficiency inverters, these DC systems don't make much sense. In most cases, springing for an inverter is probably better than buying home appliances, lights, and accessories that run on 12- or 24-volt DC. These items aren't readily available and usually cost more than equivalent 120-volt AC items.

- **Solar:** Solar panels can produce DC power. These panels need no maintenance other than an occasional cleaning. A 100-watt panel is about 9' × 9' and costs about $700.

A 100-watt solar panel installed in an area sunny enough to produce power 10 hours per day will generate 1 kW per day, or 365 kW per year. Most utilities charge less than a dime per kW. This means that 365 kW from the power company costs about $36.50. It therefore takes 19 years for the $700 solar panel to pay for itself. And this doesn't account for installation charges or the interest you could've earned by investing your $700 instead.

- **Water (*hydroelectric*):** Water-wheel motion can very effectively turn a generator if your home and property include a stream or creek with a sufficient waterfall. A waterfall distance of about 10' with ample volume can be captured at the high mark and piped though a wheel or turbine that turns the generator. A flow of 15 cubic feet of water per minute though the turbine with a 10' head produces about ¹⁄₁₀ of a kilowatt. A 300-watt low-head water turbine-generator costs about $750. I suspect these systems may require some kind of permit from the environmental oversight authority.

From a purely financial standpoint, green power systems only make sense if the cost of bringing conventional utility power to the home is excessive. Most utilities charge large installation fees to set and wire poles or trench in underground power lines if your home is more than 1,000' from the nearest service line, so take this into consideration when you look at green power systems. Often these fees are a lot more than the purchase of an independent power system. If you need to use fuel backup along with green power, the fuel's cost may be higher over the long run. The power companies' usage charge for power is relatively cheap.

Calculate your alternative power costs over at least a ten-year span. When calculating, you may want to consider the environmental cost savings of clean air and clean water.

Power from two or more environmentally friendly sources can be combined. Figure 15-2 shows a general diagram for charging batteries with solar and wind power, as well as with a backup generator. You can control the generator automatically to start when the battery voltage is below 11 volts on a 12-volt battery bank. If the wind and solar sources can supply the load and keep the battery voltage above 11 volts, you need to start the generator only to test reliability and for maintenance.

External combustion steam systems

Another method of producing power is by steam. Most utilities use steam to produce their power. Their power plants may use nuclear power, oil, coal, or wood to produce steam, which then drives steam turbines. With the cost of traditional fuels escalating we would not be surprised to see steam power used in some home power systems in the future. The steam boiler could be fired by virtually anything that burns. The exhaust steam from the turbine could also be used to heat the house. But for now, home steam power systems are a thing of the future.

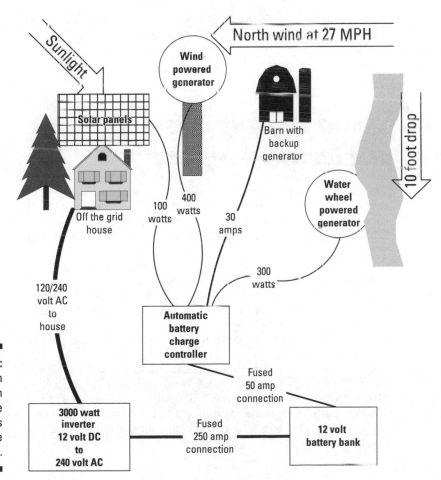

Figure 15-2: Green power from multiple sources can be combined.

Internal combustion systems

The most common type of backup system is a generator running on an internal combustion engine. For homes, these generators typically range in size from 4 kWto 25 kW. Some are portable units so you can drag it out of the garage and hook it up temporarily during an outage. Others may be permanent and start automatically during an outage, although you usually have a lag time between when the power goes out and the generator starts. The most efficient internal combustion generators run on diesel fuel, although propane or natural gas-fueled units are more common.

Diesel fuel deteriorates with age. This happens with gasoline-powered generators, too. Some fuel additives can extend diesel's or gasoline's shelf life, but this means added expense and maintenance. If your area typically only has infrequent, short-duration power outages, then a natural gas or propane generator probably makes more sense.

Color Plate 10 (turn to the color insert pages in this book) shows an 80-kW Katolight backup generator. This unit is a bit larger than most, which allows you to see more detail. This generator is controlled by an automatic transfer switch, which is described in the next section.

Interfacing Backup Systems to Your Electrical System

The easiest way to interface a backup power source is to simply unplug your refrigerator or lamp from the wall and plug it into the backup generator. But this isn't very convenient, so in this section we describe how to interface directly between a backup system and your home's electrical system.

If your backup system connects directly to your regular electrical system, the interface must be interlocked so that the backup can't connect to the utility's system and back feed electricity. *Back feeding* power into the utility's distribution system could kill or injure a lineman trying to restore your power. The utility company may want to approve the interface to ensure the interlock is fail safe. Make sure the interface is installed by a qualified, experienced electrician.

Some manual transfer switches meet the interlock requirement. A manual switch usually costs less than $200 and only connects to a few of the home's electrical circuits. One popular unit uses two breakers to energize a separate standby panel. One breaker connects to the generator, and the other to the utility power. The breakers are mechanically interlocked so that turning on one breaker turns off the other one.

Whole-house manual transfer switches are also available. Install these between the meter socket and the home distribution panel. The transfer switch has the same current rating as the electrical service, which is generally 100 or 200 amps. A whole-house manual transfer switch is rare because of its expense, and an automatic transfer switch doesn't cost that much more.

Automatic switches are nice because as the name implies, they start the generator and switch to the backup power source automatically when there's an outage. Two types of automatic transfer switch installations are possible:

✔ **Circuit-specific:** This type of switch installation, shown in Figure 15-3, usually switches power to a separate standby panel when the normal power goes out. The standby panel has circuits for some critical loads, but not for the whole house.

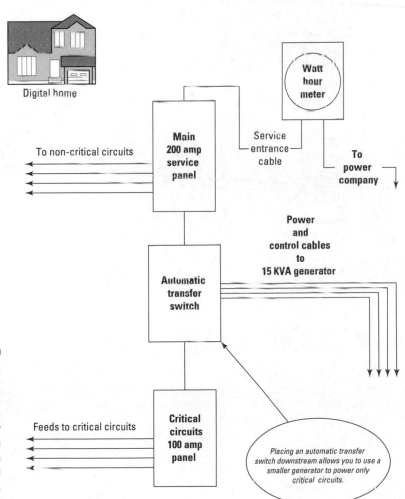

Figure 15-3:
This switch installation automatically transfers power to critical circuits.

✔ **Whole house:** Surprise! This type of switch installation, shown in Figure 15-4, transfers the entire home's electrical system over to back-up power when necessary. This switch must have the same current rating as the home's electrical service. A 200-amp automatic transfer switch costs about $500.

A service-transfer switch — whether manual or automatic — must be listed by Underwriters Laboratory and marked as, "Suitable for Use as Service Equipment." This marking (often abbreviated *SUSE*) is sometimes referred to as a *Susie label.*

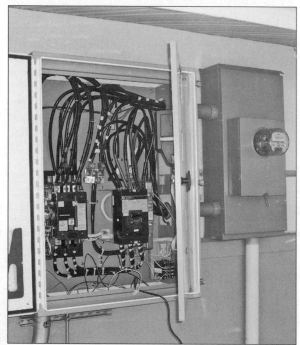

Figure 15-4:
This switch transfers power for the whole home.

Alternative Energy Systems

Some alternative energy sources — such as solar or wind — don't have to just be for emergencies. You can use them every single day to reduce your utility bill or provide electricity where utility service isn't available.

Alternative power systems usually have more than one means of generating electricity. Most are equipped with a *solar array* (more than one solar panel grouped to work together). Although the solar panels are expensive, they also have three outstanding advantages:

- ✔ Solar panels are silent because they have no moving parts.
- ✔ Solar panels are relatively maintenance free.
- ✔ Solar panels have a long life.

Wind-powered generators are also available, but are sometimes noisy, potentially hazardous to birds, and require some maintenance. Whether you have a wind generator or solar panels, the power source charges batteries. The batteries may be 12-volt or 24-volt units, and are arranged in a battery bank that powers an inverter. The inverter provides the home with 120-volt AC power.

If you're building a home and plan to install a battery bank and inverter, install it near the beginning of construction. Without an inverter and battery bank, you'll be running a generator all day, every day to provide power for construction activities. With the inverter and battery bank installed, the generator only has to run three or four hours a day to provide round-the-clock power. This spares you from the noise, fuel cost, and generator wear.

Choosing an inverter

Inverters convert the DC power stored in batteries to the AC power that most household appliances need. Inverters for alternative power systems typically range from 500 watts to 5,000 watts. A 500W inverter powers just a few lights and receptacles. The 5,000W inverter can handle the whole house. Inverters typically cost about $1 per watt. Popular voltages for inverter inputs are 12- and 24-volt DC. Better-quality inverters are always vigilant and have a search mode that conserves power. At least one manufacturer's inverter can connect to a second inverter in series, giving you 120-/240-volt power like most utility companies provide.

Usually a generator is connected directly through the inverter. But if you install a manual bypass switch, you can connect your electrical system to the generator in case the inverter fails.

Caring for batteries

If the weather's nasty for a long time, you could run out of power if you rely solely on solar or wind to charge your alternative power system's batteries. For this reason, it's a good idea to also have a generator, just in case. In northern climates, the generator can probably supply most of the power in winter. For these northern applications, an 1,800-RPM water-cooled diesel generator is usually the best choice because it provides longevity and efficiency. We recommend installing a meter to monitor the batteries, and possibly an alarm that automatically starts the generator when the batteries run low. Some inverters include this feature.

Lead-acid storage batteries draw a lot of current while charging, especially when the batteries are very discharged. This draw tapers off as the batteries near full charge. This makes for poor efficiency when using a generator to fully charge batteries. On the other hand, the batteries become *sulfated* if they aren't *topped off* (fully charged) every couple of months. This sulfation permanently robs some of the battery's ability to store a charge. As the battery discharges, the sulfuric acid (H_2SO_4) combines with the lead (PB), leaving lead sulphate ($PbSO_4$) and water (H_2O). If left discharged for three months or more, the $PbSO_4$ becomes set and the SO_4 doesn't completely recombine with the H_2O to get H_2SO_4.

Battery talk

Four 6-volt batteries connected in series add up to 24 volts. A large-capacity 2-volt battery may be two to three times larger than a car battery and weigh more than 200 pounds. A 2-volt, 2,000 ampere-hour battery can cost about $600. *Ampere-hour* is a battery's capacity rating — how much charge it can hold. A typical automobile battery has a 100 ampere-hour rating. A battery's capacity is proportional to the number of plates or amount of plate area immersed in the acid inside the battery. In most cases this means a higher-capacity battery is also physically bigger. We say "in most cases" because some batteries have very large voids in the bottom. Manufacturers may advertise this as an *extra-large sediment chamber.*

A battery's state of charge is measured by a *hydrometer* or *refractometer.* A hydrometer costs about $15, and a refractometer costs about $100. A refractometer — shown in the following figure — is more accurate and much easier to use than a hydrometer. These instruments measure the specific gravity of the battery's electrolyte. The specific gravity of electrolyte in a fully charged lead-acid battery is 1.265. A dead battery has a specific gravity of 1.190. Specific gravities are ratio comparisons of the material's density compared to pure water, which has a specific gravity of 1.0. Reichert, which is online at www.reichert.com, makes refractometers.

Batteries come in these common voltages:

- 2 volts
- 6 volts
- 12 volts

If your power system will be inactive for long periods — for example, your mountainside cabin sits vacant for weeks at a time — a single solar panel can do an excellent job of topping off the batteries and thus reducing or eliminating sulfation.

While charging and especially while equalizing, batteries give off hydrogen (H) gas. (*Equalizing* is the process of fully charging a battery.) Hydrogen, the lightest gas in the universe, is colorless, odorless, and flammable when mixed with air in concentrations of 4 to 75 percent. In concentrations of 15 to 59 percent it's highly explosive. While equalizing, keep the batteries vented and don't smoke near them. Just the spark from disconnecting a booster cable from an automobile battery while it's charging can blow up the battery, as many folks have unfortunately discovered.

A lead-acid battery stored at room temperature will completely self-discharge in about three months. Because chemical reactions slow down at lower temperatures, a battery stored at 0°F will barely show any discharge after being stored for a year. A fully charged battery will freeze at −75°F, while a half-charged battery with a specific gravity of 1200 will freeze at −17°F. So, while batteries hold a charge longer at lower temperatures, they also perform better at warm temperatures (to a point; if battery temperature reaches 125°F, the battery may be ruined).

Store a fully charged battery outside in the cold or in a freezer. If you store the battery outside, remember to disconnect one of the cables. You may have heard an old wives' tale about placing a battery on a board to store it; this isn't necessary.

When you're dealing with lead-acid batteries, remember that acid is *in* — and sometimes *on* — the battery case. If battery acid (also called *electrolyte*) gets on your skin, simply wash it off with water. If you don't wash it off, your skin will become reddened. Acid can burn a hole in your clothes. However, if the acid gets in your eyes, the damage will be much more extensive. Remember to always wear eye protection when handling battery electrolyte.

Electrolyte is diluted sulfuric acid, which is colorless and odorless, and thus easily mistaken for water. You can neutralize sulfuric acid with baking soda. If a battery looks wet, find out if sulfuric acid is present before you handle the battery by sprinkling baking soda on the wet surface. If the moisture contains sulfuric acid, the baking soda will produce a neutralization reaction that can be seen as a fizz.

Part V
Extending Technology to Outdoor Living Spaces

Oh, it's really nice looking. I just thought you'd be more comfortable working in the house.

In this part . . .

Technology doesn't have to stop at the back door. Sunshine, fresh air, and your favorite technologies can be combined with a little effort and some wire. The chapters in this part help you design and wire outdoor places and spaces, light your way across the garden, cook coddled eggs on the patio while watching the sun rise, and surf the Web to be sure it really was a red-necked phalarope that just flew over the rock garden. This part covers solar and low-voltage wiring, along with what it takes to bring electric services, phones, and networks to an outbuilding.

Chapter 16

Wiring Outside the House

- -

In This Chapter

▶ Considering wiring requirements for screened rooms

▶ Powering your deck or patio

▶ Lighting your garden or yard

▶ Wiring outbuildings for light and power

▶ Wiring a sauna building

▶ Powering water pumps for a well or waterfall

- -

Some people like to go outside to get away from all the high-tech complexities of modern life. Some people want to be out in the beautiful weather but are stuck inside, working.

Your digital home doesn't have to end at the exterior walls. If you wish to extend the value and enjoyment of technology to the outdoors, this chapter is for you. Installing some basic wiring for power and other electronic conveniences is easy. In this chapter, we show you how to install devices and wiring in sunrooms, open areas, gardens, outbuildings, and more.

Powering Sunrooms

Sunrooms — also commonly called *screened-in porches, patio enclosures,* and *Florida rooms* — are indoor/outdoor rooms with these features:

- ✔ Coverage by the house's roof
- ✔ One or more doors to the main house
- ✔ One or more doors to a deck, patio, or yard

Typically, two or three walls are shared with the main house and are covered by stucco or other siding material; the other wall(s) are screened, sometimes glassed in, and may have one or more sliding glass doors. The floor in the sunroom may be concrete, teak wood, or outdoor carpeting. To meet electrical code, sunrooms are considered outdoor spaces because at least one side is open to the elements (or only separated from the weather by screens).

Sunrooms allow you to enjoy the outdoor breeze without the bugs, they provide a place for children to play, and they're a nice place to eat in the fresh air. The following sections show you how to wire sunrooms.

Installing power and lighting

You can run wiring in sunrooms much like indoor wiring. Use Romex nonmetallic cable for the wiring on shared walls (walls shared with the main house). You can feed light switches for the sunroom with Romex *if* the switches are inside the home and not in the screened area. Protect switches in the sunroom with weatherproof covers (or weatherproof boxes with weatherproof covers) in the non-shared walls. The wiring to weather-exposed switches must be underground feeder (UF) cable, conduit with rain-tight fittings, or PVC conduit.

Other electrical components in the sunroom also need special consideration:

- ✔ **Lighting fixtures:** The fixtures should be marked for use in damp locations. Any fixtures marked for use in wet locations can also be used here. Most recessed fixtures are suitable for use in damp locations, but always check the specifications to be sure.

- ✔ **Electrical receptacles:** Any receptacles mounted on an exterior house wall can use indoor wiring methods (such as Romex) but must be protected by weatherproof covers. Electrical receptacles installed on exposed walls must be fed by UF cable or conduit. The receptacles must have weatherproof covers and be GFI protected.

- ✔ **Circuit loading:** If you're only considering a few light fixtures, you can power them from one of the house circuits. If you only have a few receptacles, you can connect them to the exterior outlet circuit. However, if the sunroom has a lot of outlets or you plan to install appliances that draw a lot of current, run a separate circuit from the panel just for this area.

- ✔ **Electrical devices and appliances:** A lot of the equipment and appliances popular in sunrooms aren't rated for damp-area use. These items may include TVs, computers, radios, and electric grills. Move these things into the house on rainy days, or at least cover and unplug them.

Bringing entertainment to the sunroom

For fun in the shade, you may want to bring some of your electronic entertainment and communication systems out to the sunroom.

Consider first the audio speakers. Ideally, you should use weatherproof speakers in any exposed area. However, because weather exposure in a sunroom should be minimal, you can get away with installing standard speakers if you recess them a few inches from the surface of the ceiling. Keep the speakers; make sure the speaker installation area doesn't get damp.

If you want to install an intercom in your sunroom (see Chapter 7 for more on intercom systems), use the same type of station designed for exposed door-answering units. These units are inexpensive and weather resistant. Mount the intercom unit flush in a common wall with the house, and wire to it using standard indoor wiring.

You can install TV cable outlets, network drops, and phone outlets in sunrooms if you do so on a common wall with the house. Again, use standard indoor wiring. You must also install weatherproof plates on these receptacles. If the installation location is exposed to the elements, use wire such as underground feeder (UF), which is approved for damp locations. The boxes should be weatherproof as well.

Electrifying Patios and Decks

Patios and decks don't usually have roofs, and they may only share one wall with the house, if not be completely detached from the home. Because of the increased exposure, wiring to patios and decks is a little more challenging than wiring a sunroom. But don't let the added challenge stop you from adding some power outlets or lighting to your decks and patios! At a bare minimum you will probably want an electrical outlet to plug in a griddle or rotisserie for the gas grill.

If the patio is adjacent to the house, the easiest solution for power is to use GFI-protected receptacles on an exterior house wall. If the patio is away from the house or the layout requires power at the patio's outside edge, follow these steps:

1. **Run UF Romex underground from the house to the receptacle location.**

   The Romex should be buried at least 18". The wire can be directly buried.

2. **Install a 4" × 4" treated post in the ground on which to mount the receptacle.**

   For detailed installation, see the text accompanying Figure 16-1. If you can use an existing post, such as a roof or deck rail support, you don't need to install one.

3. **Mount a weatherproof box on the post (or on the existing roof or deck railing).**

   The wire from the switch to the light in Figure 16-1 goes out the back of the weatherproof switch box via a hole drilled through the post at a downward angle. The angle prevents water from running into the switch box.

4. **Install PVC conduit from the box down to below grade, and run the wire through the conduit up to the box.**

5. **Install a GFI receptacle in the box, and use a waterproof outlet cover.**

In addition to a power receptacle, you may want to include some lighting for your deck or patio. If you have a roof overhead, you may want follow the sunroom example and use recessed lighting on a dimmer switch. Just make sure that any switch you use on a deck or patio is equipped with a weatherproof cover.

An inexpensive yet very functional installation is shown in Figure 16-1. Here, a simple 4" × 4" treated post has been installed with two receptacles and a light fixture next to a picnic area at a remote cottage. The mostly transparent "in use" cover is open to show the two receptacles. The wire is then stapled to the back of the post, out of site in this view. Through another hole drilled at an upward angle, the wire enters the light fixture's box. A PVC conduit protects the UF Romex to about 1' underground. For stability, the 4" × 4" post extends about 2' into the ground. The light fixture has a base slightly wider than the post, making it necessary to install a square piece of treated plywood so that the fixture fits flush.

To stabilize the 4" × 4" post in Figure 16-1, a 3'-long treated 2" × 6" board is fastened horizontally to the post with galvanized or stainless-steel screws, forming a T. The 2" × 6" is buried just a few inches below grade. This makes for a very stable installation once all the holes are backfilled. This stabilization method saves you from having to buy and mix concrete. Use a bubble level to make sure the 4" × 4" is straight before backfilling.

Figure 16-1:
This installation brings light and power to an outdoor area.

Lighting Your Garden

Gardens don't have to be enjoyed exclusively in daylight. With some accent lighting you can beautify your yard and gardens at night as well. Garden lights are usually powered by either solar cells or electrical power. Shop around to see which type fits your needs and budget. In this section, we focus on low-voltage lights that run on electrical power, because those lights require special wiring consideration.

Most garden lights are 12 volts. This means that your system must have a transformer that transforms the 120/240-volt power from your house to the 12-volt power used by the lights. As you plan your garden lighting, you have to select a transformer that can handle the load that the system uses. To plan and install your garden lighting, follow these steps:

1. **Select a transformer that can handle more than the total load of all your lights.**

   Most garden light fixtures range from 4 to 50 watts per light. Add up the total wattage required by all the lights, and then choose a transformer with a higher-rated capacity. Also, make sure you choose a transformer designed for damp areas; most garden-light transformers are rated for weather exposure.

An oversized transformer doesn't cost any more money to operate. A 1,000-watt transformer with 200W of lighting connected to it draws close to the 200W load. We recommend limiting the load on the transformer to a maximum of 80 percent of its rated wattage capacity.

2. **Choose low-voltage wiring that can handle the amperage drawn by your lights.**

   At 12 volts, a 50W lamp draws 4.2 amps. Self-sealing, moisture-resistant, low-voltage cable comes in the following sizes and the maximum wattage for each is shown here:

   - 16 AWG: 150 watts maximum

   - 14 AWG: 200 watts maximum

   - 12 AWG: 300 watts maximum

   Total up the wattage as you wire in the lamps, being careful not to exceed the wire's rated capacity. Each pair of wires can power as many lamps as you like, but don't go over the wire's or transformer's capacity.

3. **Install the wiring between the transformer and lights.**

   For large lamp loads, run several wires to groups of lights or install multiple transformers.

   Low-voltage garden-light wiring has no minimum burial depth. You can run it on the surface, but consider burying it at least a few inches for appearance and safety. When burying the wire, run it where you're not going to damage it while tending your garden. Running the wire next to the building or along the sidewalk edge may help you remember where it is many months after installation. You may want to diagram the wiring, especially if someone else ever helps pick weeds.

4. **Connect the transformer to a GFI-protected, weatherproof outlet.**

How are you going to control those lights? You can turn garden lights on and off manually, with timers, or with light sensors. See Chapter 5 for more on controls and automation.

Delivering Electricity to Outbuildings

Most *outbuildings* fall into one of two popular categories: unattached garages and pole barns. *Pole barns* tend to have dirt or gravel floors, while garages usually have cement floors. But no matter what kind of outbuilding you have — a guest cottage, office, studio, or yurt — running power to outbuildings on your property must be done carefully, especially if you plan to run high-load equipment like compressors, air conditioners, and welders in the building.

As with a house electrical service (see Chapter 2), you must be able to turn off outbuilding power with six or fewer hand operations. You can bring power to outbuildings numerous ways; we cover five of these. Each method is defined by the size and type of wire used to feed the service. The five methods follow. See Chapter 2 for definitions of wire types.

- ✔ **12-2 or 10-2 with ground UF Romex:** Run from the house panel to a single-pole switch for the outbuilding, and then wire from that switch to the building's lighting and receptacles. The single-pole switch satisfies the disconnect requirement. The burial depth for 12-2 or 10-2 UF Romex is a minimum of 12" below grade when fed from a 20-amp GFI circuit. If the circuit isn't GFI protected, the burial depth must be at least 18". The maximum power available from this method is only 2,400 watts.

- ✔ **12-3 or 10-3 UF with ground Romex:** Run from the house panel to a two-pole switch for the outbuilding, and then wire from the switch to the lighting, receptacles, and equipment powering the building. The two-pole switch satisfies the disconnect requirement. An 18" burial depth is required. For this option, the feeder is 20-amp, 240-volt service fed from a two-pole breaker in the house panel. Maximum power available from this method is increased to 4,800 watts.

  In either of the preceding options, you can use a 30-amp breaker for the outbuilding if the feeder wire is 10 AWG. If the feeder is 30 amp, you must put a breaker panel in the outbuilding with either 15- or 20-amp breakers to supply the lighting and outlets. 14 AWG or 12 AWG wire should supply the circuits within the outbuilding; 10 AWG feeder wire has less voltage drop than smaller-gauge wire.

- ✔ **2/2/4 or 2/2/2** *Underground Residential Distribution (URD)* **aluminum cable:** Run this cable from the house panel to a service panel in the outbuilding. The outbuilding panel usually has a 100-amp rating. The panel has to be either a main lug panel with fewer than six circuit breakers, or a panel with a main disconnect to satisfy the disconnect requirement. The neutral connection bar in this panel must be bonded (using the supplied bond screw) to panel. You must ground this panel by connecting it to the water piping (if present) and with ground rods as detailed in Chapter 2. The URD cable must be run in PVC or rigid conduit in any exposed areas. An 18" burial depth is required for direct burial cable. Maximum power available from this method is a whopping 24,000 watts.

  The panel in the house that feeds the outbuilding panel should have a two-pole breaker on the feeder line. This breaker should be rated for 100 amps or fewer. We generally use a 40-, 50-, or 60-amp breaker. These sizes accommodate 2 AWG wire and cost about the same. Of course 70-, 80-, 90-, or 100-amp breakers also accommodate 2 AWG wire, but each one is progressively more expensive. Use a larger breaker only if you need that much power.

- ✔ **4/0-4/0-2/0 or 4/0-4/0-4/0 URD aluminum cable:** Like the preceding option, this involves a run from the house panel to a service panel in the garage or outbuilding. All of the grounding and cable-protection provisions mentioned for 2/2/4 and 2/2/2 runs apply here as well. A panel fed by 4/0-4/0-2/0 or 4/0-4/0-4/0 URD cable has a 150- or 200-amp rating. The feeder breakers in sizes larger than 100 amps use four spaces in the house panel. Maximum power available from this method is a watt-hour meter spinning 48,000 watts.

✔ **Overhead or underground service installed on the garage or outbuilding:** You can have electric service installed directly to the outbuilding, as described for residences in Chapter 2. In some cases this is the only electric service on the property, and the house is powered from the outbuilding. If the utility service connects to your outbuilding first, in the outbuilding install a feed-through panel rated at 125, 150, or 200 amps. Maximum power available from this method is 48,000 watts.

Figure 16-2 shows conduit passing through the home's perimeter framing and down the side of the home's foundation. The conduit ends between a few inches and a foot underground. On the outbuilding, the wiring normally doesn't run on the exterior — you bring it up through a piece of conduit in the building floor as shown in Figure 16-2. A 90-degree sweep elbow brings the cable up from its horizontal run. Install this conduit prior to pouring any foundation slab. The conduit can range in size from ¾" to 2", depending on the wire feeder you use.

If you use the last wiring option given in the preceding bulleted list (the 4/0 option), you may use a 200-amp, eight circuit, weatherproof Square D like the one shown in Figure 16-3. Square D makes this panel in 125-, 150-, and 200-amp sizes. Notice the two large feed-through lugs on the bottom of the black removable interior. These lugs are connected to the incoming large lugs on top through the 200-amp breaker. The incoming and outgoing neutrals are connected to the two center lugs on top. This outbuilding panel is fed directly from the utility company through an overhead or underground meter socket to the panel.

Retrofitting power to existing outbuildings

It's possible to retrofit electrical service in an existing outbuilding, although the installation obviously isn't as easy as with new construction. Your first challenge is getting power into the outbuilding. If the building has a concrete floor, you have to use a large roto-hammer to drill a hole in the concrete to accommodate the feeder wire.

It isn't necessary to install a conduit in the drilled hole through the concrete, but a conduit should start where the wire protrudes from the concrete. Stabilize the conduit by fastening a hub to the concrete or to a piece of treated lumber into which you have drilled a hole to accommodate the conduit. Fasten the treated lumber to the floor using concrete nails or anchor bolts, or by using a power driver.

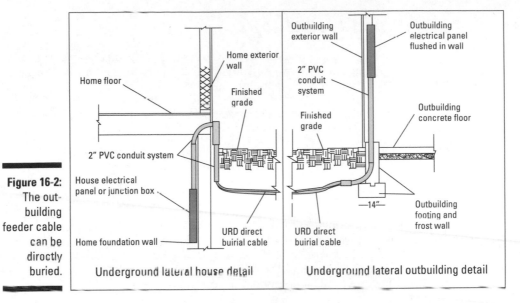

Figure 16-2:
The out-
building
feeder cable
can be
directly
buried.

Home floor

Home exterior
wall

Finished
grade

2" PVC conduit system

House electrical
panel or junction box

Home foundation wall

URD direct
buirial cable

Underground lateral house detail

Outbuilding
exterior wall

Outbuilding
electrical panel
flushed in wall

2" PVC
conduit
system

Finished
grade

Outbuilding
concrete floor

URD direct
buirial cable

14"

Outbuilding
footing and
frost wall

Underground lateral outbuilding detail

Figure 16-3:
This
200-amp
Square D 200
panel can be
installed in
your out-
building.

Wiring in workshops

Believe it or not, the National Electrical Code doesn't specify where your outlets should be and how many you should have in garages and outbuildings. We suggest the following for installing outlets:

- ✔ **Garage:** Install at least one receptacle on each wall, except for the wall with the garage door.

- ✔ **Workshop:** In a work area (whether in a garage or a separate outbuilding), install several outlets or a couple of quad-density outlets per wall. You may also want to include some 15- or 20-amp 120-volt combination receptacles.

Some 120-volt equipment draws more than 12 amps; they have 20-amp plugs. The maximum draw for a tool or appliance is 80 percent of the connecting cord's rating. Eighty percent of 15 amps is 12 amps, and 80 percent of 20 amps is 16 amps. Any 120-volt device requiring more than 1,440 watts (12 amps × 120 volts) must use a 20-amp rated or larger plug, or it may use 240 volts.

All 15- and 20-amp 120-volt receptacles in garages and outbuildings must be GFI protected. The receptacle for the garage door opener is exempt from this requirement.

If you plan to use any 240-volt equipment, install 15- or 20-amp combination receptacles fed by 12-2 Romex. Figure 16-4 shows a 240-volt 15/20-amp duplex receptacle. The 240-volt receptacle is on the left. The receptacle in the middle is a standard 15-amp, 120-volt receptacle, and the receptacle on the right is a 120-volt 15/20-amp combination receptacle. This type of 120-volt receptacle is easily confused with the 240-volt receptacle because they're mirror images of each other. Also shown in Figure 16-4 are the four cord-matching end configurations that plug into each receptacle.

Sizing conductors for welders in workshops

If you plan to do any welding in your workshop, you have some wiring decisions to make. Welders have current multipliers that allow reducing the size of the conductors that feed them. This multiplier is based on the welder's duty cycle. Most consumer welders have a duty cycle of 20 percent. The current multiplier for a welder with a 20-percent duty cycle is .45.

For calculating welder supply conductors using the electrical code's allowable derating multipliers, you need the following:

```
Name Plate Current Rating × Derating Multiplier =
          Allowable Conductor Current Rating
```

15 amp 240 volt

15 amp 120 volt

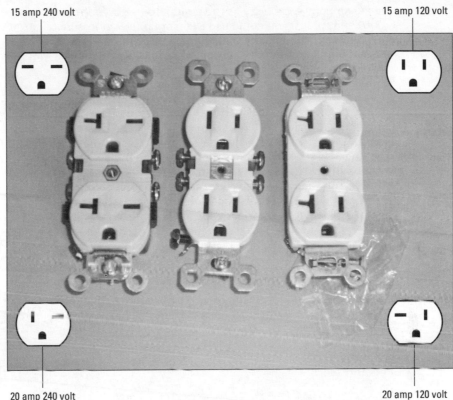

Figure 16-4:
These 120-
and 240-volt
receptacles
are common
(and not-so-
common).

20 amp 240 volt

20 amp 120 volt

For example, if the name plate rating on a welder with a 20-percent duty cycle is 50 amps, you multiply the 50 amps times .45 to get 22.5 amps. The conductor size for 22.5 amps is 12 AWG wire. The 75°C current rating for 12 AWG wire is 25 amps. This size wire is the minimum.

The welder's duty cycle is determined by the manufacturer and is required to be indicated on the electrical rating tag or name plate. The *duty cycle* is the number of minutes in a ten-minute period that the welder can produce current without overheating. A 20-percent–rated welder can be used two minutes out of ten.

The code allows you to use a circuit breaker as large as 200 percent of the welder's rated primary current. You can use a breaker in the range of 20 to 100 amps in the panel feeding the 12 AWG wire to the welder receptacle. The welder receptacle would be rated 50 amps to accommodate the factory-installed 50-amp plug. The code allows this plug and receptacle to be the same amperage capacity as the conductor, so if you're supplying your own cord end (plug), you could use a 20-amp plug. On this installation we suggest using wire a little heaver than the minimum allowed and using a much smaller breaker than the maximum permitted. The welder would have a 10 AWG wire fed with a 40- or 50-amp breaker.

Using a breaker that's too large can be dangerous. In Color Plate 15 (shown in the color insert pages in this book), the tip of a soldering gun has been replaced by a piece of 12 AWG wire. I pulled the trigger and measured the current with a clamp-on ammeter. Initially the current was about 115 amps, but in a few seconds it had dropped to 98.1 amps, as shown in the figure. Although the trigger was only on for a few seconds, the wire was too hot to touch. You want the circuit breaker to trip long before the wire is heated to the point where its insulation is destroyed. Most breakers trip in about an hour if just slightly overloaded, and that's plenty of time to protect the wire if the breaker rating is 200 percent or less of the conductor rating. Carrying 100 amps on a 12 AWG wire is 400 percent of the conductor rating.

Sizing conductors for air compressors in workshops

If your work requires an air compressor, some wiring decisions are in your future. Compressors also have a current multiplier to determine the conductor current rating.

Unlike welders, using these multipliers is mandatory. Use this formula for a compressor:

```
Name Plate Full Load Current × 125 Percent = Current Wire
            Rating
```

For example, the full load current rating of a 5 HP compressor is 28 amps. To calculate the proper conductor current rating, you multiply the 28 amps times 1.25; you get 35 amps. The 75°C rating of 10 AWG wire is 35 amps. A 10 AWG wire is the minimum conductor in this case. The circuit breaker rating can be as much as 250 percent of the name plate full load current rating. In this case, we have 28 amps times 2.50, giving us 70. You could use a maximum of a 70-amp breaker on this compressor.

Sometimes you need the larger breaker on a motor to prevent false tripping from the motor's high starting current. In this case we suggest using a 60-amp breaker because it's more common than the 70-amp breaker, and the 70-amp breaker costs twice as much. Square D breakers sized from 15 to 60 amps are the same price.

Lighting outbuildings

You're probably going to want to install some lighting inside and outside your outbuilding, whether it's a garage or pole barn.

If your detached garage has power, code requires you to have a switch-controlled light that illuminates the exterior of the entrance door, sometimes referred to as the *man door*. (The code doesn't consider an overhead garage door to be an entrance door.) This outside fixture is typically a coach light. The required switch for the exterior lights may also control the interior lights if you wish.

You have some options when it comes to choosing interior light fixtures:

- ✔ Porcelain lamp with an incandescent bulb
- ✔ Fluorescent tube

Fluorescent lights usually give better light and are more energy efficient.

If you install florescent lights in an outbuilding in colder climates, use high-output florescent fixtures with low-temperature ballasts. We recommend florescent fixtures that hold two high-output 8' lamps. Four of these fixtures installed in a 24' × 24' building gives an average lighting intensity level of 80 footcandles at the floor. (1 footcandle is equal to the light intensity from a burning candle at a distance of 1'.) Eighty footcandles is plenty for most uses. See Chapter 10 for more about lighting.

To control your lighting, you may want to install a three-way switch between the house and the outbuilding. You can leave the switch on to light your way to the house at night. We describe three-way light switches in Chapter 4, but because you're wiring between the house and an outbuilding, you must take into account two special considerations:

- ✔ Run a three-conductor UF cable between the switch box in the house and the lighting circuit in the outbuilding. Alternatively, you could install an X10-style remote control, as described in Chapter 5.

- ✔ Code requires that you be able to turn off all power in the outbuilding at its service disconnect location. Any three-way outbuilding switches in the house must receive power from an outbuilding circuit, not from a house circuit. You can meet this code requirement in the house if the home-service disconnect kills the outbuilding power. If the house and outbuilding are fed from independent services, one of the three-way switches is going to bring power to one of the buildings that can't be turned off by killing the power to that building. This three-way switch should be plainly marked that it receives power independently. This alerts workmen that the switch remains energized even if this building's power is turned off.

Installing network, phone, TV, and intercom service

Just because your outbuilding is away from the house doesn't mean you have to forgo things like telephone, computer networks, cable TV, and intercoms. When adding any of these communications systems to your outbuilding, follow these installation tips:

- ✔ Use direct burial UF-rated communications cables for the runs between your house and the outbuilding.

- ✔ You can bury the communications cable in the same trench as power wires; however, at least 1' of separation should be between the power wires and other low-voltage wires. The low-voltage communication wires are installed after partially backfilling the trench over the electrical power wires.

- ✔ If you install the wires in conduit, use rigid, IMC, or PVC conduit. PVC conduit is the cheapest and easiest to work with.

    Even if you use a conduit, the wiring must be rated for direct burial because conduit isn't considered waterproof.

- ✔ All low-voltage systems can share the same conduit with each other, but *never* include the low-voltage wires in the same conduit as the electrical feeds.

For network, phone, TV, and intercom wiring inside the outbuilding, follow the same rough-in procedures used for in-home installations. You may use burial-rated wire for interior installations in outbuildings.

Wiring for sheds

In potting or storage sheds, you may need to use any or all of the following devices:

- ✔ Vacuum cleaner
- ✔ Small power tools
- ✔ Task lighting
- ✔ Fixed or overhead lighting
- ✔ Dehumidifier or heater
- ✔ Refrigerator

Many of the very small buildings would be adequately served by using 12-2 or 10-2 with ground UF Romex to run from the house panel to a single-pole switch for the outbuilding, and then wiring from that switch to the building's lighting and receptacles. This wiring option is covered in the "Delivering Electricity to Outbuildings" section, earlier in this chapter.

Sometimes, you're faced with the dilemma of having to run two pieces of equipment simultaneously and wondering if a single 20-amp circuit will be enough. As we stated earlier in this chapter, any electrical item with a standard 15-amp plug draws a maximum of 80 percent of 12 or 15 amps. By plugging in two items that draw the maximum 12 amps, you have 24 amps on the 20-amp breaker feeding this usage. In this example, the breaker may trip after 30 minutes to 1 hour, or it may never trip. The breaker does protect the circuit conductors, so trying this isn't problematic if tripping a breaker is just a nuisance. If you recognize this challenge in the design stage, we recommend bringing in enough power to handle all the loads with some capacity to spare.

Installing Saunas

Saunas generally have two rooms: one for changing and the other for steaming. Some designs may also include a third room for a shower. Figure 16-5 shows a typical sauna layout including a shower and toilet in separate rooms. This sample layout has ventilation fans in the shower and in the changing room. Individual switches, separate from the lighting switches, control these fans. The sauna building needs circuits for lighting and receptacles, as well as a circuit for an electric sauna stove. The best way to accomplish this is to install a separate 100-amp service panel for the sauna building, as described earlier in this chapter.

The steam portion of a sauna can involve temperatures of 145°F to 194°F. Some people like to run from a sauna and jump into cold water or roll in some snow for a fast cool down, while others prefer a slower cool-down period. Although saunas have been used and enjoyed since about the year 1100 across many cultures, high temperatures and extreme temperature changes are unsafe for some people. Before building, buying, and using a sauna, check with your physician to make sure that a sauna is safe for you.

Selecting a sauna stove

The size of the circuit you need for the sauna stove depends on the stove's current rating. The stove size — expressed in kilowatts (KW) — depends on the steam room cubic volume. A 6' × 8' room that has an 8'-high ceiling has a volume of 384 cubic feet. You need about 1 KW for every 50 cubic feet of room volume. In this example, a 384-cubic-foot room needs 7.68 KW, so you should choose a sauna stove with a rating of 7 or 8 KW. Choosing the right size stove is an important step in planning your sauna. An improperly sized stove will be difficult, if not impossible, to properly control.

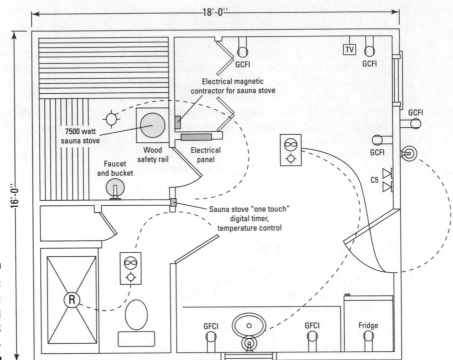

Figure 16-5:
Your sauna
outbuilding
may look
like this.

For our 384-cubic-foot sauna, we chose a 7.5 KW ILO-brand stove made by
A&L Fabricating of Dollar Bay, Michigan. The manufacturer says this stove
will service a sauna steam room from 217 to 420 cubic feet. Dividing 7,500
watts (7.5 KW) by the circuit voltage of 240 equals a 31.25-amp load. Because
this is a continuous load, we must multiply the current times 125 percent to
determine the conductor size. 125 percent of 31.25 amps is 39 amps. This
means that a 40-amp breaker and 8 AWG should be used to supply the stove.

Here are the formulas to plug into:

```
Stove Wattage ÷ Circuit Voltage = Amp Load

Current × 125 Percent = Conductor Size
```

Any load expected to be on for three hours or more is considered *continuous*.

Supplying power

The sauna building should use a 6-circuit, 120/240-volt, 100-amp electrical panel. The panel should have a two-pole 40-amp circuit for the sauna stove, a 15-amp lighting circuit, and a 20-amp receptacle circuit. To install the panel and electrical service, follow these general steps:

1. **Install the electrical panel flush with the closet wall with the front of the panel facing the changing room.**

   In these steps, we assume the layout for the sauna you're constructing is similar to the one shown in Figure 16-5.

2. **Place the stove's contactor in the closet.**

   The *contactor* is a control relay that provides power to the sauna stove's heating element when the digital thermostat calls for more heat. The contactor is supplied with a painted enclosure. Mounting the contactor in the closet makes it easy to run 8-3 Romex from the electrical panel to the 4" × 4" box in the steam room that the stove is wired to. This box needs a two-gang plaster ring with a raise to match the wall finish. Mount the box about 1' above the floor behind the sauna stove. Both the box and the plaster ring should be metal to ensure a good ground on the stainless steel plate that you install when connecting the stove later.

3. **Connect high-temperature wire between the contactor and the stove's heating elements.**

   The stove manufacturer provides about 6' of high-temperature wire connected to the heating elements and a ground wire. These wires come out of a threaded hole in the lower part of the stove, near the base. The wires are enclosed in about 2' of flexible, weatherproof metal conduit (such as Sealtite) which you supply. Install a stainless-steel blank plate on the plaster ring, and punch a hole through which to connect the conduit.

4. **Calculate the sauna's lighting and receptacle load.**

   Consider the total *volt amps (VA)* for everything in the building. In the example shown in this chapter we have a 288 square feet building. For a sauna building, calculate the general building current load at 3 VA per square foot. This gives a total load of 864 VA. With a 120/240-volt service, divide the total volt amps by the 240 volts, which equals 3.6; then round up to 4.0. This adds 4 amps to the feeder wires' load. Adding the sauna stove's calculated load of 39 amps (from the preceding section) brings the total load to 43 amps. To accommodate the 43-amp load, you need a minimum of a 50-amp breaker to power the feeder to the sauna building.

Installing the sauna stove control

High-quality sauna stoves should include an electronic digital thermostatic control. To complete installation of the sauna and controller, follow these steps:

1. **Install a three-gang electrical box outside the entrance to the steam room to house the controller.**

2. **Run the low-voltage wiring for the controller between the stove's contactor and three-gang box.**

   The manufacturer should provide the control wiring with the stove.

3. **Mount the thermistor in the steam room.**

   The *thermistor (thermo-resistor)* is a heat-reactive resistor that monitors and reports the temperature to the stove control.

Figure 16-6 shows a 9-kilowatt ILO sauna stove, contactor, digital controller, and coils of control wire. The controller is push-button with a digital readout.

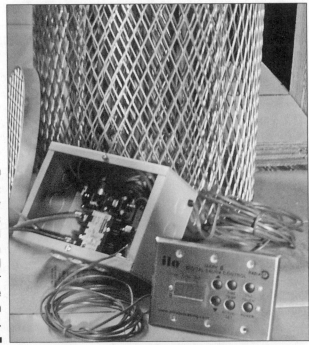

Figure 16-6:
High-quality saunas should include a digital controller and all the installation wiring.

Wiring near Pools and Hot Tubs

Homeowners don't normally install their own pools. You may, however, want to make some improvements to or near existing pools or hot tubs.

With all the aquatic frolicking that occurs in and around pools, it should come as no surprise that electricity must follow stringent requirements near pools:

- ✔ Anything electrical within 20' of a pool must be GFI protected.

- ✔ A GFI-protected receptacle must be in the pool area. The receptacle must be at least 10' but not more than 20' from the pool wall.

- ✔ Any light switches in the pool area must be 5' or more from the pool, and they must be GFI protected.

- ✔ No light fixtures are to be installed over a pool, or over a 5' border zone around the pool.

- ✔ No sound equipment or speakers supplied by 120-volt power can be located within 5' of a pool.

- ✔ Overhead service conductors must be at least 10' horizontally from the edge of the pool walls

Unlike pools, homeowners often install hot tubs. Regardless of where you install your hot tub — on a deck, on a patio, or inside a building — some electrical requirements must be met.

Some hot tubs are dual-voltage or triple-voltage rated. They operate on 120, 208, or 240 volts. Most hot tubs are actually 240-volt appliances, but if they are supplied with less voltage, the heater capacity is reduced. Hot tub pumps usually run on 120 volts. The heater element resistance is not linear. A heater that draws 4 KW at 240 volts draws only about 1 KW at 120 volts. When calculating the electrical feeder requirements for the hot tub, you have to decide what voltage to use and then check the manufacturer's current rating for that voltage. The tub manufacturer specifies the circuit size you need for each allowable voltage.

Some hot tub manufacturers use two 120-volt, 2 KW heaters connected in series, yielding a total draw of 240 volts. In 120-volt operation, only one of these heaters is used. This gives the tub a 2 KW rating at 120 volts and a current draw of 16.6 amps. You must use a 20-amp, 120-volt GFI outlet because the current exceeds the allowable for a standard 15-amp receptacle.

Once you determine the feeder size for your hot tub, you have to actually install the feeder circuit. Special considerations follow:

- Regardless of the location of the tub, the wire must be rated for the installation chosen.

- You must install a power disconnect for the tub. The disconnect must be easily accessible and within sight of the hot tub; however, it must also be at least 5' away from the tub.

- The tub circuit must be GFI protected unless the tub is certified to have integral GFI protection.

- You may want 120-volt power near the tub for sound systems or weatherproof spa entertainment centers. Power and cable TV wiring must be rated for outdoor use. AT least 5' must be between 120-volt receptacles and the hot tub. As well, your entertainment equipment must also be at least 5' away from the hot tub and must be GFI protected.

- Any receptacles located within 10' of the hot tub must be GFI protected.

Pumping Water on Your Property

If your home isn't on a city water system, you probably have an electric well pump supplying water pressure for your plumbing. You may also have other kinds of water pumps around your property, such as those for garden waterfalls or built-up waste drain fields. The following sections introduce you to the special issues you must consider when installing different kinds of water pumps.

Powering well pumps

Submersible pumps are one of the few electrical installations that don't require a within-sight disconnect. Also, unlike most other wiring you do near water, pump wiring isn't GFI protected because of the likelihood of false trips. The wire down the well casing to the pump is usually a twisted, open, waterproof conductor supplied by the well-drilling company. The wire supplying power to the pump runs to the pump along with the water supply line, and the wiring enters the house with the supply line as well. A disconnect is required at this location to service the pressure switch.

The wiring must suit the pump voltage, length of the run, and depth of the installation. Short to moderate runs may use 12-2 or 10-2 UF Romex, but no matter how long the run, you should carefully calculate the size needed. Smaller wire causes more voltage drop. You want to keep the voltage drop to less than 5 percent of the circuit voltage.

The formula for calculating voltage drop over copper wire follows:

```
(2 × Length in Feet) × Amps × 10.4 ÷ CMA = Voltage Drop
```

Multiply by 2 the length of the run in feet from the service panel in the house all the way to the pump — including the run from the house to the pump, and the wire running down the well to the pump itself. Now multiply this by the pump's amp rating, multiply by 10.4 (the voltage drop constant for copper wire), and divide it all by the Circular Mill Area (CMA) of the wire. The CMA for 12 AWG is 6,530. The CMA of 10 AWG is 10,380. For example, this is the calculation for a 150' run to a 20-amp pump using 10 AWG wire:

```
(2 × 150) × 20 × 10.4 ÷ 10,380 = 6 volts
```

The calculation for a 150' run to a 20-amp pump using 12 AWG wire follows:

```
(2 × 150) × 20 × 10.4 ÷ 6,530 = 10 volts
```

A 240 volt ¼ horsepower pump running at full load draws about 5 amps. The full load starting current may be as high as 20 amps. If the total power run is 150', the voltage to the motor is reduced from the 240 to 230 volts with 12 AWG wire, or 234 volts with 10 AWG wire.

Figure 16-7 shows a typical wiring installation for a submersible pump with a schematic diagram inserted on the left. Follow these steps to install the wiring for your pump:

1. **Run the UF Romex wire from the pump along the water supply line though the wall to the location for the 4" × 4" box.**

   The wire should enter the house along with the water line and continue unbroken to the pressure switch.

2. **Mount a 4" × 4" box and pull the pump wire and the power wire from the panel into the back of the box.**

   In Figure 16-7, a handy box has been used instead of a 4" × 4" box.

3. **Install a ¾" flexible conduit between the 4" × 4" and tank pressure switch.**

   This conduit will contain the two wires from the pump, a pair of load wires from the switch, and a ground wire.

4. **Connect the wires from the pump and the load wires from the toggle switch to the tank pressure switch.**

   The pressure switch turns the pump on when the water pressure reaches the low-set level; it turns the pump off when the water pressure reaches the high-set level. This action maintains the pressure within the desired *pounds per square inch (PSI)* range. The pressure tank shown on the right in Figure 16-7 reduces the frequency of pump cycling. Because the inlet and outlet are in the tank bottom, a volume of air is compressed as the tank fills. This compressed air supplies the pressure until the pressure drops below the low-pressure setting; then the pump turns on again, repeating the process.

5. **Connect the power wires from the panel and the load wires to the pressure switch to the two-pole toggle switch mounted in the 4" × 4" box.**

6. **Connect the four ground wires together and install the toggle switch mounted on the 4" × 4" raised cover.**

   If you can only see three ground wires, you forgot to add a ground pigtail to ground the 4" × 4" box.

The two-pole switch turns the pump off for maintenance work or when you don't need it for long periods of time. During normal operation the tank pressure switch turns the pump on and off to meet the demand for water.

If you look closely at the wiring diagram in Figure 16-7 you can see that if the power-in wires and the pump wires are reversed, the system would still work. That's because there are two double-pole switches in series. If both switches are on, the pump will work. However, hooking up the wiring backwards defeats an important function of the switch, which is to cut off power to the pressure switch for maintenance.

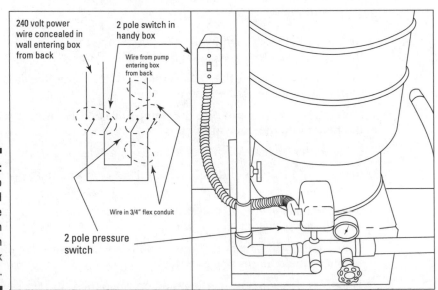

Figure 16-7: The pump wiring and pressure switch installation should look like this.

240 volt power wire concealed in wall entering box from back

2 pole switch in handy box

Wire from pump entering box from back

Wire in 3/4" flex conduit

2 pole pressure switch

Installing garden and waterfall pumps

Small waterfall pumps are usually in small lined pools or 5-gallon plastic buckets. The pumps are usually supplied with a 6' power cord.

To power a waterfall or other garden pump, install a GFI receptacle near the pump location. You can install this receptacle on a short piece of treated 2" × 4" just above ground level. The receptacle should use a weatherproof box and an in-use weatherproof cover. An *in-use cover* is hooded, keeping the receptacle dry when the cord is plugged in. The circuit to this receptacle should be supplied with 12-2 UF Romex.

As with other garden wiring, code requires a burial depth of at least 12" for pump receptacles if the conductors are protected by a GFI, and 18" if not protected by a GFI. This prevents the wire from being damaged by power tillers or other garden tools.

You may also want to light your garden waterfall. See the earlier section, "Lighting Your Garden," for more information.

Using waste system pumps

Some homes may have a built-up or engineered drain field to which waste-water must be pumped. These pumps are also sometimes called *lift stations.* Such drain fields are usually mandated by the County Health Department if the grade-level soil doesn't *percolate* (or pass liquid through a porous substance) sufficiently. Improper percolation is normally due to a high water level in the area. When the County Health Department does its *perk test,* it's assessing the soil's ability to drain.

Wastewater pumps are sometimes equipped with alarms to alert you to a problem. The alarm is a good feature, and required by building codes in most states. When shopping for a waste pump, look for one that has an alarm or can have an alarm easily added. These pumps are usually about 1/2 horsepower and operate at 120 volts. Supply them with a 20-amp circuit fed by 12-3 UF Romex. The alarm circuit usually requires two more conductors to connect to a failure-alarm float switch.

Chapter 17

Outdoor Electronics

· ·

In This Chapter

▶ Bringing stereo to the patio

▶ Waterproofing power outlets for the deck or patio

▶ Selecting outdoor speakers

▶ Putting in a home weather station

· ·

*I*t seems that way too much time is spent indoors these days, and one reason may be because computers, TVs, and video games are inside. But you can use many types of electronic devices outside. Technology has come a long way since the first battery operated picnic-table TVs, and you can have your electronic cake and eat it, too.

In this chapter we discuss some of the devices you can use outside, special product choice considerations, and outdoor wiring. We cover some practical considerations and ideas for bringing some elements of the digital age to your patio.

Designing around the Weather

When installing wiring for electronic devices outside the home, make sure that the wiring is safe, provides reliable connections, and is attractive (or at least inconspicuous). Two basic strategies exist for bringing power and communications wiring to the great outdoors:

▶ **Overhead:** Overhead wiring is usually less than ideal, not only because it's unsightly but also because you must maintain at least 10' of clearance underneath. However, overhead runs may be okay if they run under eaves or along porch or deck rails.

> ✔ **Underground:** For most outside installations, underground is usually the best choice. Underground cables are out of sight and out of mind.

When running overhead or underground wiring, make sure the cable is approved for the specific installation. All outdoor cabling should be waterproof. If it will be run overhead, it should be rated for sunlight exposure; if run underground, it should be rated for direct burial.

Running wires in bulkheads

One way to protect your wiring from the weather is to use a protective barrier such as a wall or roof. Such barriers are often called *bulkheads*.

Chapter 16 explains that one of the easiest ways to protect wiring to an outside area is to use exterior house walls that share the area where you'll use power or communications. Your home's exterior walls are good bulkheads for protecting wiring. Look for other potential bulkheads such as half walls built along decks and patios. Use these bulkhead wall cavities for wiring or mounting boxes for outlets or electronics. Follow the same Chapter 3 rules for roughing in when wiring in bulkheads. Also be mindful that you can use conduit for exterior wiring.

Wiring directly to the point of use

You can run outdoor wiring directly to a point of use even if there isn't a wall or other bulkhead around.

All outdoor wiring should be rated as weatherproof. We recommend running exposed wiring in a PVC conduit.

All outdoor receptacles must meet the following requirements:

> ✔ Outlets must be standard GFI outlets.
>
> ✔ Receptacle boxes and covers must be weatherproof.
>
> ✔ Use weatherproof in-use covers for receptacles in continuous use. *In-use covers* are hooded, allowing you to plug in a cord with the cover closed. Figure 17-1 shows an in-use outlet cover. The manufacturer claims it

works on 14 different receptacles types. The transparent hooded cover has holes on the bottom to allow cords to exit with the cover closed. To the right of the cover is a single-gang weatherproof box to which an in-use cover is usually fastened.

✔ Use exposure-rated connectors for outdoor Ethernet and USB connections. Use jacks and plugs rated for dust and water exposure. Connectors rated as IP67 are dust proof and rated for immersion in 1 meter of water. IP68 connectors are dust proof and can withstand immersion for extended periods and being under pressure.

Many of the devices and cords you want to use outside may not be rated for outdoor use. Take these things indoors after you use them, or at least cover and unplug them.

Another way to protect outdoor outlets is to mount them so they face the ground, deck surface, or patio and are protected by an overhang or roof. But even in this case, down-facing outdoor receptacles must be GFI protected.

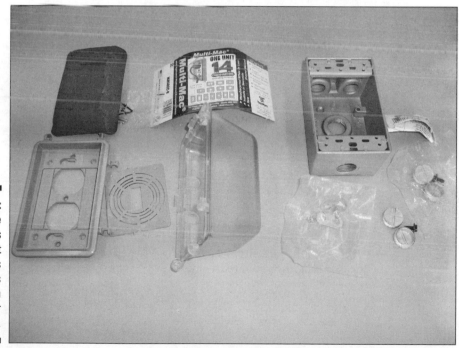

Figure 17-1:
In-use covers protect receptacles and devices from weather exposure.

Using Electronic Devices in Outdoor Kitchens

If you do a lot of cooking and entertaining outside, you may want an elaborate outdoor kitchen area where you can use just about any electric kitchen device. Wiring for an outdoor cooking area can run the gauntlet from powering your grill for an electric charcoal igniter, to a multipurpose kitchen, dining, and entertainment area. For the more upscale outdoor kitchen and dining, calculate the power needs just as you would for indoor cooking areas.

You might want to use some of these goodies in your outdoor kitchen:

- **Electric grill:** While most outdoor chefs cook with charcoal and gas, you may want to consider an electric grill. If you're a charcoal purest, you'll be happy to know that combination electric/charcoal grills are available. Most electric grills draw a lot of current (as much as 20 to 30 amps or more, depending on the surface size), so make this an important consideration when planning your wiring.

- **Refrigerator or warming trays:** If you intend to include these items in your outdoor kitchen, include their current draw in your load calculation to determine feeder sizes and circuit breaker ratings. Use GFI-protected breakers for all outdoor kitchen circuits.

- **Lighting:** The possibilities are nearly endless and may include over- and under-cabinet lights, dimmers, and overhead (or string) lights. All of the lighting fixtures should be weatherproof or rated for use in damp areas. All of the wiring must be rated for the use you employ, which can include direct burial, waterproof, or sunlight resistant.

- **Convenience receptacles:** Some items may serve double duty, working in both your outdoor and indoor kitchens — toasters or your favorite electric carving knife. Provide some outlets (GFI protected, of course) for these devices.

As with all electrical systems, add up the anticipated loads and install a feeder line to accommodate the loads. For just a few electrical appliances, you may run several feeds from the house. For heavier, more elaborate installations (including electric grills and large lighting loads), run a feeder to a weatherproof panel and run all outdoor kitchen loads from this panel.

Wiring Outdoor Theaters or Sound Systems

We think stereo sound is a must outdoors. And if you're fortunate enough to live in a warmer climate, a full outdoor home theater — complete with 5.1 or 7.1 channel surround sound — isn't out of the question. The faux rock speakers available at many electronics retailers are a good choice for outdoor sound. You can put them in the garden, next to decks, or along walkways.

The best sound sources are at or near ear level, so rock speakers work best in areas such as sloped rock gardens. Other low-mount locations provide suboptimal sound quality, but you may decide that suboptimal stereo is better than none at all.

Exposed speakers must tolerate water or be protected from rain, snow, sleet, and hail by a weatherproof enclosure. Fortunately, many manufacturers supply outdoor-rated speakers such as the Niles Audio OS5.3 or OS5.5. As you compare brands and models, remember to include the following things, and see Chapter 9 for more information:

- Frequency response of the speakers in your comparison
- Anti-corrosion materials
- Other durability features, such as mounting brackets that tolerate strong wind loads or finishes that are resistant to sunlight.

If you don't get outdoor-rated speakers, you can still protect them in other ways, such as recessing them or mounting them under roofs.

Speaker wire used outdoors should be rated for outdoor use. Wires not rated for direct burial will short out, possibly causing damage to your amplifier when constantly exposed to wet or damp conditions. As always, use boxes, wire, and cable rated for its intended use.

Controlling outdoor theaters or sound systems

Creating an outdoor theater or sound system doesn't mean you have to buy another whole set of equipment. Leverage the indoor electronic devices you already own by incorporating them into a multi-source, multi-zone sound system that extends to your patio or deck. Chapter 9 describes multi-zone systems in greater detail.

To control your multi-zone entertainment system from your outdoor theater or sound system, install the control and faceplate supplied by the multi-zone system's manufacturer in a two-gang box in your outdoor area, and run Cat 6 cable between the box and the central control unit. Once connected, you can play CDs, radio, or another audio source and control the selection and volume from the remote control panel. To protect the panel in an exposed area, install a hinged see-though plastic cover that you can lift when you want to press the buttons. Alternatively, install the panel in a recess in an exterior wall which is then covered by a small 12" × 12" cabinet door. Use *spar* (marine) varnish to protect the door.

Planning the theater space

Bringing audio to an outdoor space is relatively easy because of the wide availability of weatherproof speakers. Outdoor video is a little trickier, especially if you don't want to place an expensive, weather-sensitive TV outside.

In one notable installation we have seen, the homeowner built a patio next to the family room. A very large flat-screen TV was installed in the family room, and then the homeowner installed a large picture window in the shared wall between the family room and the patio. The picture window allowed people on the patio to clearly see the TV inside the family room. With outdoor speakers and controls, this made for a complete patio theater.

Feel free to be creative with your outdoor theater plan, if not a little bit crazy. Just be sure to follow the wiring basics, keep safety in mind, and adhere to your community's electrical or building codes.

Installing a Home Weather Station

Home weather stations and temperature monitors are popular additions to the digital home. Weather reports on TV and radio are great, but they usually can't tell you what's happening right now outside your house.

When you're selecting a home weather station, look for a system with these features:

✔ **Solar power:** Solar-powered weather stations eliminate the need to run power wires to your roof or another hard-to-reach location. See Chapter 15 for more information about solar power.

✔ **Wireless data transmission:** Along with solar power, wireless data transmission eliminates the need to run a lot of wires. Information flows wirelessly from the weather station to a monitoring panel inside your home.

✔ **Internet Protocol (IP) server:** An *IP server* allows you to connect the outputs from the weather monitoring station to your home's Ethernet network. Once connected and configured, the server module lets you monitor the weather readings using a Web browser on any networked computer in your house. If you have a static IP address for your home (as described in Chapter 12), you may even be able to use the Internet to monitor the weather conditions at your home from anywhere in the world.

WeatherHawk makes home weather stations that have most of the features in the preceding list. They also sell an IP server module that connects to the outputs from the weather station, and the server module supplies information to your computer's Web browser over your home's Ethernet network.

Once you connect a home weather station to your home network, computer software can monitor the weather station input, and use it to automate actions within the home. For example, the software can turn on the air conditioner when the outside temperature exceeds 76°F. See Chapter 13 for more on home automation software.

The typical computer hookups include the sound card's sound output and microphone input, Ethernet network communications, and USB ports. . Connecting computer electronics beyond this may require other standard and even non-standard interfaces. The standard interfaces include RS-232, RS-422, and RS-485. Often the connections for these devices can be over common twisted-pair wire such as Cat 6, and in other instances you have to use shielded cables with very precise connections from and to certain pin numbers on the devices' connections. Closely follow the manufacturer's instructions for connections, pin outs, and cable types when wiring to install any specialized equipment with non-standard wiring requirements.

Just for fun: Wiring a traffic signal in your driveway

Working with wiring, electrical devices, and controls can be very, well, practical most of the time. But armed with some knowledge and practical know-how gained from reading this book, you can undertake some projects that are more for amusement and personal satisfaction than for functionality. One such attention-grabbing project: a traffic-control signal light that a Marquette, Michigan homeowner installed. (Flip to the full-color insert pages in this book and check out Color Plate 12 to see a photograph of the traffic signal.)

Understanding how the signal works

Junkyards and recycling centers offer many antique traffic signals. If the controls weren't salvaged (or salvageable), use three interval timers to control the light. Turn to the full-color insert pages in this book and take a look at Color Plate 13 to see a diagram of the three interval timers. Interval timers cost less than $100 each.

In the diagram shown in Color Plate 13, all of the neutrals are shown as dashed lines. Ignore the neutrals; they just provide the return path. The time-delay relays, the signal lights, and the pilot lights all need a connection to the neutral. When troubleshooting, make sure that a neutral wire is present and connected everywhere one is needed.

Pilot lights on the panel cover are for timing adjustment, because the stop-signal lamps are normally out in the driveway, out of control panel range. The relays are 11-pin plug-in time-delay relays with an instant contact. You can adjust the delay time from 0 to 60 seconds. The instant contacts are on the right of each relay in

the diagram, and the timed relay contact is on the left. NO denotes a contact that's normally open, and NC denotes a contact that's normally closed when no power is applied to the relay. Think of the relays as a pair of three-way switches. (See Chapter 4 for more about three-way switches.)

In the figure shown in Color Plate 13, all contacts are shown in the NC position, where no power is applied. Connected means a wire is connected from one pin to another pin to make the necessary circuits. Contact or Contacted means a relay's contacts are closing to make a connection from one pin to another inside the relay.

Wiring in the logic

Wiring is the secret to a properly functioning traffic signal light. The logical relay connections determine the operating sequence of the three lights. Trace the power wire in the figure shown in Color Plate 13 to see how the system works:

1. The power source is connected to pin 1 of relay #3, which is the common pin. Pin 1 contacts pin 4, which is the NC time-delay contact on relay #3.

2. The power wire leaves relay #3 at pin 4 and connects to pins 11 and 2 on relay #1.

3. When pin 2 is energized, the instant NO contact operates and contacts pin 11 to pin 9.

4. Pin 9 powers pin 1, which contacts pin 4 until the relay times out.

   The green signal light illuminates and stays on until relay #1 times out.

5. When relay #1 times out, the NC contact opens and contacts pin 1 to pin 3.

6. Pin 3 connects to pins 2 and 11 on relay #2.

7. When pin 2 is energized, the NO contact closes and contacts pin 11 to pin 9.

8. Pin 9 powers pin 1, which is contacted to pin 4 and turns on the yellow light.

   The yellow light stays on until relay #2 times out.

9. When relay #2 times out, pin 1 contacts pin 3, which powers pins 2 and 11 of relay #3.

10. The NO contact on relay #3 closes, contacting pin 11 to pin 9 and illuminating the red light.

    The red light stays on until relay #3 times out.

11. When relay #3 times out, the incoming power to relay #1 is opened and thus turned off.

    This turns off all the relays, including relay #3 and the red light. As soon as relay #3 loses power, the NC contacts pin 1 to pin 4, restarting the sequence.

Building the control enclosure

The controls for your traffic light should be in a secure, protected area such as a garage or wiring closet. You can see a photograph of the control enclosure for the traffic light in Color Plate 14; see the full-color insert pages in this book.

As you can see in the figure, the homeowner added a time clock to control the operating times, so the signal light is only on between 7:00 a.m. and midnight. The diagram shown in Color Plate 13 only has three relays. This four-relay wiring is nearly identical to the three-relay layout we described, except that when the red light relay times out, it operates the fourth relay, which opens the power to the system.

Remember: Even though a traffic light is just a fun project, you must select the devices and install wire in accordance with the National Electrical Code. See Chapters 2, 3, and 16 to figure out the details for wire size, use ratings, circuit breaker sizing, grounding, and wiring methods.

Part VI
The Part of Tens

The 5th Wave   By Rich Tennant

Okay—you were right, I was wrong. F5 opens the garage door, and F6 backs the car out.

In this part . . .

The chapters in this part contain top-ten lists of ageless secrets concerning the wiring arts and sciences. You may want to commit certain items to memory, or at least refer to these lists whenever you need them.

Here you find ten wiring Web sites worth visiting often, and ten mistakes you don't want to ever make. Finally, read ten ways to find out what's awry, so you can come to the rescue and mend the predicament for all time.

Chapter 18

The Ten Best Wiring Web Sites

The sites in this chapter help you solve problems, discover more about products, or just read more about interesting home-wiring topics. Some of the sites are purely commercial, while some aren't trying to sell you anything. We listed these particular sites not because we endorse these companies or products over others, but because we believe the information on these sites is of value to anyone building or upgrading a digital home. These sites have a lot of free value-added information that complements this book, and we like that.

As a consumer of digital products and services, always do your homework, comparison shop, and make informed choices before you buy.

Wiring Devices

www.leviton.com

This Web site is valuable from a number of perspectives. The site's rich in information about products, from wiring devices and controls to more advanced systems like networking, voice, and data. Its wealth of educational material complements the product information. This site is great for the professional electrician or the do-it-yourselfer.

Wire and Cable

www.belden.com

Along with cable product information, the Belden Web site has a link to what they refer to as "Cable College," a must for anyone doing Cat 6 terminations for digital or communications wiring. Links on this site take you to valuable tables, color-code lists, and glossaries of industry terms. It also includes pictures of properly terminated and tied wiring. These pictures are very useful to someone running network cable for the first time.

Home Electronics

```
www.pioneerelectronics.com
```

Pioneer Electronics is a manufacturing leader in home electronics. Their Web site is not only a great place to learn specifically about their offerings, but gives you a good idea of the vast array of products offered by the entire industry.

Home Security

```
www.adt.com
```

ADT is a home-security company that provides 24-hour monitoring. Their Web site offers personal safety tips along with information on their pre-packaged systems, monitoring services, and system installation services.

```
www.brinks.com
```

Brinks also provides installation and 24-hour monitoring. They have a great checklist to help you compare any number of local or national home security companies.

Networking and Electronics Technology

```
www.iec.org/online/tutorials/
```

The IEC was founded in 1944 by universities and engineering societies as a nonprofit organization focused on educational topics for the U.S. electronics industry. If you want to learn about the H.323 standard, or more about cable modems than any average Joe or Jane should know, or you want to find out how Internet Television works, then this site is for you. The tutorials section includes a wealth of information that is highly technical yet is written and illustrated in a way that anyone can easily learn from it.

Networked Video Surveillance

www.axis.com

If you want information about cameras and basic surveillance technologies, this site has it. It takes some drilling down to find some of the information, but the rewards are there. Start with the Solutions button at the top of the page and work your way in from there.

Solar and Alternative Energy

www.solartoday.org

SOLAR TODAY is a bimonthly magazine published by the American Solar Energy Society. The Useful Links tab lists a literal who's who in alternative-energy technologies, from solar panels and standalone solar lighting to wind energy.

Digital Home Media

www.digitalhomemag.com

The *Digital Home Magazine* Web site is a great place to find breaking news and feature articles about cutting-edge products. On our most recent visit, a great article called "HomePlug AV: Return of the Wired Network" talked about using a product named HomePlug AV to stream video from a home theater to a bedroom.

Outdoor Living

www.hgtv.com

To use the Home & Garden Television (HGTV) site, go to the home page search window and type in a term. For example, if you type *outdoor,* you get page after page of articles about outdoor living, including tips about building outdoor kitchens and dining rooms, and articles about smaller projects such as mounting ceiling fans in outdoor spaces. If you're designing a new home or remodeling your current home and want to expand your living outdoors, spend some time checking out this site.

Remodeling and Repair Projects

www.thisoldhouse.com

This Old House is a popular home-improvement show that you can watch on your local PBS station. On the show's home page, click Electrical and Lighting, and then click the Browse All Articles link. You find a number of easy-to-understand articles on home-wiring improvement projects. Find the "15 Milestones That Changed Housing" article by Dan Cray, and then imagine how someone 20 years from now might write about digital innovations included in the modern digital homes of today.

Chapter 19

The Ten Biggest Wiring Mistakes

*W*iring your home properly makes it safer and more livable. Unfortunately, home wiring is often sabotaged by a few common mistakes. Sometimes these mistakes are the result of ignorance or laziness. Other times, they're just plain old blunders.

This chapter introduces you to ten of the most common mistakes people make when home wiring. We present them so that you know how to best avoid making these mistakes. So sit back and absorb this list of ten things you *don't* want to do.

Not Leaving Enough Slack

One thing that clearly separates a professional, workmanlike wiring job from an amateurish one is the amount of wire slack left in junction and device boxes. Overall neatness is hampered when you try to make quality connections using wires that are too short. And if repair work needs to be performed later, the short wires add time and hassle to the job.

The problem of not having enough slack on the conductors in a box is often a result of not installing a large-enough box in the first place. One popular manufacturer offers a 32" × 32" two-gang box, which we feel is too small. (See

Chapter 3 for information on calculating box fill.) A larger-capacity box gives you room to be neat *and* leaves enough room for wire slack. The largest nail-on plastic boxes we found had the following capacities:

- Single-gang box with 22" × 22"
- Two-gang box with 41" × 41"
- Three-gang box with 57" × 57"
- Four-gang box with 68" × 68"

Try to leave at least 8" of slack on each wire if possible. Having generous slack and choosing a box of sufficient volume allows you to neatly lay all of the bare ground wires in the back of the box first, followed by layering the neutral conductors. This leaves enough space to neatly fold the power wires under the installed devices.

Not Paying Attention to Details

Wiring a home for lighting, appliances, computer networks, and other electronic equipment is a huge job. A momentary lapse in attention while doing this work can cause damage to your equipment or even create a hazard for the home's residents.

Follow these basic rules as you work:

- Avoid doing electrical work while you're tired, fatigued, or under the influence of certain beverages.
- Always follow safety procedures, and exercise care with every connection you make to ensure that you're doing the installation correctly.
- Pay attention to color codes on wire connections or cables.
- Read equipment installation instructions, heed the warning labels, and read the information on allowable environmental factors to ensure they match your installation and use conditions.
- Work closely with other trades. If you're doing the work yourself, coordinate your activity and installation of electrical, communication, and plumbing to avoid the potential for conflicts. For example, if a plumber runs a vent pipe straight up from the center of a vanity, this may conflict with a lighting box you were planning to install.

Including Lighting Loads on Receptacle Circuits

Article 210 of the National Electrical Code (NEC) discusses branch circuits. This code section requires the receptacle circuits in the kitchen, dining room, laundry, and bath to exclusively serve only the power receptacles in those respective rooms, and not be connected to the lighting or power receptacles in other locations. We recommend that you keep receptacle and lighting circuits separate throughout the entire house, not just in the rooms and areas mentioned in the NEC. Only make exceptions in light-use cases such as bedroom closet lights or outside lights where the only available wiring is a receptacle circuit.

Lighting in a home is usually fairly reliable because of the stable loads on the circuit. It is really annoying for occupants to have the lights go out when a fault or overload causes a GFIC or breaker trips off line. Such lights-out scenarios are prevented when the lights are wired on their own circuit breakers, separated from the varying loads caused by the items that may be plugged into the room outlets.

Ignoring Physics

Ignore the physics of your installation work at your own peril. The first clue that you or your installer might be doing something to challenge the physics of an installation is when you say or hear the phase ". . . that should be good enough." When you hear or say this, it's time to extend your "Uh oh, here comes trouble" antennae. Carefully consider the risk you're about to accept. Then don't accept the risk: Have it done right or take the time to do it right yourself. Following are some laws of physics you will contend with as you wire your home.

Gravity

As an installer, you must concern yourself with securely attaching wires and components, and this means finding suitable mounting locations. If you live in an area that gets lots of snow, anticipate and avoid areas where ice may form and fall onto your service entrance. In areas with harsh winter weather, power companies prefer that you install meter sockets on the gable end of the building. Sometimes the gable end is the most visible, and the power company's preference may need to come second. Following our recommendation for a well-placed through-the-roof mast avoids this problem and works well on any style of pitched roof.

Attach all components securely and use large-enough screws for the job. If you attach a meter socket to a single stud using one pair of vertical holes, the holes on the other side will be about 6" away from any support. In most modern construction, the wall itself is not very sturdy. Often, it is only vinyl siding over insulation. The easiest way to secure the other side of the meter socket is to install backers inside the wall. The backer should be a 2" × 6" piece of lumber cut to fit between the studs, and then placed against the outside wall and nailed in place. If the wall has 1" insulation, use ¼" × 3" lag bolts to mount the meter socket through the siding and installation into the 2" × 6" backer.

Use pre-placed backers behind drywall to secure surface-mounted fluorescent lights. For a drywall-finished mechanical room with a lot of equipment to mount, it may prove easier to just sheet the entire wall space with ½" or ¾" plywood before the drywall is hung. This takes a lot less time than measuring out and installing a large number of backers. And if the layout changes between design and installation, the full wall sheeting provides more mounting flexibility.

Wind

The risk of swaying tree branches hitting or falling on overhead service wires in a heavily wooded area may be avoided if you run the cable into the site from another direction with fewer trees. Look at all your options and deal with potential problems before making the wiring runs. When installing anything outside, be wary of wind exposure and fasten every wire and component in a suitable fashion. Be especially wary of *chaffing*, which can occur if the wind causes a wire to vibrate or move against any object.

Water

Falling water, rising water, and condensation are all issues to consider when you select locations to mount or use electrical devices, or the wires that bring power or communications signals to them. Water in any electrical apparatus degrades it by causing corrosion and rust. Excess water can also cause shorts that trip GFI circuits and breakers. Avoid installing electrical items in wet areas, if possible. If you can't avoid doing so, use weatherproof wiring, methods, and materials.

Fire

Excessive heat from things like chimneys, stoves, furnaces, and heaters can cause problems for wiring and connected devices. Avoid making general runs near high-heat sources. When making direct connections to heat-generating appliances or fixtures, always use wire appropriately rated for such service.

Avoid running network, sound, and communications wires through ventilation ducts in your home. If using ventilation ducts for network cabling is unavoidable, make sure that you use Category 6 Ethernet *communication plenum*-rated (*CMP*-rated) cable with 100-percent fluorinated ethylene propylene sheathing. The plenum-rated cable is required if you're running through ventilation ducts.

Installations Not Designed for Use and Abuse

Someone could kick or step on anything that protrudes from the wall, including junction boxes you've mounted too low. Installations of conduits within easy reach may become an inappropriate point on which people lean, swing, or hang. These problems can hurt the people in your home, and shorten the service life of your expensive installations. You can tell people, "Don't lean on that," until you're blue in the face, but unless you have eyes in the back of your head, this probably isn't a good plan for reducing damage.

Consider typical use and abuse when you choose locations and mounts. Securely mount high-abuse items (such as video cameras), or mount them in locations less likely to receive abuse (such as from the ceiling).

Improperly Interpreting the National Electrical Code

Article 230.9 of the NEC states that open service conductors shall be at least 3' away from any window. The operative word here is *open,* which means not in a raceway or a wire cable assembly with a protective outer jacket. When conductors leave a conduit or service entrance cable to connect to an overhead drop with exposed conductors, they are considered open. This applies whether the *window* has the ability to open or not.

A manufactured-home factory in our area won't place a service within 3' of a window, even if it is a mast-type through-the-roof service entrance, which clearly isn't the meaning of this requirement. The company even includes basement windows (if the manufactured home is placed on a basement) in this misinterpretation.

The open-conduit requirement mentioned here is just one example of a code-reading mistake you can make by not paying attention to the code's heading or not reading all of the exceptions. For example, requirements for voltages over 600 volts are different from the requirements if the voltage is less. It's *not* okay to read a section of code requirements for high voltages and then try to apply those rules to lower voltages.

Always be sure your understanding of the code is accurate and seek professional assistance and guidance if you don't fully understand the code. Pay particular attention if your compliance with the code rests on one or more allowable exceptions. We recommend that you buy an electrical code book or — better yet — the handbook of the code book. The handbook includes every article the code book contains, but it also explains and clarifies many of the articles and includes many illustrations.

When Grounding Is Not Grounding

Electrical grounding is supposed to do two things:

- Trip the circuit's breaker if the hot wire accidentally touches any metal surface that should be grounded.
- Provide some degree of lighting protection.

The ground conductor connected to a ground rod, although grounded, doesn't clear an electrical fault. The ground has to be solidly connected to the neutral conductor at the electrical panel to clear a ground fault (also known as *tripping the breaker*). When lightning strikes your electrical service, the service grounding carries the lightning to the earth. When this happens, the ground's potential (voltage) at the grounding point spikes, and every ground connected to the service ground spikes also. A lightning strike can be hundreds of millions of volts and generate currents of 100,000 amps or more for about ¹⁄₁₀ of 1 second.

Grounding is the most misunderstood topic in the electrical industry. In a continuing education course Paul recently took as a licensing requirement, the topic of auxiliary grounding was covered. Some designers require ground rods on steel light poles. The presenter indicated how foolish he thought this was. His point of discussion was that the required grounding conductor that ran with the circuit conductors also grounds the steel pole. The grounding conductor is useful, and it is necessary to trip the breaker when a power-to-ground fault occurs. A frayed wire or failed ballast could cause a fault and energize the pole, causing a shock hazard if no ground wire traces back to the service grounding point.

A driven ground rod by itself won't necessarily carry enough current to trip a breaker when a fault occurs, because ground's soil (earth) is such a poor conductor. If the ground conductor leading back to the panel becomes opened, the ground rod lessens, but doesn't eliminate the potential between the pole and ground by raising the potential of the earth in the vicinity of the ground rod.

On the other hand, the pole is a lightning rod waving to passing electrical storms shouting, "Strike here!" If lightning strikes a light pole without an auxiliary ground rod, the voltage between the steel pole and ground can be tens of thousands of volts. A person walking or standing near the pole could be in serious danger. Add an auxiliary ground rod to increase the ground potential and it reduces the hazard. A person actually touching the pole is still in some danger, but those in proximity are much safer. In this case the ground rod — although not required by code — is useful and adds some degree of safety. This anecdote just reinforces our contention that grounding is often misunderstood, even by those teaching it. The advice we offer? Supplementary ground rods add some safety. During a thunderstorm, don't use power tools or wired telephones; using indoor cordless phones is okay. Recent evidence shows that using cell phones outdoors may also attract lightning. What you heard as a child ("Stay away from metal and plumbing during lightning storms") is still very good advice.

If you have any light poles, lighted flag poles, TV/ham radio antenna towers, wind generators, metal weather vanes, digital weather stations, or the like at risk for lightning, please read and heed the information on proper grounding.

Ignoring the BOCA or IRC Codes

Although amusing reading at times, code books aren't intended for your entertainment, nor are they merely suggestions. And the NEC mentioned earlier in this chapter isn't the only code you must heed. Other important code books include the *BOCA (Building Officials and Code Administrators)* and *IRC (International Residential Code)*. Both building codes have specifications intended to prevent the various mechanical and electrical trades from weakening the basic building structure through improper drilling or cutting, or from modifications that reduce fire ratings and impair safety.

Take the time to review the section in Chapter 3 on drilling framing and joists. It sometimes takes a little ingenuity and measuring to avoid drilling through a bottom plate into the top of a joist for wires that have to be run down into a basement or crawl space.

 On pre-manufactured trusses, it is vital to avoid drilling through or near the flanges, although 2X lumber is a little more forgiving if drilled properly. Sometimes the wire can be run along the wall around a corner, and then brought down. If you can't avoid drilling down into multiple joists of 2X lumber, drill at a 70@dg angle to come out high on the side of the joist. Drill as small a hole as comfortably fits the wire.

Not Following Your Own Consistency Rules

Throughout the text we have set up a number of suggested rules to follow when planning and wiring your house. These rules have been developed over many years of experience, and a few of them were adopted from advice from friends in the trade. These rules have served us well, saving time and providing our customers a good, consistent job. Set your methods and performance standards and follow them. Set consistent quality standards for your work and take pride in it. Modify your rules only after careful and thorough consideration of the "what-if" consequences of the changes you make.

Wiring systems are all about details, rules, and following correct instructions. Take your time, do the job right, and savor your success.

Minimizing Wiring Runs and Circuit Counts

All too often homeowners and builders will treat the electrical and communications wiring as the budget item to reduce. Going down that path will seriously limit the options for fully automating and enjoying your home.

Running wires in new construction projects will never be cheaper than when the walls are open. Also keep in mind that the wire itself is one of the least expensive components of the project. Don't get caught up in the trap of reducing cost during the wiring phase by making fewer wire runs than you anticipate using. Your home is more versatile and useful if the wiring you need is put in place during the original construction. This applies to a lesser extent in remodeling projects, but it still applies. The cost and difficulty of wiring later after all the drywall is in and the paint is dry will be greater.

In some cases you can compensate for not having the wires by using wireless technologies. Using wireless has tradeoffs with security, configuration, and costs.

Plan your implementation well and think in terms of your home serving your needs over the coming decades. Anticipate the potential for your changing needs and wire for them now.

Chapter 20

Ten Troubleshooting Tips

Troubleshooting is said to be part art, part science, and part luck. You have to come up with the luck component entirely on your own; we can't provide that. Perhaps a four-leaf clover embroidered over your shirt pocket will help? But we *can* help you with the science — and maybe some of the art — of troubleshooting. Essentially, *troubleshooting* is a repeatable process that you can apply to any problem. You methodically eliminate possibilities until you're left with only the solution. The artistic elements of troubleshooting will come, but usually only with the insight gained from experience.

Even though the spotlight of this book is on wiring, networking, and deploying digital equipment in your home, this chapter's ten troubleshooting concepts could help you solve almost any type of problem. It doesn't matter if the problem is with a lawn mower, car, sound system, or computer — a seasoned troubleshooter should follow certain steps. The tips presented here are generic enough to apply to most problems, although in this case we've tailored somewhat to residential electrical systems.

Collect the History

When something breaks, your first step is to determine the chain of events that led up to the failure. If you were there when the problem occurred, you have a head start. But if you weren't there, you may have to become a detective (like Columbo or Sherlock Holmes). In these cases you can borrow some key interrogatives from the press corps:

✔ Who

✔ What

  ✔ Where
  ✔ How
  ✔ When
  ✔ Why

Some of the questions may get immediate answers from people who were there. Sometimes no one can provide history. You may come upon the problem yourself, or you may be called in by someone who has no idea what happened. You may find clues, but what appears to be a clue may not be useful information at all. The following sections go over each of the questions you should ask as you start troubleshooting.

Who witnessed the point of failure?

Knowing who was there when the breakdown occurred allows you to quiz those witnesses: What was happening right up to the point of failure? For example, knowing that a high-wattage heater was plugged in and turned on just as the room lights went out might help explain why the breaker for that room tripped offline.

If more than one person was present, keep in mind that any two peoples' perceptions and attention to details varies. Quiz everyone so you can collect as much of the story as possible.

What was happening at the time?

Strong winds can find weak connections on overhead power lines, so knowing there were 90 mph wind gusts when the room lights were flashing on and off may help explain what happened.

The circumstances leading up to a failure often help you focus your energies on the most likely cause. If you're driving down the expressway and your car starts to miss and jerk before the engine quits altogether, that event could point to an empty fuel tank, a clogged fuel filter, or a loose ignition wire that finally fell off.

Whatever the problem may be, knowing all the circumstances leading up to the failure is helpful. All the collected information may not be relevant to the failure. Once you've collected the circumstantial evidence, begin the analysis. Investigate each item on your list for relevance. For each item on the list, ask yourself if it could have been the definite cause of the malfunction.

Where was the device when it failed?

This question may not always apply, particularly in the case of fixed equipment. But for portable devices, the location could be important. For example, suppose you used a power drill inside the house to drive screws on a new bookcase, and then you went outside to mount a flagpole hanger. The drill failed when you tried to install the flagpole hanger. What could be the cause? Why did it work in the house and not outside?

The problem may not be the drill's failure. Suppose the power cord wasn't long enough to reach the work area, so you connected two cords and ran them across a flowerbed. The two cords joined together at the flowerbed, and while you were drilling the sprinkler system came on. The doused cord might have caused a GFI circuit to trip.

Environmental factors can cause problems with sensitive electrical equipment. Always consider environmental factors in your troubleshooting process.

How did it fail?

Pushing devices can lead to damage and failure. Knowing how the failure appeared may help explain which component stopped working. If you overload a drill motor, excessive heat and smoke may pour from the vents. If you spin the starter on a stalled car for too long, the starter motor may overheat and throw solder from its windings. So when the witness tells you the starter motor quit after trying to start the motor for over ten minutes, and that there was a pungent smell right before the starter motor quit working, that's good data.

When did the failure occur?

Knowing the exact time of a breakdown can provide clues. Can the failure be linked to some other event, like an electrical storm or high winds? Was another major appliance running on a timer?

Why did it fail?

Troubleshooting's ultimate goal is to understand why the equipment, controls, or wiring failed. By understanding why the failure occurred, you can avoid it or eliminate the possibility of future failure.

Understand the Process

To troubleshoot any system or equipment, you must first understand what makes the item work in the first place. In other words: How does it operate normally? How does it work when it's working correctly?

Take, for example, a gasoline engine. If you've never encountered engine trouble in a car, lawn mower, or chain saw, it's probably only a matter of time before you do. A gasoline engine must have the following things to run:

- ✔ Fuel
- ✔ Spark
- ✔ Air
- ✔ Compression

Suppose your backup gasoline-powered generator fails. If you want to troubleshoot, you must know how that generator works. That means knowing the four necessary items, and then working through each to find out why the motor will not start and run. Learn how your home works and arm yourself with manuals, diagrams, and notes you made during construction and installation.

Plan the Approach

Haphazard, random, and *subjective* aren't good terms when you're troubleshooting wiring or electrical components.

- ✔ **Make a list.** The system and your knowledge of it help you plan your approach by making a checklist of diagnostic tasks. If you aren't familiar with the system or equipment, do some research. A checklist made by an expert can save you time and gives you steps with which to start.

- ✔ **Check out the manual.** Real troubleshooters aren't afraid to read the directions.

- ✔ **Group tasks.** Use logic, of course, and convenience. If you're in the neighborhood of X, you might as well check Y because it's within easy reach.

- ✔ **Be inclusive.** This is the most important part. All the related wiring, controls, devices, and systems that feed into or from the failed device must be on your checklist.

Follow Safety Procedures

Whenever you troubleshoot, first stop and think about the safety risks. Haste in troubleshooting can quickly harm you and those working with you. Finding and fixing the problem is never worth risking injury to people or the destruction of expensive equipment. Safety should always come first.

Every trade or profession has a list of safety procedures. Electricians know that energized wires bite, burn, and even kill. Federal *Occupational Safety and Health Administration (OSHA)* electrical safety standards apply equally to novices and professionals alike. About 24 states have adopted their own electrical safety standards as well. Whenever working with potential hazards, take the time to learn and heed all the safety procedures required for your safety and those working with you.

Some of the most common and important safety precautions to take when working around electricity include

- Always follow lock-out/tag-out procedures when working on any of the circuits in your home. When you work on a circuit, lock the circuit out and place a tag on it stating that you're the only one authorized to reenergize the circuit. If other people on the job site are also working on the same circuit, they must lock it out and tag it also. When their work is completed, they remove their tags. The last person to complete work and remove the last remaining tag can safely reenergize the circuit.

- Always use appropriate protective equipment, including eyewear, air filtration masks when needed, and clothing appropriate to the tasks.

- Always take your time. A good troubleshooter realizes that staying safe and living to troubleshoot another day are more important than getting things done quickly.

Eliminate the Obvious

You're at the neighbor's barbeque and the center cut is on the rotisserie. For some reason, halfway through cooking the motor stops on the rotisserie. What could be the problem? Should you start taking the motor apart, or should you first follow the cord around the corner of the house to see if the kids accidentally knocked the cord out of the wall? While you're at it, look inside the house to see if the lights are still on, and peer across the street to see if the neighbor's lights are on, too. These clues help you identify a power outage or tripped breaker.

Whatever device or system you're checking, take some time to review all the potential causes of the failure, no matter how obvious and unlikely they may seem. Otherwise, you're going to look pretty silly for tearing apart the rotisserie motor, when the problem was that the cord was unplugged.

Begin at the Beginning

Troubleshooting electrical or digital devices can often begin at either end of the circuit. A number of factors help determine the starting point, not the least of which is your comfort zone for working on the failed device. To find a problem, you must be methodical and begin at one end of the process and proceed through, checking each stage, one by one, until you find the point of failure.

When the lights don't light, where do you start troubleshooting? If only one light is out, it's probably a bulb. If other electrical items don't work, maybe a single circuit is out. If all lights are out, look for the presence of lighting in the neighborhood to see if there's a larger power outage. Start at the beginning, where you may find the most obvious causes and the easiest item to replace.

Avoid the Replacement Trap

An old adage says, "The best way to fix your broken car is to lift up the radiator cap and then drive another car underneath it." Needless to say, we don't seriously recommend this approach.

As you troubleshoot a problem, it's very easy to replace widget A and see what happens. Widget A becomes thingamabob B, and before you know it you've replaced doodad Z and it still doesn't work. You've just wasted a lot of time and money and you still have trouble to shoot. Sure, you've eliminated components A to Z as causes, but this isn't the most efficient way to go about fixing things.

When troubleshooting devices with multiple components, don't haphazardly replace components just because you *think* they might be the problem. The original problem may actually end up destroying the new parts. Use testing and logic to determine the problem, and only replace suspect parts when you have fairly solid evidence that the component in question is, in fact, the real cause of the trouble.

Check the Vital Signs

When you visit the doctor's office, the nurse usually starts by checking your weight, temperature, blood pressure, pulse, and breathing. The nurse checks your vital signs to make sure they're normal. Checking vital signs is an important step in troubleshooting any wiring system or electronic device as well.

You need to know things like voltage, current draw, and operating temperature ranges before you can test them. For example, house wiring is supposed to be 120 volts. If you check a circuit and the voltage is only 10 volts, you have a vital clue as to the source of the problem.

Most digital devices in your home should have instruction manuals that include troubleshooting procedures and normal vital signs. Store these manuals in a safe place, and refer to them when you have problems.

Eliminate the Cause

Replacing a blown fuse or restarting a circuit breaker doesn't eliminate the cause of the problem; it only treats a symptom. As the troubleshooter, you must solve the problem, not just treat the symptom. The goal of troubleshooting is to find the underlying cause, make the repairs, and take steps to prevent a recurrence.

Once you've isolated what needs repair or replacement, take care when making the repair. Always follow safety precautions by turning off power and shutting down equipment before making any repairs. Disconnecting wires on live circuits is dangerous, and it can cause damage to the equipment because of voltage spikes. Always use the Off switch or breaker to power down the equipment or circuit you're working on.

Verify the Repair

Verification is your final step and provides quality control for the troubleshooting process. Being certain your efforts have actually found and fixed the problem is the mark of a serious troubleshooter. A pro wants to be certain that it's really good to go when she says, "It's good to go." Use every feature after a repair. If, for example, you just replaced a bad switch on a four-way circuit, test every other location on that circuit.

Part VII
Appendixes

The 5th Wave — By Rich Tennant

"That's it! We're getting a wireless network for the house."

In this part . . .

The first two appendixes in this part contain information that didn't fit into a chapter earlier in this book but is nonetheless worth knowing. Those of you who are do-it-yourselfers or professionals should put Appendixes A and B in your toolbox and ride to the job site with them every day. The last appendix in this part describes the contents of the CD that's included with this book.

Appendix A

Product Sources

. . . .

*O*nce your projects are designed and budgeted, take your supplies list, climb into the F150, and go shopping for tools, wire, equipment, and hardware. We like the idea of using local businesses whenever possible, but you can't always get everything you need at the local hardware store. This appendix provides a handy list of national suppliers for all of the widgets, thingamabobs, or whatchamacallits that your project needs. The companies listed here should have shelves full of the stuff required for your project.

Big-Box Stores

Big-box stores are so called because their buildings usually look like, well, big boxes. Inside those big boxes are almost anything you might need for your project. Big-box hardware stores offer almost anything you may need for a construction project, from lumber and drywall to electrical components, finish materials, and even appliances. Big-box electronics stores offer a wide selection of cool electronic gadgets.

Best Buy

www.bestbuy.com

Best Buy sells electronics. There you can find computers, networking supplies, appliances, home theater components, and much more.

Circuit City

www.circuitcity.com

Circuit City is an electronics store where you can find home theater components, computers, networking supplies, and much more.

The Home Depot

www.homedepot.com

The Home Depot sells home-improvement items. It carries appliances, building, electrical, and gardening supplies, lighting, tools, plumbing, and so on.

Lowe's

www.lowes.com

At Lowe's you can find appliances, home décor, lighting, gardening items, all sorts of building supplies, tools, and more.

Small-Box Stores

Just because a store is big doesn't mean it has everything. You may have to visit smaller, more specialized stores for unusual parts and equipment.

Micro Center

www.microcenter.com

Micro Center carries all sorts of electronics, from plasma TVs to PCs.

RadioShack

www.radioshack.com

RadioShack carries all kinds of small electronics. You can also find cables and electronics parts there.

Wholesale Electric and Contractor Suppliers

Electric and contractor suppliers cater mainly to licensed trade professionals and building and construction contractors. As a do-it-yourselfer, these companies can provide you with the specialized products on a cash-and-carry, list-price basis. The suppliers are great sources for those hard-to-find items that the local hardware or big-box store doesn't have.

Do your homework and know exactly what you want when visiting a local branch of a major supplier; that helps ensure that you maintain a good relationship with the staff. When items are out of stock, the store will order them, but you may be required to give a deposit up front.

Crescent Electric Supply Company

`www.cesco.com`

Crescent Electric Supply Company supplies wire, cable, service equipment, electrical devices, and lighting fixtures.

GE Supply

`www.gesupply.com`

GE Supply is where you can find electrical products from GE, as well as hundreds of other manufacturers.

Graybar Electric Company

`www.graybar.com`

Graybar provides networking, telecommunications, and electrical products.

Home Automated Living

`www.automatedliving.com`

Home Automated Living (HAL) provides the voice-recognition technology and software program that enables you to automate your home by speaking to a computer, which in turn controls electrical devices.

WESCO International

www.wescodist.com

WESCO is one of the largest distributors of electrical supplies and equipment. It supplies lighting, distribution equipment (such as circuit breakers and transformers), wire, and cables.

Appendix B

What Mr. Ohm Wanted
You to Know

• •

*P*robably more than once you heard a math teacher say, "Someday you'll need these math skills in real life!" Now pay attention, because your math teacher was right. Basic mathematics ensures you're using the right type of wire and other components.

This appendix tells you a little bit about the formulas, terms, and calculations involved with home wiring. We can't turn you into a professional electrician with this one appendix, but we can give you enough information to impress your friends and wire your own home.

Using the Basic Ohm's Law Formula

The basic formula for Ohm's Law is stated as follows:

```
I = V/R
```

- ✔ I is current.
- ✔ V is voltage.
- ✔ R is resistance.

Some people use E for electromotive force in place of V, but either is okay. With simple algebra you can derive that $V = I \times R$ and $R = V/I$. This defined relationship between current, voltage, and resistance allows you to predict mathematically the electrical circuit's behavior. When 1 volt is connected to a circuit that has a resistance of 1 ohm, the current flowing is 1 amp.

The diagram in Figure B-1 is a basic DC-series electrical circuit. If you change any one of the values, one or both of the remaining values change to keep the relationship equal.

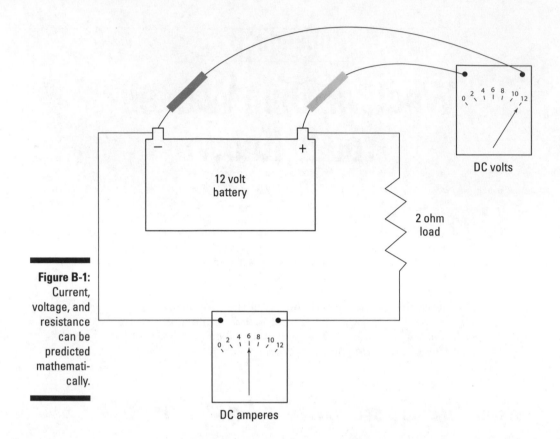

Figure B-1:
Current,
voltage, and
resistance
can be
predicted
mathemati-
cally.

The following sections describe calculations used in DC-powered circuits. For AC power (which most home power circuits use), the voltage and current aren't always in phase with each other. Calculations for AC circuits must include the power factor, which we describe in the section "Measuring power in AC circuits" later in the appendix. See Chapter 2 for an explanation of the difference between AC and DC power.

Measuring current in amps

An *ammeter* is just like a piece of wire. High current flows through the meter. The ammeter adds a miniscule amount (essentially zero) of resistance to the circuit. The ammeter functions by reading the tiny voltage drop across the meter's own very low internal resistance. At full scale, this voltage drop may be .050 volts (50 millivolts).

Who was Mr. Ohm?

Georg Ohm was a German physicist born March 16, 1787. He observed and recorded the relationship between current, voltage, resistance, and temperature in electrical conductors. He found that the current through a wire is proportional to the square of the wire's diameter, and inversely proportional to the wire's length at a given temperature.

In spite of the fact that today we refer to electrical resistance as *ohms,* Georg Ohm spent most of his life in poverty. Ohm published his findings in 1827, but at first his theory made him an object of ridicule. His very significant contribution to science was dismissed throughout most of his own lifetime, although by 1840 the scientific community began to understand its significance. He was eventually honored by being granted a professorship in experimental physics at the University of Munich. He died five years later at the age of 65. The symbol for ohms is the Greek capital letter omega: Ω.

Measuring electromotive force in volts

Unlike the ammeter, the *voltmeter* is essentially an open circuit. It adds a high resistance load to the battery. The resistance in this example may be as high as 240,000 ohms, or 20,000 ohms per volt (240,000 ohms ÷ 12 volts = 20,000). In Figure B-1, the battery supplies 12 volts, and a 2-ohm load (resistance) is connected across the battery. This causes 6 amps of current to flow as measured on the ammeter.

Calculating Electrical Values

Not all electrical values in a wiring circuit need to be measured, and in some cases you can't take measurements directly. Instead, you can use published or known values and calculations. The following sections show you how to calculate various electrical values.

All the electrical calculations described in this appendix can be arranged in a pie chart. (See the Ohm's Law chart on the Cheat Sheet at the front of this book.) This chart provides an easy way to find the various electrical measurement formulas without having to remember or go through all the algebraic manipulations.

Calculating power in watts

Instantaneous electrical power is expressed in watts, and is the product of current times voltage.

```
Power = I × V
```

In the sample circuit shown in Figure B-1, the voltage is 12 volts and the current is 6 amps. That gives a power rating of 72 watts.

Ohm's Law states that $E = I \times R$ (or $V = I \times R$). Substitute $I \times R$ for V in the $P = I \times V$ formula, and you have $P = I \times I \times R$ or $P = I^2 \times R$. Using the readings from the example in Figure B-1, the current is 6 amps and the resistance is $2 \, \Omega$. Doing the math, the result is $6 \times 6 \times 2 = 72$ watts of power for this circuit.

Calculating energy use in watt-hours

Often, power use includes a time element. The power used in your home is measured in watt-hours, or more accurately *KWH (kilowatt-hours)*. If you used 72 watts of power for 1 hour, that equals 72 watt-hours. If you use that same amount for a whole day, that equals 1.728 KWH ($72 \times 24 \div 1,000 = 1.728$).

Measuring power in AC circuits

When determining power values in AC circuits, you must include the power factor in your calculations. The *power factor,* a number between 0 and 1, is the cosine of the angle at which the current leads or lags the voltage. This angle represents the relative time differential between when voltage and the current change *polarity,* or direction, in the circuit. AC circuits feeding regular incandescent light bulbs and heating equipment are resistive loads, and don't contribute to power factor. However, circuits feeding electric motors and light fixtures with ballasts (such as fluorescent and HID lights) have a lagging power factor.

Sometimes you need to include power factor to calculate power requirements when voltage and current are out of phase. For example, it takes twice as much amperage to do the same work when the power factor is at 0.5 instead of 1.0. This phase differential is caused by an inductor and can be corrected with a capacitor or a synchronous motor.

The best way to explain power factor is to graph it by tracking it through one full cycle of current flow. Figure B-2 begins to graph the power line (marked with a P), when both the voltage line (marked with a V) and the current line (marked with an I) are positive.

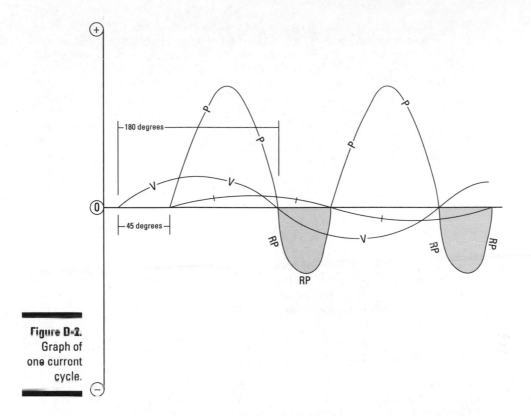

Figure B-2.
Graph of
one current
cycle.

The Ohm's Law chart (on the Cheat Sheet at the front of this book) reveals that the power used is voltage times current. That formula works fine until the voltage becomes negative. Now you have a positive current times a negative voltage, giving you a negative power. This is impossible, because there's no such thing as negative power. This power is called *reactive power*. This condition exists until (for 45°) the current also goes negative. Now you have a negative voltage times a negative current, yielding a positive power. The negative values of the current curve at the beginning of the graph are omitted for clarity. The reactive power present at the beginning of the graph is omitted because you are only tracking one current cycle. The reactive power is graphed below the 0 line with cross-hatching and is marked RP. You can easily see that if the voltage and current were *in phase* (lined up with each other), the power curve would be much larger and there would be no reactive power. The power factor in this chart is .707, which is the cosine of 45 degrees. If the current in this example were 141 amps at a power factor of 1 (referred to as *unity*), the current would only have to be 100 amps to produce the same power.

Turn to the full-color insert pages in this book and check out Color Plate 16 to see a photograph of a power factor meter taking a measurement; the power factor meter reading in the photo is about .94. The *Power Factor Meter (PFM)* needs a current and voltage input to produce a reading. A load is on the cord to the left. The PFM compares the *relationship* (phase angle) between the load's current with the circuit voltage. We're using an adapter plugged into the cord from the GFI. The adapter does two things: It gives you a place to connect the PFM's voltage leads, and it separates the conductors within the adapter to the load. One side of the line runs around the loop that the PFM jaw clamps to. If you just clamp the PFM jaw around the cord, it measures the current in both directions and the in-flowing and out-flowing currents cancel each other out.

Using the NFPA Wire Properties Table

The *National Fire Protection Association (NFPA)* has sponsored the *National Electrical Code (NEC)* since 1911. The original code document was developed in 1897 as a result of united efforts by various insurance, electrical, architectural, and allied building and construction interests.

One of the most handy parts of the NEC is Wire Table Number 8, which is used primarily for calculating the voltage drop on a wire run over any given distance. This table is included here as Figure B-3. Various parts of this book refer to wire properties that are consistent with this table. The most frequently used column in the table is the Area (Circular Mils) column. This number is used with one of two formulas to calculate the voltage drop for electrical power circuits over various wire sizes. The number isn't really the cross-sectional area of the wire, but rather the product of the square of the diameter of the wire expressed in mils. (A *mil* is a unit of measure equaling $\frac{1}{1,000}$ of 1", and is most often used to express the thickness of wire, sheet metal, and plastic films.)

In an electrical circuit, ideally you keep the total voltage drop to less than 5 percent. The electrical service to your house is assumed to have a voltage drop of up to 2 percent from the transformer to your service panel. This assumes other loads are on the electrical service besides the circuit you're concerned with. This means that your branch circuits should keep voltage drop to 3 percent or less.

The formula for determining voltage drop in single-phase circuits follows:

```
VD = 2L × K × I ÷ CM
```

To calculate voltage drop, use the following terms and values:

- ✔ VD is voltage drop expressed in V (volts).
- ✔ L is one-way length of the wire run expressed in feet.

✔ CM is the circular mils from Wire Table Number 8.

✔ I is the maximum current expressed in amps.

✔ K is a constant multiplier for the wire type you're using:

- For copper conductors at 75°C, K = 12.9

- For aluminum conductors, K = 21.3

Table 8. Conductor Properties

Size (AWG or kcmil)	Area (Circular Mils)	Conductors				Direct-Current Resistance at 75°C (167°F)		
		Stranding		Overall		Copper		Aluminum
		Quantity	Diameter (in.)	Diameter (in.)	Area (in.2)	(ohm/1000 ft)	Coated (ohm/1000 ft)	(ohm/1000 ft)
18	1620	1	–	0.04	0.001	7.77	8.08	12.8
18	1620	7	0.015	0.046	0.002	7.95	8.45	13.1
16	2580	1	–	0.051	0.002	4.89	5.08	8.05
16	2580	7	0.019	0.058	0.003	4.99	5.29	8.21
14	4110	1	–	0.064	0.003	3.07	3.19	5.06
14	4110	7	0.024	0.073	0.004	3.14	3.26	5.17
12	6530	1	–	0.081	0.005	1.93	2.01	3.18
12	6530	7	0.03	0.092	0.006	1.90	2.05	3.25
10	10380	1	–	0.102	0.008	1.21	1.26	2
10	10380	7	0.030	0.116	0.011	1.24	1.29	2.04
8	16510	1	–	0.128	0.013	0.764	0.786	1.26
8	16510	7	0.049	0.146	0.017	0.778	0.809	1.20
6	26240	7	0.061	0.184	0.027	0.491	0.51	0.808
4	41740	7	0.077	0.232	0.042	0.308	0.321	0.508
3	52620	7	0.087	0.26	0.053	0.245	0.254	0.403
2	66360	7	0.097	0.292	0.067	0.194	0.201	0.319
1	83690	19	0.066	0.332	0.087	0.154	0.16	0.253
1/0	105600	19	0.074	0.372	0.109	0.122	0.127	0.201
2/0	133100	19	0.084	0.418	0.137	0.0967	0.101	0.159
3/0	167800	19	0.094	0.47	0.173	0.0766	0.0797	0.126
4/0	211600	19	0.106	0.528	0.219	0.0608	0.0626	0.1
250	–	37	0.082	0.575	0.26	0.0515	0.0535	0.0847
300	–	37	0.09	0.63	0.312	0.0429	0.0446	0.0707
350	–	37	0.097	0.681	0.364	0.0367	0.0382	0.0605
400	–	37	0.104	0.728	0.416	0.0321	0.0331	0.0529
500	–	37	0.116	0.813	0.519	0.0258	0.0265	0.0424
600	–	61	0.099	0.893	0.626	0.0214	0.0223	0.0353
700	–	61	0.107	0.964	0.73	0.0184	0.0189	0.0303
750	–	61	0.111	0.998	0.782	0.0171	0.0176	0.0282
800	–	61	0.114	1.03	0.834	0.0161	0.0166	0.0265
900	–	61	0.122	1.094	0.94	0.0143	0.0147	0.0235
1000	–	61	0.128	1.152	1.042	0.0129	0.0132	0.0212
1250	–	91	0.117	1.289	1.305	0.0103	0.0106	0.0169
1500	–	91	0.128	1.412	1.566	0.00858	0.00883	0.0141
1750	–	127	0.117	1.526	1.829	0.00735	0.00756	0.0121
2000	–	127	0.126	1.632	2.092	0.00643	0.00662	0.0106

Notes:

1. These resistance values are valid only for the parameters as given. Using conductors having coated strands, different stranding type, and especially, other temperatures changes the resistance.

2. Formula for temperature change: R2 = R1 [1 + a(T2 - 75)] where: a cu = 0.00323, a AL = 0.00330

3. Conductors with compact and compressed stranding have 9 percent and 3 percent, respectively, smaller bare conductor diameters than those shown. See Table 5A for actual compact cable dimensions.

4. The IACs conductivities used: bare copper = 100%, aluminum = 61%

5. Class B stranding is listed as well as solid for some sizes. Its overall diameter and area is that of its circumscribing circle.

FPN: The construction information is per NEMA WC8-1992. The resistance is calculated per National Bureau of Standards Handbook 100, dated 1966, and Handbook 109, dated 1972.

Figure B-3: NEC Wire Table Number 8.

This table is used by permission from the NFPA.

In some chapters in this book, we use 10.2 as the copper wire constant. This is the constant for copper at 60°C rather than 75°C. We believe 10.2 is more realistic in most instances.

Most houses are supplied from single-phase 120/240-volt circuits. *Single phase* is supplied from a single alternating source of power or from one phase of a three-phase source. Some circuits, such as those supplying multiple-horsepower motors, are usually three-phase circuits; they require a different formula for determining voltage drop. Three-phase power sources or line transformers are configured in wye (Y) or delta (Δ) configurations. In a three-phase circuit, the voltage and current cycle from each individual phase are separated by 120°. The formula for three-phase circuits follows:

```
VD = 1.73L × K × I ÷ CM
```

Notice that in three-phase circuits, the 2L (two times length) changes to 1.73L. The 2L in single phase is just the one-way length doubled to account for the circuit's total length. On a three-phase circuit, the return path for each phase wire is through both of the remaining three-phase conductors. The return conductors operate 120° out-of-phase with each other. This accounts for the 1.73L as opposed to 2L.

If the sample circuit carries 15 amps at 120 volts over 45' of 14 AWG copper wire, the calculation looks like this:

```
(45 × 2 × 10.2 × 15) ÷ 4110 = 3.57 volts
```

The voltage drop is 3.57 volts, but you can round up to 3.6 volts. Since this is a 120-volt circuit, divide 3.6 by 120 and you get .03, or 3 percent:

```
3.6 ÷ 120 = .03 = 3%
```

Add this to the assumed 2-percent voltage drop for the service, and this circuit is within the allowable 5-percent total voltage drop.

```
.03 + .02 = .05 = 5 %
```

One of the main reasons for calculating voltage drop is to determine the needed wire size in circular mils to keep the voltage drop to 3 percent or less. To solve the equation for circular mills, VD and CM just change places, resulting in this new formula:

```
2L × K × I ÷ VD = CM
```

If your maximum allowable voltage drop is 3.6 volts, and you're running 50' of copper conductors for a 20-amp maximum load circuit, the calculation looks like this:

```
(2 × 50 × 10.2 × 20) ÷ 3.6 = 5,666 circular mils
```

As you look at Wire Table Number 8 from the NEC (shown in Figure B-3) notice that no wire has exactly 5,666 circular mils, but the next larger size wire is 12 AWG with 6,530 circular mils. However, even though the calculation works out to 12 AWG wire, remember the 80-percent maximum loading rule: The circuit's maximum constant load mustn't exceed 80 percent of the wire's capacity. Therefore, you should use the next larger wire size, which is 10 AWG.

Selecting Conductors

This NFPA NEC table indicates the allowable current-carrying capacity for a conductor at various insulation temperature ratings. When many current-carrying wires fill a conduit or run together, the current and induction cause the conductors to heat up. Overheating eventually destroys the insulation, causing electrical shorts, which will cause breakers to trip.

When you purchase wire or cable, the specifications should list the following things:

- ✔ Wire size
- ✔ Use-type rating
- ✔ Insulation's maximum temperature rating

Table 310-16 (included here as Figure B-4) from the NEC indicates the maximum amperage a conductor can handle without overheating and exceeding the insulation's maximum temperature rating. The table also lists the maximum over-current protection (circuit breaker or fuse) that may be used on a feeder run. Use this table as a starting point for choosing conductors. The ratings in NEC Table 310-16 are for three or fewer conductors in a raceway or cable. The following sections provide additional guidance for conductors in various situations.

Regardless of your conductor size, you mustn't exceed amperage and temperature ratings for the circuit breakers. Most circuit breakers are rated at 75°C.

Table 310-16. Allowable Ampacities of Insulated Conductors Rated 0 Through 2000 Volts, 60°C Through 90°C (140°F Through 194°F) Not More than Three Current-Carrying Conductors in Raceway, Cable, or Earth (Directly Buried), Based on Ambient Temperature of 30°C (86°F)

Size	Temperature Rating of Conductor (See Table 310-13)						Size
	60°C	75°C	90°C	60°C	75°C	90°C	
	(140°F)	(167°F)	(194°F)	(140°F)	(167°F)	(194°F)	
AWG or kcmil	Types TW, UF	Types FEPW, RH, RHW, THHW, THW, THWN, XHHW, USE, ZW	Types TBS, SA, SIS, FEP, FEPB, MI, RHH, RHW-2, THHN, THHW, THW-2, THWN-2, USE-2, XHH, XHHW-2, ZW-2	Types TW, UF	Types RH, RHW, THHW, THW, THWN, XHHW,	Types TBS, SA, SIS, FEP, FEPB, MI, RHH, RHW-2, THHN, THHW, THW-2, THWN-2, USE-2, XHH, XHHW-2, ZW-2	AWG or kcmil
	COPPER			ALUMINUM OR COPPER-CLAD ALUMINUM			
18	—	—	14	—	—	—	–
16	—	—	18	—	—	—	–
14*	20	20	25	—	—	—	–
12*	25	25	30	20	20	25	12*
10*	30	35	40	25	30	35	10*
8	40	50	55	30	40	45	8
6	55	65	75	40	50	60	6
4	70	85	95	55	65	75	4
3	85	100	110	65	75	85	3
2	95	115	130	75	90	100	2
1	110	130	150	85	100	11	1
1/0	125	150	170	100	120	135	1/0
2/0	145	175	195	115	135	150	2/0
3/0	165	200	225	130	155	175	3/0
4/0	195	230	260	150	180	205	4/0
250	215	255	290	170	205	230	250
300	240	285	320	190	230	255	300
350	260	310	350	210	250	280	350
400	280	335	380	225	270	305	400
500	320	380	430	260	310	350	500
600	355	420	475	285	340	385	600
700	385	460	520	310	375	420	700
750	400	475	535	320	385	435	750
800	410	490	555	330	395	450	800
900	435	520	585	355	425	480	900
1000	455	545	615	375	445	500	1000
1250	495	590	665	405	485	545	1250
1500	520	625	705	435	520	585	1500
1750	545	650	735	455	545	615	1750
2000	560	665	750	470	560	630	2000

CORRECTION FACTORS

Ambient Temp. (°C)	For ambient temperatures other than 30°C (86°F), multiply the allowable ampacities shown above by the appropriate factor shown below.						Ambient Temp. (°F)
21–25	1.08	1.05	1.04	1.08	1.05	1.04	70-77
26–30	1	1	1	1	1	1	78-86
31–35	0.91	0.94	0.96	0.91	0.94	0.96	87-95
36–40	0.82	0.88	0.91	0.82	0.88	0.91	96-104
41–45	0.71	0.82	0.87	0.71	0.82	0.87	105-113
46–50	0.58	0.75	0.82	0.58	0.75	0.82	114-122
51–55	0.41	0.67	0.76	0.41	0.67	0.76	123-131
56–60	—	0.5	0.71	—	0.58	0.71	132-140
61–70	—	0.33	0.58	—	0.33	0.58	141-158
71–80	—	—	0.41	—	—	0.41	159-176

Figure B-4: Table 310-16 from the NEC.

This table is used by permission from the NFPA.

Limitations for using small conductors

Smaller conductors handle less amperage than larger conductors do, so special rules apply when using small conductors. These rules define the maximum breaker or fuse size to use with given conductor sizes. The special rule says that unless specifically permitted in other sections of the electrical code, the over-current protection (circuit breaker or fuse) mustn't exceed the following:

- ✔ AWG 14 copper wire: 15 amperes
- ✔ AWG 12 copper wire: 20 amperes
- ✔ AWG 10 copper wire: 30 amperes
- ✔ AWG 12 aluminum and copper-clad aluminum wire: 15 amperes
- ✔ AWG 10 aluminum and copper-clad aluminum wire: 25 amperes

Don't forget to adjust the size of a circuit's over-current protection using correction factors such as ambient temperature and the number of applied conductors. For information on correction factors, see the NEC tables in Figures B-3 and B-4.

Bundling conductors together

If you have more than three current-carrying conductors in a cable, conduit, or raceway, you have to adjust, or *derate,* the conductors' ampacity ratings by the percentages in Tables B-3 and B-4. You must derate them if they meet *any* of the following criteria:

- ✔ You're running separate cables through the same drilled hole.
- ✔ You're running separate cables through the same conduit.
- ✔ You're running separate cables together for 24" or more.

The NEC provides separate tables for installations that involve constant loads and load diversity. *Load diversity* means that not everything is turned on at the same time. Many circuits in your home are considered to have load diversity, so use the adjustments listed in Table B-1. In situations where the conductors carry a constant load, use Table B-2 instead.

Table B-1	NEC Table B-310-11 Adjustment Factors for More than Three Current-Carrying Conductors in a Raceway or Cable with Load Diversity	
Number of Current-Carrying *Conductors*	*Percent of Values in Tables as* *Adjusted for Ambient Temperature* *if Necessary*
4–6	80
7–9	70
10–24	70*
25–42	60*
43–85	50*

* These factors include the effects of a load diversity of 50 percent.

Table B-2	NEC Table 310-15(b)(2)(a) Adjustment Factors for More than Three Current-Carrying Conductors in a Raceway or Cable	
Number of Current-Carrying *Conductors*	*Percent of Values in Tables 310-16* *Through 310-19 as Adjusted for* *Ambient Temperature if Necessary*
4–6	80
7–9	70
10–20	50
21–30	45
31–40	40
41+	35

Most modern conductors have a 90°C insulation temperature rating. To derate conductors, follow these steps:

1. **Determine how many conductors are run together.**

   Suppose, for example, that you have 20 conductors sharing a couple of holes, so they run together for more than 24".

2. Refer to Table B-1 to determine the derate percentage.

According to Table B-1, if these conductors have load diversity, you should derate the conductors by 70 percent. Copper 14 AWG wire with a 90°C rating can normally carry 25 amps.

3. Multiply by the percentage

In this example, multiply by 70 percent (0.7) to get 17.5 amps.

4. Round down to the small conductor limitation.

In this example, the largest breaker you can use on this circuit is 15 amps. Even though the calculation works out to 17.5 amps, in this case the small conductor limitation applies, so the maximum breaker size is limited to 15 amps.

Using non-metallic cable (NMC)

The maximum ampacities of *non-metallic cable (NMC)*, or Romex, mustn't exceed the 60°C ratings. You can use higher temperature ratings for derating calculations, but the final ampacity rating of the wire size and circuit breakers for Romex runs can't exceed the 60°C ratings.

Converting between Celsius and Fahrenheit

Conductors and breakers are usually rated in Celsius, but if you live in the United States you're probably more comfortable with the Fahrenheit system. You may not always have your math crutch (a calculator) at your side, but you can still perform quick Celsius-to-Fahrenheit conversions using a stubby pencil and paper. Simply use the magic number 40:

1. Add 40 to the known temperature.

This applies whether you're converting from Celsius (C) to Fahrenheit (F) or vice versa.

2. Multiply that number as follows:

- To convert from F to C, multiply by $\frac{5}{9}$ (0.5555).
- To convert from C to F, multiply by $\frac{9}{5}$ (1.8).

3. Subtract 40.

To quickly find the Celsius temperature for 120°Fahrenheit, the math looks like this:

```
120 + 40 = 160 × ⁵/₉ = 88.8 - 40 = 48.8
```

To convert 100°Celsius to Fahrenheit, the formula looks like this:

```
100 + 40 = 140 × ⁹/₅ = 252 - 40 = 212
```

Ethernet Length Limits

Throughout this book, we recommend that you use four-pair, copper, Cat 6 cable not only for Ethernet computer networks, but for a variety of other uses. We recommend Cat 6 because it's easy to work with, is readily available, can handle high frequencies, and is easy to terminate (with the right tool). Cat 6 cable can be terminated into a RJ-45 plug connector, or into a punch-down block on an outlet jack.

Cat 6 is versatile, but it isn't without limitations. Chief among its limitations is run length when used for transmitting Ethernet data packets. If you have to run a Cat 6 network cable for more than 100 meters (328') — say, to your artist studio on the back 40 — you may need to use special kinds of Ethernet cable. The Base T standards for Ethernet cabling assume a limit of two segments, or 200 meters. The 10 Base 2 thin Ethernet standard allows three segments for a total distance of 555 meters using repeaters. Thin Ethernet cable is similar to TV cable, and with the right crimping tool a do-it-yourselfer can easily install it. Table B-3 lists Ethernet cabling standards and the limitations associated with each.

Use plenum-rated cable if the cable runs though air ducts.

Table B-3	Maximum Ethernet Cable Lengths		
Ethernet Standard	*Cable Type*	*Distance One Segment*	*Connector Type*
10 Base 5	Thick Ethernet	500 m (1,640')	AUI
10 Base 2	Thin Ethernet	185 m (606')	BNC
10 Base T	Twisted Pair, UTP Cat 3, 4, 5, or 6	100 m (328')	RJ-45
100 Base TX	Twisted Pair, UTP Cat 5 or 6, or STP	100 m (328')	RJ-45

Ethernet Standard	Cable Type	Distance One Segment	Connector Type
1000 Base T	Twisted Pair, UTP Cat 5 or 6	100 m (328')	RJ-45
10 Base F	Fiber Optic	Varies by fiber type & sub-specification	Varies; see the three following examples
FL	Fiber	1,000–2,000 m (3,280–6,561')	Varies by equipment
FB	Fiber	2,000 m (6561')	Varies by equipment
FP	Fiber	500 m (1,640')	Varies by equipment

Appendix C

About the CD

System Requirements

Make sure your computer meets the following minimum system requirements. If your computer doesn't match up to most of these requirements, you may have problems in using the contents of the CD.

- ✔ A PC with a Pentium 500 MHz or faster processor (1 GHz or faster is recommended)

- ✔ Microsoft Windows 98, Windows Me, Windows 2000, Windows XP Home Edition, or Windows XP Professional versions (Windows 2000 or XP is recommended)

- ✔ At least 256MB of total RAM (for best performance, 512MB or more of RAM is recommended)

- ✔ A minimum of 80MB of free disk space; the installation uses 50MB

- ✔ A sound card on your PC connected to a microphone and speakers

- ✔ A CD ROM drive

In order to use certain features in HALbasic, you also need to have

- ✔ A phone line connected to a HAL Voice Portal (for telephone features)

- ✔ An Internet connection (to allow HAL to access data on the Internet)

Note: If you plan to purchase and use the optional HALdmc, you need to have Microsoft Windows Media Player 9 or later installed on your PC and additional disk storage for storing the music files. The HALvoices option requires 400MB of free disk space.

If you need more information on computers and Windows basics, check out these books published by Wiley Publishing, Inc.: *PCs For Dummies,* by Dan Gookin; *Windows 98 For Dummies, Windows 2000 Professional For Dummies, Microsoft Windows ME Millennium Edition For Dummies, Windows XP For Dummies,* all by Andy Rathbone.

Using the CD with Microsoft Windows

To install HALbasic from the CD included with this book, follow these steps:

1. **Insert the CD into your computer's CD-ROM drive.**
2. **The HALbasic Install Menu screen should automatically appear. If it doesn't appear, follow these steps:**
   a. Double-click the My Computer icon on your desktop. (You can also find My Computer on the Start menu.)
   b. Double-click the drive letter for the CD ROM drive containing the HALbasic CD.
   c. Find the icon labeled Install Menu and double-click it.
3. **When the Install Menu appears, select the Install HALbasic option.**

   This will bring up the HAL Installation Wizard and step you through the various screens.
4. **Follow the installation wizard's prompts.**

   After you finish the installation wizard, the HAL Setup Wizard automatically begins.
5. **Complete the HAL Setup Wizard by answering the various questions.**

   When the setup wizard is completed, the HALbasic program begins, prompting you to register the software.

   Registration is required to activate the one-year software license. You must provide a valid e-mail address because the registration number is e-mailed to that address.

   After you complete the registration process, HALbasic launches, and you can begin to enjoy the benefits of the HAL home automation software!

What You'll Find

HALbasic, from Home Automated Living, Inc.
14401 Sweitzer Lane, Suite 600
Laurel, MD 20707
www.automatedliving.com

The HALbasic program is an entry-level version of the home automation software introduced in Chapter 13. The version included on the CD is a fully functional, one-year user license that must be registered prior to use. HALbasic
enables you to use some of the neat things discussed in the book, such as
time- and voice-based control of lights and devices within your home that are
equipped with X10 or X10-compatible controllers though any one of multiple
supported X10 interfaces. (To use additional controllers or features, consider
upgrading to HALdeluxe or HAL2000.)

HALbasic also allows you to use voice commands to control many aspects of
your Internet experience. Getting the latest stock quote, checking the weather
forecast for your destination city, or checking prime time TV listings by voice
commands are all possible with the HAL software.

HALbasic offers other features such as voice mailboxes, directory information, notification services, and more.

If You've Got Problems (Of the CD Kind)

HALbasic will work on most computers that meet or exceed the minimum
system requirements. Regrettably, your computer may differ, and some programs may not work properly for some hard to discover reason.

The most likely problems are that you don't have enough memory (RAM) for
the programs you want to use, or you have other programs running that are
affecting installation or running of a program. If you have problems, you
might try one or more of the following suggestions, and then try using the
software again:

- **Turn off any antivirus software that you have on your computer.**
  Installers sometimes mimic virus activity and may make your computer
  incorrectly believe that it is being infected by a virus.

- **Close all running programs.** The more programs you're running, the less
  memory is available to other programs. Installers also typically update
  files and programs. So if you keep other programs running, installation
  may not work properly.

✔ **Have your local computer store add more RAM to your computer.** This is, admittedly, a drastic and somewhat expensive step. However, if you have a Windows 98 or later PC, adding more memory can really help the speed of your computer and allow more programs to run at the same time.

HAL's Web site lists a number of support services and frequently asked questions at `www.homeautomatedliving.com/support.shtml`. For additional support, registered HAL users can telephone Home Automated Living's Technical Support department at 301-498-7000. The Technical Support department is open Monday through Friday from 10:00 AM to 7:00 PM Eastern time.

Index

● *M* ●

• *Q* •

surveillance system, 175, 178–179, 207, 231–233
temperature range, 176
weather protection, 176, 180
Web-based, 179
wireless, 179, 181
wiring, 181
zooming, 178
virtual private network (VPN), 202, 232
voice
  gateway, phone, 112
  home automation voice control, 206, 208, 209–212, 213
Voice over Internet Protocol (VoIP), 112–116
volt, 22, 25, 39, 321
volt amp (VA), 25, 27
voltage drop (VD), 275, 324–325, 326–327
voltmeter, 321

• *W* •

W (watt), 25, 322
WAN (wide-area network), 114
waste system pump, 277
water
  alarm, high water, 229
  hydroelectric power backup, 244
  pipe, connecting ground to, 41
  pump, 240, 274–277
  steam power backup system, 245
  well, wiring considerations when house connected to, 41, 42
watt (W), 25, 322
watt-hour, 25, 322
weather. *See also* temperature
  electrical receptacle, weatherproof, 256
  electrical service weather head, 36
  home weather station, 284–285
  lightning protection, 300–301
  switch, weatherproof, 256
  video camera weather protection, 176, 180
  wiring, weatherproof, 298

WeatherHawk home weather station, 285
webcam, 179, 188, 232–233
welder, wiring, 264–266
well
  pump, 240, 274–277
  wiring considerations when house connected to, 41, 42
WESCO International, 318
wet-bar sink electrical receptacle, 46
wide-area network (WAN), 114
Wiley Publishing, Web site, 2
wind power backup system, 244, 249
window
  alarm system window sensor, 223–224, 225, 236
  wiring under, 55
Windows 98 For Dummies (Rathbone), 336
Windows 2000 Professional For Dummies (Rathbone), 336
wireless
  alarm system, 230–231
  home automation system, 212
  home network, 199–200
  home weather station, 285
  Institute of Electrical & Electronics Engineers (IEEE) 802.11 standards, 192, 199
  Internet connection, 192
  microphone, 212
  video camera, 179, 181
Wiremold receptacle strip, 49
wiring. *See also* cabling; circuit; conductor
  air compressor, 266
  alarm system, 224–225, 233–234
  aluminum, 34, 325, 329
  American wire gauge (AWG), 24, 37
  backboard, 39
  backup power system, 246–248
  basement, 57
  bathroom, 60
  bedroom, 60, 61–62, 226
  box, supporting wire near, 55, 58
  Brown and Sharpe (B&S) Wire Gauge, 24
  bulkhead, 280
  cable, distance from, 13–14

BUSINESS, CAREERS & PERSONAL FINANCE

0-7645-5307-0

0-7645-5331-3 *†

Also available:
- Accounting For Dummies †
  0-7645-5314-3
- Business Plans Kit For Dummies †
  0-7645-5365-8
- Cover Letters For Dummies
  0-7645-5224-4
- Frugal Living For Dummies
  0-7645-5403-4
- Leadership For Dummies
  0-7645-5176-0
- Managing For Dummies
  0-7645-1771-6

- Marketing For Dummies
  0-7645-5600-2
- Personal Finance For Dummies *
  0-7645-2590-5
- Project Management For Dummies
  0-7645-5283-X
- Resumes For Dummies †
  0-7645-5471-9
- Selling For Dummies
  0-7645-5363-1
- Small Business Kit For Dummies *†
  0-7645-5093-4

HOME & BUSINESS COMPUTER BASICS

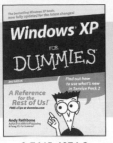

0-7645-4074-2

0-7645-3758-X

Also available:
- ACT! 6 For Dummies
  0-7645-2645-6
- iLife '04 All-in-One Desk Reference
  For Dummies
  0-7645-7347-0
- iPAQ For Dummies
  0-7645-6769-1
- Mac OS X Panther Timesaving
  Techniques For Dummies
  0-7645-5812-9
- Macs For Dummies
  0-7645-5656-8

- Microsoft Money 2004 For Dummies
  0-7645-4195-1
- Office 2003 All-in-One Desk Reference
  For Dummies
  0-7645-3883-7
- Outlook 2003 For Dummies
  0-7645-3759-8
- PCs For Dummies
  0-7645-4074-2
- TiVo For Dummies
  0-7645-6923-6
- Upgrading and Fixing PCs For Dummies
  0-7645-1665-5
- Windows XP Timesaving Techniques
  For Dummies
  0-7645-3748-2

FOOD, HOME, GARDEN, HOBBIES, MUSIC & PETS

0-7645-5295-3

0-7645-5232-5

Also available:
- Bass Guitar For Dummies
  0-7645-2487-9
- Diabetes Cookbook For Dummies
  0-7645-5230-9
- Gardening For Dummies *
  0-7645-5130-2
- Guitar For Dummies
  0-7645-5106-X
- Holiday Decorating For Dummies
  0-7645-2570-0
- Home Improvement All-in-One
  For Dummies
  0-7645-5680-0

- Knitting For Dummies
  0-7645-5395-X
- Piano For Dummies
  0-7645-5105-1
- Puppies For Dummies
  0-7645-5255-4
- Scrapbooking For Dummies
  0-7645-7208-3
- Senior Dogs For Dummies
  0-7645-5818-8
- Singing For Dummies
  0-7645-2475-5
- 30-Minute Meals For Dummies
  0-7645-2589-1

INTERNET & DIGITAL MEDIA

0-7645-1664-7

0-7645-6924-4

Also available:
- 2005 Online Shopping Directory
  For Dummies
  0-7645-7495-7
- CD & DVD Recording For Dummies
  0-7645-5956-7
- eBay For Dummies
  0-7645-5654-1
- Fighting Spam For Dummies
  0-7645-5965-6
- Genealogy Online For Dummies
  0-7645-5964-8
- Google For Dummies
  0-7645-4420-9

- Home Recording For Musicians
  For Dummies
  0-7645-1634-5
- The Internet For Dummies
  0-7645-4173-0
- iPod & iTunes For Dummies
  0-7645-7772-7
- Preventing Identity Theft For Dummies
  0-7645-7336-5
- Pro Tools All-in-One Desk Reference
  For Dummies
  0-7645-5714-9
- Roxio Easy Media Creator For Dummies
  0-7645-7131-1

* Separate Canadian edition also available
† Separate U.K. edition also available

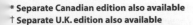
 WILEY

SPORTS, FITNESS, PARENTING, RELIGION & SPIRITUALITY

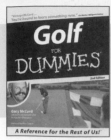
0-7645-5146-9

0-7645-5418-2

Also available:

- Adoption For Dummies
  0-7645-5488-3
- Basketball For Dummies
  0-7645-5248-1
- The Bible For Dummies
  0-7645-5296-1
- Buddhism For Dummies
  0-7645-5359-3
- Catholicism For Dummies
  0-7645-5391-7
- Hockey For Dummies
  0-7645-5228-7

- Judaism For Dummies
  0-7645-5299-6
- Martial Arts For Dummies
  0-7645-5358-5
- Pilates For Dummies
  0-7645-5397-6
- Religion For Dummies
  0-7645-5264-3
- Teaching Kids to Read For Dummies
  0-7645-4043-2
- Weight Training For Dummies
  0-7645-5168-X
- Yoga For Dummies
  0-7645-5117-5

TRAVEL

0-7645-5438-7

0-7645-5453-0

Also available:

- Alaska For Dummies
  0-7645-1761-9
- Arizona For Dummies
  0-7645-6938-4
- Cancún and the Yucatán For Dummies
  0-7645-2437-2
- Cruise Vacations For Dummies
  0-7645-6941-4
- Europe For Dummies
  0-7645-5456-5
- Ireland For Dummies
  0-7645-5455-7

- Las Vegas For Dummies
  0-7645-5448-4
- London For Dummies
  0-7645-4277-X
- New York City For Dummies
  0-7645-6945-7
- Paris For Dummies
  0-7645-5494-8
- RV Vacations For Dummies
  0-7645-5443-3
- Walt Disney World & Orlando For Dummies
  0-7645-6943-0

GRAPHICS, DESIGN & WEB DEVELOPMENT

0-7645-4345-8

0-7645-5589-8

Also available:

- Adobe Acrobat 6 PDF For Dummies
  0-7645-3760-1
- Building a Web Site For Dummies
  0-7645-7144-3
- Dreamweaver MX 2004 For Dummies
  0-7645-4342-3
- FrontPage 2003 For Dummies
  0-7645-3882-9
- HTML 4 For Dummies
  0-7645-1995-6
- Illustrator CS For Dummies
  0-7645-4084-X

- Macromedia Flash MX 2004 For Dummies
  0-7645-4358-X
- Photoshop 7 All-in-One Desk Reference For Dummies
  0-7645-1667-1
- Photoshop CS Timesaving Techniques For Dummies
  0-7645-6782-9
- PHP 5 For Dummies
  0-7645-4166-8
- PowerPoint 2003 For Dummies
  0-7645-3908-6
- QuarkXPress 6 For Dummies
  0-7645-2593-X

NETWORKING, SECURITY, PROGRAMMING & DATABASES

0-7645-6852-3

0-7645-5784-X

Also available:

- A+ Certification For Dummies
  0-7645-4187-0
- Access 2003 All-in-One Desk Reference For Dummies
  0-7645-3988-4
- Beginning Programming For Dummies
  0-7645-4997-9
- C For Dummies
  0-7645-7068-4
- Firewalls For Dummies
  0-7645-4048-3
- Home Networking For Dummies
  0-7645-42796

- Network Security For Dummies
  0-7645-1679-5
- Networking For Dummies
  0-7645-1677-9
- TCP/IP For Dummies
  0-7645-1760-0
- VBA For Dummies
  0-7645-3989-2
- Wireless All In-One Desk Reference For Dummies
  0-7645-7496-5
- Wireless Home Networking For Dummies
  0-7645-3910-8

HEALTH & SELF-HELP

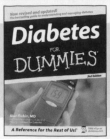

0-7645-6820-5 *†

0-7645-2566-2

Also available:
- Alzheimer's For Dummies
  0-7645-3899-3
- Asthma For Dummies
  0-7645-4233-8
- Controlling Cholesterol For Dummies
  0-7645-5440-9
- Depression For Dummies
  0-7645-3900-0
- Dieting For Dummies
  0-7645-4149-8
- Fertility For Dummies
  0-7645-2549-2

- Fibromyalgia For Dummies
  0-7645-5441-7
- Improving Your Memory For Dummies
  0-7645-5435-2
- Pregnancy For Dummies †
  0-7645-4483-7
- Quitting Smoking For Dummies
  0-7645-2629-4
- Relationships For Dummies
  0-7645-5384-4
- Thyroid For Dummies
  0-7645-5385-2

EDUCATION, HISTORY, REFERENCE & TEST PREPARATION

0-7645-5194-9

0-7645-4186-2

Also available:
- Algebra For Dummies
  0-7645-5325-9
- British History For Dummies
  0-7645-7021-8
- Calculus For Dummies
  0-7645-2498-4
- English Grammar For Dummies
  0-7645-5322-4
- Forensics For Dummies
  0-7645-5580-4
- The GMAT For Dummies
  0-7645-5251-1
- Inglés Para Dummies
  0-7645-5427-1

- Italian For Dummies
  0-7645-5196-5
- Latin For Dummies
  0-7645-5431-X
- Lewis & Clark For Dummies
  0-7645-2545-X
- Research Papers For Dummies
  0-7645-5426-3
- The SAT I For Dummies
  0-7645-7193-1
- Science Fair Projects For Dummies
  0-7645-5460-3
- U.S. History For Dummies
  0-7645-5249-X

Get smart @ dummies.com®

- **Find a full list of Dummies titles**
- **Look into loads of FREE on-site articles**
- **Sign up for FREE eTips e-mailed to you weekly**
- **See what other products carry the Dummies name**
- **Shop directly from the Dummies bookstore**
- **Enter to win new prizes every month!**

* Separate Canadian edition also available
† Separate U.K. edition also available

Available wherever books are sold. For more information or to order direct: U.S. customers visit www.dummies.com or call 1-877-762-2974.
U.K. customers visit www.wileyeurope.com or call 0800 243407. Canadian customers visit www.wiley.ca or call 1-800-567-4797.

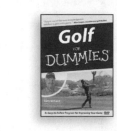